2ND EDITION

INSURANCE MATTERS

Englisch für Kaufleute
für Versicherungen und Finanzen

von

Willi Fensel

Uwe Krabbe

Keith Purvis

in Zusammenarbeit mit der Verlagsredaktion

BWV

Cornelsen

Verfasser/innen:	Willi Fensel, Nürnberg Uwe Krabbe, Nürnberg Keith Purvis, München Irene Eckart, Flensburg (KMK *mock exam*) Willi Fensel und Barbara Jaik, Nürnberg (KMK *exam practice*)
Berater:	Dr Katharina Höhn, BWV, München Ingo Klohn, Allianz Deutschland, München
Verlagsredaktion:	Merlene Griffin
Redaktion:	James Abram, Salzburg
Redaktionelle Mitarbeit:	Hannah Hudson, Oliver Busch (Wörterverzeichnisse)
Bildredaktion:	Gertha Maly
Umschlagfoto:	Gettyimages/Paul Conrath
Umschlaggestaltung:	Katrin Nehm
Layout und Technische Umsetzung:	Sabine Theuring, Berlin
Erhältlich ist auch:	Audio-CD ISBN 978-3-06-020088-7 Handreichungen für den Unterricht (+ CD-ROM) ISBN 978-3-06-020090-0

www.cornelsen.de

Die Links zu externen Webseiten Dritter, die in diesem Lehrwerk angegeben sind, wurden vor Drucklegung geprüft. Der Verlag übernimmt keine Gewähr für die Aktualität und den Inhalt dieser Adressen und Dateien und solcher, die mit ihnen verlinkt sind.

1. Auflage, 4. Druck 2014

Im 3. Druck wurden KMK *exam practice*-Seiten sowie ein KMK *mock exam* im Anhang eingefügt.

Druck: Mohn Media Mohndruck, Gütersloh

ISBN 978-3-06-020086-3

PEFC
PEFC/04-31-1033

PEFC zertifiziert
Dieses Produkt stammt aus nachhaltig bewirtschafteten Wäldern und kontrollierten Quellen.

www.pefc.de

Vorwort

Insurance Matters – 2nd Edition ist die komplett aktualisierte Neubearbeitung des bewährten Lehrwerks für Kaufleute für Versicherungen und Finanzen, das für die Ausbildung in Berufsschulen sowie innerbetriebliche Aus- und Weiterbildung konzipiert ist. Das Lehrwerk basiert auf Lehrplänen der Bundesländer für Berufsschulen und wurde in Zusammenarbeit mit dem Berufsbildungswerk der Deutschen Versicherungswirtschaft (BWV) e. V. herausgegeben.

Das Lehrwerk ist auf Lernende zugeschnitten, deren Englischkenntnisse den Anforderungen eines mittleren Bildungsabschlusses bzw. eines durchschnittlichen gymnasialen Grundkursabschlusses entsprechen. Darüber hinaus enthalten die Units 1–11 mit den *Extra Materials* auch anspruchsvolleren Lernstoff für Lernende mit fortgeschrittenen Englischkenntnissen. Neu an der *2nd Edition* ist auch der Bezug einzelner Übungen auf die KMK-Zertifikatsprüfung in Englisch, die in einigen Bundesländern auch für Kaufleute für Versicherungen und Finanzen angeboten wird.

Insurance Matters – 2nd Edition enthält 11 *Units* zu verschiedenen Versicherungsarten, die jeweils wichtige Aspekte des deutschen und britischen Versicherungsgeschäfts behandeln. *Unit* 12 beschäftigt sich mit einer Bewerbung im Ausland (inklusive Lebenslauf und Bewerbungsschreiben). Die *Units* sind in sich geschlossen, sodass sie in beliebiger Reihenfolge bearbeitet oder auch einzelne *Units* ausgelassen werden können. Dennoch wird empfohlen, die vorgegebene Reihenfolge einzuhalten, um eine kontinuierlichen Aufbau des Fachvokabulars zu gewährleisten.

Das Lehrwerk zielt in erster Linie darauf ab, Fertigkeiten der Kommunikation im Versicherungswesen, besonders in der mündlichen Kommunikation, zu vermitteln. Dazu werden in fallstudienartigen *Units* an der Praxis orientierte Gesprächssituationen wie Telefonate und Direktgespräche zwischen englischsprachigen Kunden bzw. Geschäftspartnern und Kauffrau/Kaufmann für Versicherungen und Finanzen simuliert. Das nötige Fachvokabular und entscheidende Redewendungen werden anhand von Übungen gefestigt, um sie später handlungsorientiert (*Role-play*) anwenden zu können. Außerdem wird der richtige Umgang mit englischsprachigen Formularen und Dokumenten sowie das Lese- und Hörverständnis und das eigenständige Verfassen englischsprachiger Geschäftskorrespondenz – Brief, Fax und E-Mail – geschult.

Das notwendige sprachliche Hintergrundwissen wird mit abwechslungsreichen Übungen vermittelt. Zu den vielfältigen Übungsformen gehören: *Information gap*, Rollenspiel, das Herausfiltern wichtiger Informationen aus Dokumenten und Broschüren, Wortschatzerweiterung durch *Working with words* und reines Hörverstehen.

Der Anhang enthält die *Partner files* mit Vorlagen zu Rollenspielen und ein Glossar der wichtigsten Begriffe des Versicherungswesens. Zwei Wörterlisten, eine nach Units gegliederte und eine alphabetische, ermöglichen das schnelle Auffinden von Vokabeln.

Neu an dem vorliegenden Druck ist die zusätzliche Vorbereitung auf die KMK-Zertifikatsprüfung. Dies geschieht anhand von KMK *exam practice*-Seiten sowie einem KMK *mock exam* im Anhang des Buches. Sie können die Hörtexte zu den KMK-Hörverstehensaufgaben anhören, indem Sie den jeweiligen Webcode auf www.cornelsen.de/matters eingeben. Die Transkripte und Lösungen zu den KMK-Materialien sind als Download auf der Cornelsen-Webseite unter *Insurance Matters – 2nd Edition* zu finden.

2 Dialog bzw. Text auf der Audio-CD

KMK Prüfungsrelevante Übungen für die KMK-Zertifikatsprüfung

Unit	Title	Contents
1	**The insurance company**	A company profile Company departments Dual system of training
2	**The insurer and its customers**	Customer attitudes Customer profiles Charts and graphs Presentations
3	**Contents and buildings insurance**	Formal and informal emails Types of building
4	**Life insurance**	Customer needs Business letters
5	**Personal accident insurance**	Parts of the body Types of injury Occupational risk
6	**Private health insurance**	Top-up benefits Enquiries about reimbursment
7	**Liability**	A liability claim A policy query Degrees of liability
8	**Motor insurance**	Types of vehicle Types of accident
9	**Financial products**	Methods of payment Types of bank account A bank statement
10	**Business insurance**	Classes of insurance A broker presentation
11	**Reinsurance**	Types of risk Balanced and unbalanced portfolios
12	**Applying for a job**	A CV A covering letter
	Anhang	
	Partner files	
	KMK exam practice	
	KMK mock exam	
	Glossary of insurance terms	
	Unit word list	
	Alphabetical word list	
	Irregular verbs	
	Acknowledgements	

Language	Extra material	Grammar	Page
Introducing people Meeting visitors Offering hospitality Talking about your job	Different channels of distribution in the UK	Simple present Present continuous	6
Describing trends The language of presentations Expressing opinions	Insurance fraud	Comparative and superlative forms of adjectives	18
Telephoning	Cutting costs on home insurance	Simple past Past continuous	28
Asking for and giving advice Doing calculations Advising a customer	Life insurance trends	Since, for, ago Present perfect (continuous) and simple past	40
Making appointments Expressing sympathy	Is accident cover just a waste of money?	Future tenses	52
Mildly disagreeing	Travel insurance	Phrasal verbs	62
Asking for repetition Asking somebody to speak more slowly	Types of liability insurance	Modal verbs	72
Advising a customer	What drives the cost of car insurance?	If-sentences	82
Discussing loans Writing and saying numbers	How we will pay in the future	Verb + infinitive or verb + ing-form?	90
Changing an appointment	Named perils and all risks property policies Just for fun	Relative clauses	100
Negotiating	Proportional reinsurance – surplus	Reported speech	112
Job interviews			122
			130
			134
			146
			150
			153
			172
			183
			184

The insurance company

John Fielding works for an Irish insurance company which has been taken over by the German insurer Proximus Versicherung AG. Proximus invites some of the Irish junior managers to attend a training programme to get to know how insurance works in Germany. John is interested in this programme and decides to take a look at his new parent company's English website.

1 A company profile

Proximus Versicherung

Search | Sitemap

Home | About us

History | Operations | Structure

History of the Proximus Group

Proximus Versicherung was founded in Dresden in 1885 as a public limited company. Its founders were Saxonian bankers and businessmen. The company provided three classes of insurance: fire, marine and liability insurance. In 1924 Proximus acquired Chemnitzer Lebensversicherung AG, which had got into financial difficulties during the great inflation. After World War II both companies moved their Head Offices to Munich.

In 1951 Chemnitzer Lebensversicherung took over the life insurance business of Amboss Lebensversicherung a.G. This mutual insurance company had been founded by several chambers of handicraft in 1930. In 1965 Chemnitzer Lebensversicherung merged with Düsseldorfer Lebensversicherung to create Proximus Lebensversicherung AG. Today Proximus Lebensversicherung AG is a leading provider of life insurance in Germany.

In 1970 Proximus Versicherung AG and Proximus Lebensversicherung AG established Proximus Krankenversicherung AG, which turned out to be very successful. In 1988 the Proximus Group branched out into financial services by acquiring the Süddeutsche Handelsbank AG and starting up a building society, Proximus Bausparkasse AG. Two years later Proximus opened its first branch office abroad in Italy. It is based in Rome.

Copyright 2007 Proximus | Legal warnings | Privacy Policy | Company data

INFO

Public limited company (plc): a company that sells shares in itself to the public. (= *AG*)
Mutual insurance company: a company that is owned by its policyholders. (= *VVaG*)

A Say if the statements are true or false. Correct the false ones.

1 Proximus Versicherung AG was founded by Bavarian businessmen.
2 In 1924 Proximus moved its headquarters to Berlin.
3 Two life insurance companies were combined in 1965 to create Proximus Lebensversicherung AG.
4 Proximus Lebensversicherung and Proximus Krankenversicherung are mutual insurance companies.
5 Proximus Krankenversicherung was founded 18 years before the Proximus Group established a building society.

B Complete the following text with words from the box. There is one more word than you need. Check its meaning.

classes | life insurance | provides | health insurance | distribution | financial services | billion | policyholders

Proximus Versicherung

Search | Sitemap

Home | About us

History | Operations | Structure

Operations

The Proximus Group offers a comprehensive range of insurance products. Within the group Proximus Versicherung ...[1] indemnity insurance and accident insurance, Proximus Lebensversicherung sells ...[2] policies and Proximus Krankenversicherung offers all types of private ...[3]. In addition Süddeutsche Handelsbank and Proximus Bausparkasse provide ...[4].

The Proximus Group serves 7.85 million ...[5] in nine European countries. The company's main ...[6] of business are life, health, motor and liability insurance. The group has 8,270 employees. It uses four channels of ...[7] to sell its products: 2,890 tied and independent agents, 70 brokers, its bank and direct selling (only in the UK and Ireland). The life insurance business amounts to 50% of its total premium income, which is €7.2 billion.

Copyright 2007 Proximus | Legal warnings | Privacy Policy | Company data

INFO Figures

When dealing with figures in English remember that commas and dots are used differently:

- **Britain/USA:** 8,270 *(Komma bei Tausendern)* 7.85 *(Punkt bei Dezimalstellen)*
- **Germany:** 8.270 *(Punkt bei Tausendern)* 7,85 *(Komma bei Dezimalstellen)*
- **Britain/USA:** one billion = 1,000,000,000 *(eine Milliarde im Deutschen)*

C Find expressions in the text below that match these definitions.

1 a company that owns and controls a smaller company
2 the office that serves as the administrative centre of a company
3 a company that is owned by another larger company; it has a separate legal form

Proximus Versicherung

Search | Sitemap

Home | About us

History | Operations | Structure

Structure of the Proximus Group

Proximus Versicherung AG is the parent company of the Proximus Group. It holds a majority stake in each of its four subsidiaries:

- Proximus Lebensversicherung AG
- Proximus Krankenversicherung AG
- Süddeutsche Handelsbank AG
- Proximus Bausparkasse AG

Proximus operates 4 regional offices *(Landesdirektionen)* in Germany that report to the company's Head Office in Munich. They are located in Berlin *(LD Ost)*, Hamburg *(LD Nord)*, Cologne *(LD West)* and Stuttgart *(LD Süd)*. Each regional office controls the activities of a certain number of local offices *(Bezirksdirektionen)* that are located in its area.

Apart from Germany, the company operates in the following countries of the European Union: Belgium, Denmark, France, UK, Ireland, Italy, the Netherlands and Poland.

Address: Proximus Versicherung AG, Luisenstraße 7, 80333 München.

KMK **D** Fassen Sie die wesentlichen Inhalte dieses Unternehmensberichts (Seiten 6, 7 und 8) auf Deutsch in der folgenden Tabelle zusammen. Verwenden Sie für Ihre Lösung ein eigenes Blatt.

Proximus Versicherung	
Rechtsform	...
Gründung	...
Historische Entwicklung (Meilensteine)	...
Unternehmenssitz	...
Mitarbeiterzahl	...
Umsatz/Prämieneinnahmen	...
Geschäftsfelder	...
Vertriebswege	...

USEFUL PHRASES Introductions

Introducing yourself

Good morning. My name is Charles Miller. — Nice to meet you (, Mr Miller).

Hello, I'm Claudia Stein from Proximus. — Pleased to meet you (, Ms Stein).

When you introduce yourself to an English-speaking colleague or business partner, give your first name and your surname, not just your surname as in German.

Introducing others

Eva, let me introduce to you Tom Smith. He is head of our London branch office. — It's a pleasure to meet you, Mr Smith.

Frank, this is Anne Wright, our head of Marketing. — Nice to meet you, Ms Wright.

2 The appointment

2 *John Fielding is now in Germany to take part in the training programme organized by Proximus Versicherung. He has just arrived at Proximus' Head Office in Munich.*

A Listen to the CD. Are the following statements true or false? Correct the false ones.

1 John Fielding has got an appointment with Monika Keller at 9.15 a.m.
2 He is staying in an apartment near the city centre.
3 He has never been to Munich before.
4 He has come to Munich for six days to visit a trade fair.
5 Michael Stratner works in the Marketing Department of Proximus.
6 Eva Hagen is the Managing Director of Proximus.
7 John Fielding's training will start at an agency and continue at Head Office later on.
8 John Fielding is introduced to Eva Hagen by Michael Stratner.

INFO Using first names

British and American business partners normally call each other by their first names. Colleagues, in particular, nearly always use first names. One exception, however, is when someone of 'low status' is talking to someone of 'high status'. For example a secretary might call the company CEO (Chief Executive Officer) 'Ms Phillips' but the CEO would call the secretary 'Mary'. Trainees should call senior members of staff by their surname until asked to use their first name.
When using surnames, use *Mr* for a man and *Ms* (pronounced 'Miz') for a woman. Use *Mrs* only if you are sure a woman is married and prefers this form of address. *Miss* is hardly ever used now.

B Which of the following phrases were used in the dialogue?

Introducing yourself

1 I'm John Fielding from Dublin.
2 My name is John Fielding. I'm from Dublin.
3 I'm Monika Keller, Mr Stratner's secretary.

Introducing other people

1 Mr Fielding, let me introduce you to Mrs Hagen.
2 Mr Fielding, I'd like you to meet Mrs Hagen.
3 Mr Fielding, this is Mrs Hagen.

Replying to introductions

1 Pleased to meet you, Mrs Hagen.
2 It's a pleasure to meet you, too, Mr Fielding.
3 Hello, nice to meet you, Mr Fielding.
4 Nice to meet you, too, Mrs Hagen.

3 Meeting visitors on arrival

A Complete the following sentences by using words from the box. Which expression is left over? Form a sentence with it.

on time | worry | late | pleasant | traffic | bags | know | mind | delayed | directions | drive

Apologizing for a delay

VISITOR Sorry I'm …[1]. The traffic here is terrible.

YOU No problem. I …[2] how it is.

VISITOR Sorry to keep you waiting. My flight was …[3] by an hour because of bad weather.

YOU Don't …[4]. I just got here a few minutes ago.

Asking about the journey

YOU How was the flight?

VISITOR The flight was very …[5]. / The flight was rather bumpy.

YOU How was the …[6]? *(If someone comes by car.)*

VISITOR Not so good. The …[7] was terrible.

YOU Did you have any trouble finding us?

VISITOR No, not at all. Your …[8] were very clear.

Offering and asking for help

YOU Can I help you with your …[9]?

VISITOR That would be great, thanks.

VISITOR Would you …[10] taking this?

YOU Not at all. / Of course not.

KMK **B** Work with a partner and role-play the following dialogue.

Student A: You are Klaus Braun. You work for Proximus Insurance. You have to pick up Mr Peabody from the airport. He is taking part in a workshop at your company.
Student B: You are Charles Peabody. You work for a British insurance company.

Klaus Braun	Charles Peabody
Begrüßen Sie Herrn Peabody und stellen Sie sich vor.	Begrüßen Sie Herrn Braun und bedanken Sie sich bei ihm dafür, dass er Sie abholt.
Fragen Sie Herrn Peabody, wie sein Flug war.	Sagen Sie, dass der Flug sehr angenehm war.
Fragen Sie Herrn Peabody, ob Sie ihm beim Tragen seines Gepäcks helfen können.	Bedanken Sie sich und geben Sie Herrn Braun einen Ihrer beiden Koffer.
Sagen Sie Herrn Peabody, dass Sie Ihren Wagen nicht weit von hier geparkt haben.	Fragen Sie Herrn Braun, ob er Sie vor Beginn des Workshops noch kurz ins Hotel bringen könnte.
Sagen Sie Herrn Peabody, dass das kein Problem ist, weil sie noch genug Zeit haben.	

4 Offering hospitality

A Match the questions or comments on the left with the appropriate responses on the right. Some of them have more than one possible answer. Then role-play the dialogue with a partner.

1 Would you like something to drink? / Can I get you something to drink?
2 How do you take your coffee/tea? / How would you like that?
3 Here you are.
4 You're welcome.
5 Help yourself to the biscuits/ cookies *(AE)*.

a Oh, thank you.
b A cup of coffee would be great / very nice.
c With milk/cream *(AE)*. Please.
d Mm, thanks. These look delicious.
e Just a glass of water, thanks.
f Milk and sugar, please.
g No, thanks, I'm fine.
h Just black, thanks.
i --- (no reply)

B What do you offer visitors to eat and drink at your company?

USEFUL PHRASES 'Bitte'

The English translation of the German word 'bitte' depends on the situation:

- *Please* is used in requests or in reply to an offer:
  Sit down, please.
  Another cup of tea? – Yes, please.
- For 'bitte schön' (when you give somebody something) you can say:
  Here you are.
- In reply to 'Dankeschön' you can say:
  You're welcome. / Not at all.

5 A questionnaire

A Interview your neighbour. Ask these questions and take notes.

1 What's your name?
2 Where were you born?
3 Where do you live?
4 How old are you?
5 Do you live on your own?
6 What are your hobbies?
7 What was the last school you attended?
8 Who do you work for?
9 Which department are you working in at the moment?
10 What plans do you have for the future?
11 Have you ever been to an English-speaking country? If yes, where and for how long?

B Now use your notes to present your neighbour to the class.

Example Hello everybody, this is Peter Müller. He was born in Berlin and lives in Nuremberg. …

6 At the agency

3

Mrs Hagen, one of Proximus' agents, and John Fielding are talking in her office.

FIELDING Mrs Hagen, I imagine being an insurance agent must be a rather challenging job. How do you manage to be successful with more and more people buying online?

HAGEN It's true that we face tough competition. But you shouldn't forget that insurance is an invisible product that needs to be explained. Customers often find it rather difficult to compare quotes from different insurers. They're also uncertain about how much cover they really need. So many consumers look for an expert to help them with their insurance needs.

FIELDING But you're not the only insurance expert that offers advice, are you?

HAGEN That's right, Mr Fielding. In our business networking is very important. In addition, you must be able to convince people that they're in safe hands with you. That's why we chose 'Service you can trust' as our motto.

FIELDING So you need to have excellent communications skills ... What about your insurance partner Proximus?

HAGEN A strong insurance partner like Proximus is essential for an agent's success. Proximus has a wide range of competitive products that enable us to offer tailor-made solutions to our customers. As a full service agency we offer personal insurance like motor and life insurance for individuals and various types of business insurance for business clients. In addition, we provide financial services like investment funds and mortgages.

FIELDING That's amazing. I suppose it takes a lot of training and experience to offer such a wide range of products. How do you manage?

HAGEN A single person can't manage it all. You need a team of qualified advisers who specialize in certain areas, so we have four departments in our agency. Claudia Zeller and Thomas Fritsch are responsible for private clients, Frank Wieland is involved in business insurance for business clients and Andrea Schleh deals with financial services. And they all get support from Anika Tauber who is in charge of office administration.

FIELDING What would I need to do to become an adviser in an agency?

HAGEN The usual way is to do a traineeship with an insurance company or insurance agency. The professional training is carried out by the dual system. The sponsoring company deals with the practical aspects and a vocational school provides the theoretical knowledge which is necessary for the qualification. After three years of training the trainees graduate as 'Kaufmann/Kauffrau für Versicherungen und Finanzen'.

FIELDING Oh, that's very interesting. It's different from the system where I come from. Do you have an insurance trainee at the moment?

HAGEN Yes, Stefan Knoll, but he's not in the office today. He goes to his vocational school every Monday.

FIELDING Could he set up his own agency after finishing his training?

HAGEN Yes, he could. But it's hard to survive. In my view you should work for an agent or broker for a few years to gain enough experience before you start your own business.

FIELDING I suppose selling insurance products is the main task of an agent but I'm sure there are other important tasks as well.

HAGEN Certainly, we're also involved in the settlement of claims. We have an agreement with Proximus that entitles us to settle claims up to €1,000. If that's the case, we investigate the claim and pay compensation, on the condition that the loss is covered by the terms of the policy.

FIELDING Does your job involve the collection of the premiums?

HAGEN No, that's organized entirely by the company's Head Office. The policyholder can choose between two methods of payment: either the insurer collects the premiums by direct debit or the policyholder transfers the premium to the insurer's account. …

A Match the German expressions with the highlighted English words in the text.

1 Ausbildung
2 Auszubildender
3 Ausbildungsbetrieb
4 Berufsschule
5 Angebote vergleichen
6 Schäden regulieren
7 Entschädigung
8 Kontakte knüpfen
9 maßgeschneiderte Lösungen
10 Versicherungsschutz

B Answer the following questions on the text.

1 Why do many consumers need expert advice when they buy insurance?
2 What is the agency's motto?
3 Explain the dual system of professional training in Germany.
4 What claims can be settled by the agency?
5 Which methods of payment are mentioned in the dialogue?

C Now do these further activities.

1 Explain the difference between a claim and a premium.
2 Look for an English translation of 'Kaufmann für Versicherungen und Finanzen'.
3 Copy and complete the following organizational chart of the company.

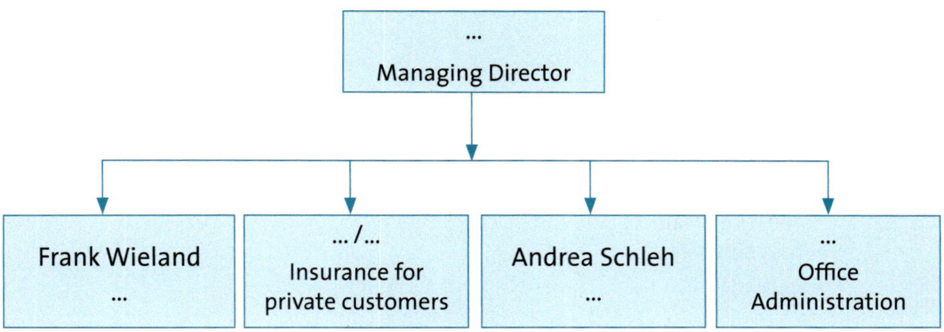

7 Talking about your job

A Use words from the box to complete Thomas Fritsch's description of what he does. Translate the word that is left over into German.

cancel | cancellation | claim | competitor | department | insurance needs | insurance policies | make | personal situation | policyholder (2x) | proposers | quotes | reviewing | settle | solution

My …[1] deals with insurance products for private customers. My job is to sell …[2]. This includes analysing the customers' insurance needs, preparing …[3] and filling in proposal forms. I also take care that …[4] are informed about their rights and duties. Apart from selling policies to new customers, I'm responsible for …[5] existing insurance contracts. Customers often need additional cover if their …[6] changes. Whether a …[7] marries, buys a house or starts their own business, it will affect their …[8]. As we always try to improve our service, it is one of my duties to contact customers who …[9] their policy. There are various reasons for cancelling an insurance policy: maybe the …[10] lost their job, maybe it's because the insurer rejected their …[11] or it's just because they got an attractive quote from a …[12]. I try to find a …[13] that makes the customer change their mind. It is also one of my duties to assist policyholders when they …[14] a claim and to investigate and …[15] claims up to €1,000.

B Work in small groups. Talk about your job:

- What are your duties?
- What do you like and dislike about your job?

Use phrases and words from the box below.

USEFUL PHRASES

Phrases for describing your duties	Adjectives for describing what you like and dislike about your job
My job involves …	interesting – boring
I'm responsible for …	demanding – undemanding
My duties include …	satisfying – unsatisfying
I'm in charge of …	varied – monotonous
Our department deals with …	useful – useless

C The insurance industry offers a lot of interesting jobs. Use the Internet to collect information about the following jobs:

- underwriter
- loss adjuster
- actuary

Explain what they do in about 50 words for each job. Use the useful phrases above.

8 Departments at Head Office

A Match the German expressions with their English equivalents:

1 EDV-Abteilung	a Underwriting Department
2 Marketing und Vertrieb	b Claims Department
3 Rechnungswesen	c Legal Department
4 Rechtsabteilung	d Public Relations Department
5 Schadenabteilung	e Mathematical Department (Actuarial Department)
6 Personalabteilung	f Accounting Department
7 Antragsabteilung	g Sales and Marketing Department
8 Öffentlichkeitsarbeit	h Personnel Department (Human Resources Department)
9 Abteilung Vermögensanlagen	i Information Technology (IT) Department
10 Mathematische Abteilung	j Investment Department

B John Fielding needs further information about Proximus Versicherung. Which department could provide the following information?

1 Last year's premium income and profit
2 Number of employees, demographic details of staff
3 Software and hardware used by the company's agents to advise clients
4 Company's revenues from investments in bonds and shares
5 Cases of insurance fraud the company had to deal with
6 Proximus' channels of distribution in the health insurance business
7 Percentage of life insurance proposals that had to be declined last year
8 Statistics to create a new tariff
9 Campaigns to promote the company's image in the public
10 Last year's claims figures in the motor insurance business

9 Role-play: networking

KMK *Bei dieser Übung sollen Sie versuchen, aufgrund weniger, stichwortartiger Vorgaben ein möglichst freies Gespräch auf Englisch zu führen.*

Partner A: Look at this page. **Partner B:** Look at File 1 on page 130.

Partner A:
Sie nehmen als Auszubildende/r an einer überbetrieblichen Fortbildungsveranstaltung in München teil, die im Hause eines internationalen Versicherungsunternehmens stattfindet. Während der Pause kommen Sie mit einer jungen Schwedin / einem jungen Schweden ins Gespräch. Sie stellen sich kurz vor und unterhalten sich mit ihr/ihm auf Englisch. Ihr Gespräch kann z. B. folgende Punkte umfassen:

- Ihre derzeitigen Aufgaben im Betrieb und Ihr Ausbildungsunternehmen;
- Ihre Freizeitaktivitäten;
- Fragen zum Heimatland des Gesprächspartners / der Gesprächspartnerin bzw. zu seinen/ihren Erfahrungen in Deutschland.

Verabreden Sie sich nach dem Arbeitstag zum Essen. Vereinbaren Sie Ort und Zeit.

Grammar review Simple present and present continuous

1 Stefan **attends** vocational school every Monday.
2 Proximus **has** 8,270 employees.
3 Ms Keller **is** a secretary.
4 Thomas Fritsch **is** just **filling** in a motor insurance proposal form for Mr Miller.
5 Mrs Hagen **owns** an insurance agency.
6 We**'re meeting** Mrs Hagen at 11 o'clock tomorrow morning.

- Das **simple present** *(einfache Gegenwart)* wird für regelmäßig wiederkehrende Handlungen (1) und Vorgänge verwendet. Außerdem dient es zur Beschreibung von Dauerzuständen, Tatsachen (2) und Berufsangaben (3).
- Signalwörter: *usually, normally, regularly, often, every week/month/...*
- Es wird aus der Grundform des Verbs gebildet. In der dritten Person *(he/she/it)* wird *-(e)s* an das Verb angehängt.
- Das **present continuous** *(Verlaufsform der Gegenwart)* wird verwendet, um zeitlich begrenzte Vorgänge oder vorübergehende Handlungen auszudrücken, die im gegenwärtigen Zeitraum stattfinden (4).
- Signalwörter: *just, now, at the moment, while, when, ...*
- Es wird gebildet aus einer Form von *to be* und der *ing*-Form des Vollverbs.
- Einige Verben, die einen Zustand und keine Handlung beschreiben, wie *need, think, know, like, prefer, want, agree, own, possess* usw., stehen in der Regel nicht im **present continuous**, sondern im simple present. (5)
- Das **present continuous** kann auch für Ereignisse in der nahen Zukunft verwendet werden, die fest geplant oder vereinbart sind. Meist erscheint dabei eine Zeitangabe (*next week* usw.) oder ein Fragewort der Zeit (*when* usw.) (6)

10 Practice

Complete these sentences with the correct form of the verb in brackets.

1 You can't speak to Mr Miller this afternoon because he … (negotiate) with a business partner.
2 Motor insurance usually … (amount to) 30% of the company's total premium income but at the moment its share … (decrease) due to the fierce competition.
3 Proximus … (not accept) health insurance applications from proposers who refuse to provide information about their state of health.
4 Agent: Sally, what … (you/do) at the moment?
Sally: I … (prepare) life assurance quotations for a few customers.
Agent: Why … (you/not/attend) the sales meeting at Head Office today?
Sally: I … (think) it's a waste of time.
5 John … (want) to make a claim this week. That's why he … (meet) a loss adjuster tomorrow.
6 … the boss still … (phone) with Head Office?
7 Agent: … (you/would/like) a cup of coffee?
Customer: No, thanks. I'm fine. I never … (drink) coffee late in the afternoon.
8 Peter: What … (you/do)?
John: I … (work) in the insurance industry.

11 Different channels of distribution in the UK

In the early days of the UK insurance industry, insurers hired agents, often on a part-time basis, to acquire business. Some agents, known as tied agents, represented a single company. Others, independent agents, worked for a number of companies. Whereas agents represented insurers, the first duty of brokers was to obtain the best cover for their clients as quickly as reasonably possible. These three distribution channels (tied agents, independent agents and brokers) exist in much the same form today. The generic term for them is intermediaries, because their role lies between the insured and the insurance company.

With the development of information technology alternative distribution channels have sprung up, including the acquisition of insurance by telephone, mail and the Internet. This is called direct selling and enables consumers to purchase insurance policies without the aid of an intermediary. In addition, insurers now use other outlets, such as banks, workplaces, associations and car dealers, to access potential policyholders.

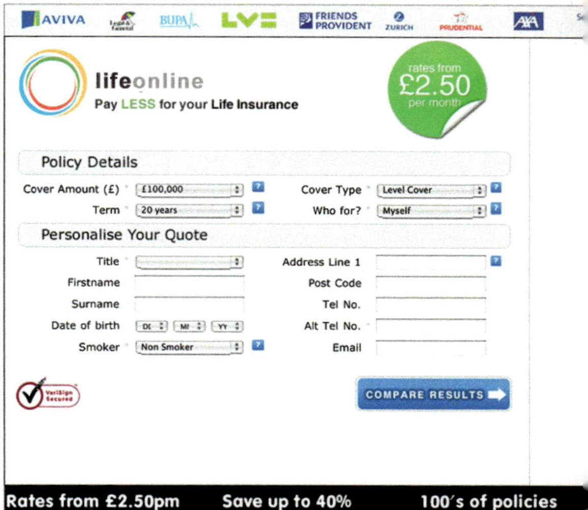

Here are some figures* that show how people's buying habits have changed in the UK insurance industry: In general insurance, the proportion of people buying insurance through brokers fell from 55% in 1997 to 34% in 2007. In contrast, 16% is now sold by banks and building societies – 10 years ago the figure was less than 5%. Direct selling amounted to 31% in 2007, retailers accounted for 10%, 8% was sold by agents.

In the life insurance business, the proportion of people buying insurance through independent financial advisers (brokers) increased from 49% in 1995 to 75% in 2007. In the same period the share of agents decreased, in 2007 it amounted to 19% of life insurance sales and direct selling accounted for the remaining 6%.

Now that insurance products are available on the Internet, online aggregators have begun to appear. Aggregators collect information on prices, generally for motor insurance and term life insurance, which are the most standardized, so that consumers can compare the cost of coverage from one company to another.

* Source: ABI, *UK insurance – key facts*

Answer the following questions.

1 What's the difference between …
  a) an independent and a tied agent? b) an agent and a broker?
2 What is an intermediary?
3 Describe how advances in information technology have influenced distribution channels and outlets of insurers.
4 Compare the trend of broker sales in general insurance with the life business.
5 Describe the importance of direct selling in general insurance and life insurance.
6 Why might consumers use an aggregator when searching for insurance?
7 What channels of distribution does your sponsoring company use?

The insurer and its customers

John Fielding is now working in the Marketing Department at Proximus' Head Office in Munich. Franz Schlemmer, the head of the Marketing Department, asks John to prepare a short presentation of the results of a survey he has just received. 2,400 insurance customers from six European countries took part.

1 Customer attitudes

John's first task is to summarize the following diagram.

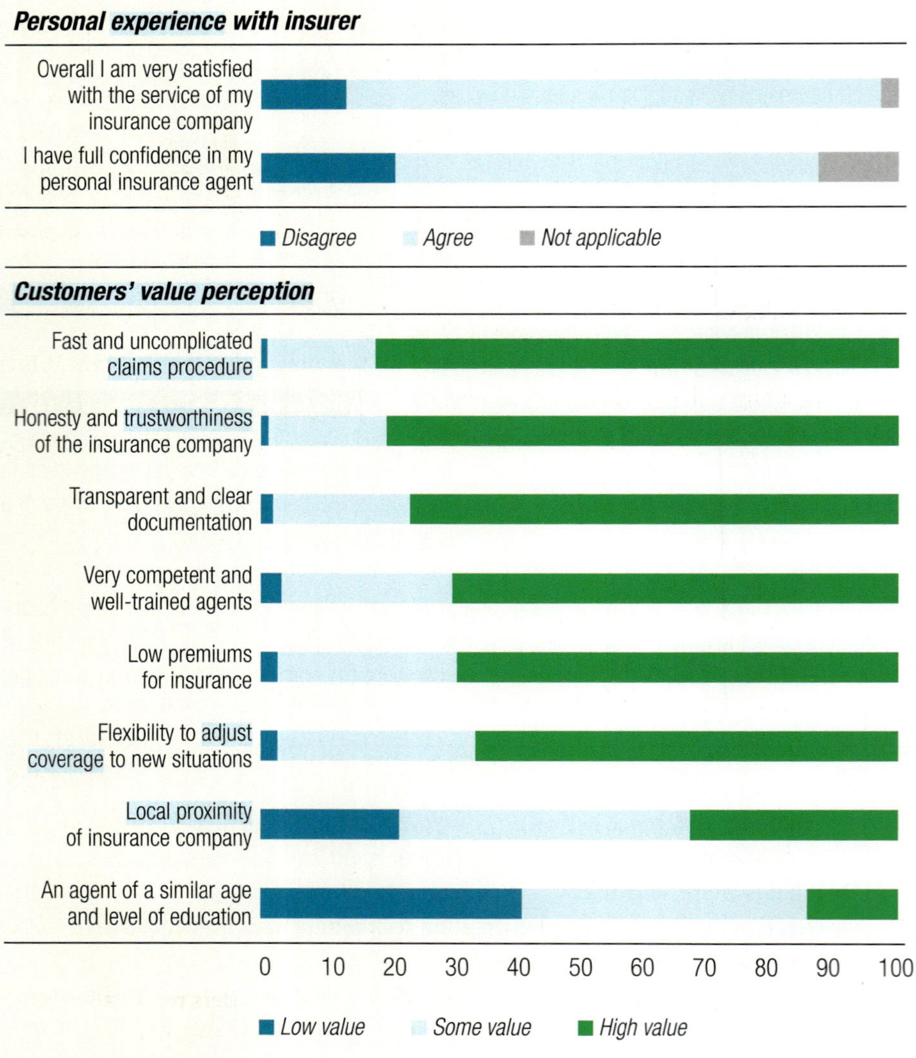

Source: IBM Institute for Business Value and I. VW University of St. Gallen 2007 Insurance Study

A Look at the diagram opposite and decide whether the following statements from John's summary are true or false. Correct the false ones.

1 Most insurance customers are very satisfied with the services of their insurance company but have no confidence in their personal insurance agent.
2 Fast and uncomplicated claims procedures are more important for insurance customers than low premiums.
3 Honesty and trustworthiness of the insurance company rank second in customers' value perception.
4 Most customers think that competent and well-trained agents are as valuable as clear and transparent documentation.
5 More than 40% of the customers place high value on the local proximity of the insurance company.
6 Less than 10% of the customers put little value on the flexibility of their insurance cover.

B Find the highlighted words in the diagram that match these definitions. Which word is left over? Define the word and form a sentence with it.

Example What buyers of a product or service consider to be important and useful.
→ customers' value perception
1 Events which happened to you that influence the way you think and behave.
2 Changing something slightly to make it more suitable for new conditions.
3 What policyholders must do in case of a loss to receive money from their insurer.
4 Being near to a certain place.
5 The quality of being reliable, honest and responsible.

C Now use the words and phrases from **B** to complete these sentences.

1 Mrs Miller decided to change her insurer because her … with her previous insurer had not always been positive.
2 Mr Green had to … his contents insurance policy when he moved to a larger flat.
3 The … of the insurer was ruined when its CEO was arrested by the police for embezzlement.
4 Before the insurance company started to sell motor insurance it tried to find out its … by doing a survey of their attitudes.
5 The … of the contents insurer requires that policyholders report a break-in to their home to the police as soon as possible.
6 With more and more customers using the Internet for information, the … of the insurer has become less important.

2 Customer profiles

John now deals with the different customer types of the survey.

Customer types	What is important for them?
Support-seeking individualists	– look for advice to find out what cover they need – are willing to shop around for transparent, personalized products – trust in people, not in the company
Product optimizers	– want high quality products and convenience – are willing to pay higher prices and provide personal data – need personalized products from a strong company
Uninterested minimalists	– want as little contact with insurers as possible – look for cheap, quick and transparent insurance – buy standardized products
Price-sensitive analysers	– shop around to get the best value for their money – want information about products, but need no advice – buy standardized products
Relationship-oriented traditionalists	– want a trustworthy adviser who tells them what cover they need – prefer to have all insurance with one insurer – want transparent and uncomplicated services

A Match the German expressions with their highlighted English equivalents in the text.

1 Produktoptimierer
2 beziehungsorientierte Traditionalisten
3 Berater/in
4 preissensitive Analysten
5 persönlich zugeschnitten
6 unterstützungssuchende Individualisten
7 desinteressierte Minimalisten
8 sich umsehen nach
9 Komfort

B These statements represent 'the voice of the customer'. Match each one with the customer types in the table above. The first one has been done for you.

Example 'I want competent help for my personal needs.'
→ support-seeking individualist

1 'I want somebody I can trust.'
2 'I want the best bargain.'
3 'I want to be left alone.'
4 'I want a great product.'

C What type of customer are you?

1 What factors are relevant for you when buying insurance? Put them on a list.
2 Number these factors according to your own priorities.
3 Exchange your list with a partner.
4 Check with the table above what type of customer he/she is.
5 Exchange your answers.

Grammar review Comparative and superlative forms of adjectives

1 The percentage of minimalists is **smaller than** that for product optimizers.
2 Our insurance company should offer **simpler** products for traditionalists.
3 Fast claims procedures are **more important than** low premiums.
4 Some customers hunt for **the cheapest** offer.
5 Uninterested minimalists require **as little** contact **as** possible.
6 Price-sensitive analysers shop for **the best** value for their money.

- Alle einsilbigen Adjektive werden mit *-(e)r* und *-(e)st* gesteigert. (1), (4)
- Einzelkonsonanten nach einem kurzen Vokal werden dabei verdoppelt: *big – bigger – the biggest.*
- Zweisilbige Adjektive mit den Endungen *-y*, *-er*, und *-le* werden ebenfalls mit *-(e)r*, und *-(e)st* gesteigert. (2) Dabei wird *-y* in *-i* umgewandelt.
- Alle anderen zwei- und mehrsilbigen Adjektive werden mit *more* und *most* gesteigert. (3)
- Einige Adjektive bilden unregelmäßige Steigerungsformen:

good	***better***	***best*** (6)
bad	***worse***	***worst***
little (wenig)	***less***	***least***
much/many	***more***	***most***

- Vergleiche bildet man mit *than* (= als) (1), (3),und *as ... as* (= so ... wie). (5)

3 Practice

Look at the pie chart and complete these sentences. Choose the right adjective and use the correct form.

1 The UK has got the (small/large) … insurance industry in Europe.
2 Germany's insurance industry is (small/big) … France's.
3 South Korea's premium income is (great/high) … the Netherlands'.
4 The combined premium income of the three (big/fast) … European countries is (little/much) … than the total of premiums written in the United States.
5 Italy's insurance market is twice (large/little) … Canada's.

Breakdown of worldwide premium income by country, 2007

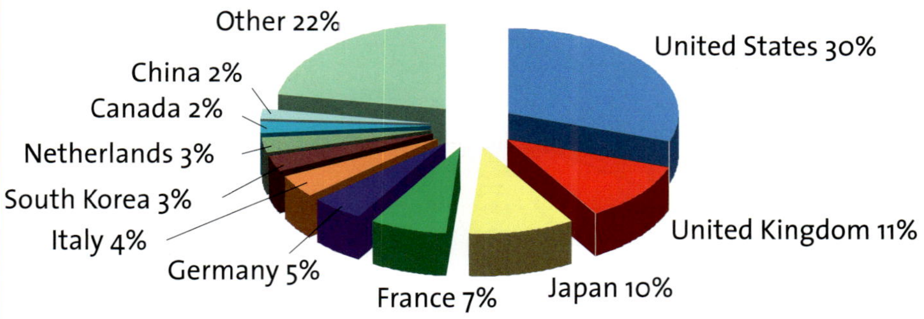

Source: Swiss Re, *Sigma* No 3/2008

USEFUL PHRASES Describing trends

upward movement ↑		horizontal movement →		downward movement ↓	
to rise/grow to go up to increase	from ... to ... by ...%	to keep stable to remain constant to even out	at ...	to fall/drop to go down to decrease	from ... to ... by ...%

You can use adverbs to indicate a degree of change.

small change	medium change	large change
negligibly, slightly	significantly, considerably	sharply, dramatically

4 Describing graphs

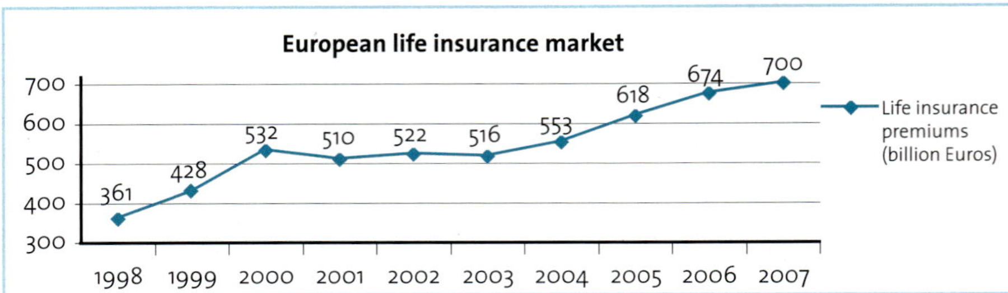

A Look at the line graph and complete the text. There are two more items than you need.

at | between | by | decrease negligibly | drop significantly | from | grow considerably | increase slightly | remain constant | rise sharply | to

As you can see from this chart, in 1998 the total premium income of European life insurers stood ...[1] €361 billion. During the following two years it ...[2] and at the end of 2000 it amounted to €532bn. In 2001 however, life premiums ...[3] to €510bn. Then they ...[4]. But only for one year, because in 2003 life premiums ...[5]. From 2004 onwards the premium income ...[6]. In 2007 the growth rate slowed down, but the premiums still went up ...[7] €26bn ...[8] €674bn ...[9] €700bn.

B Now write your own description of the following line graph.

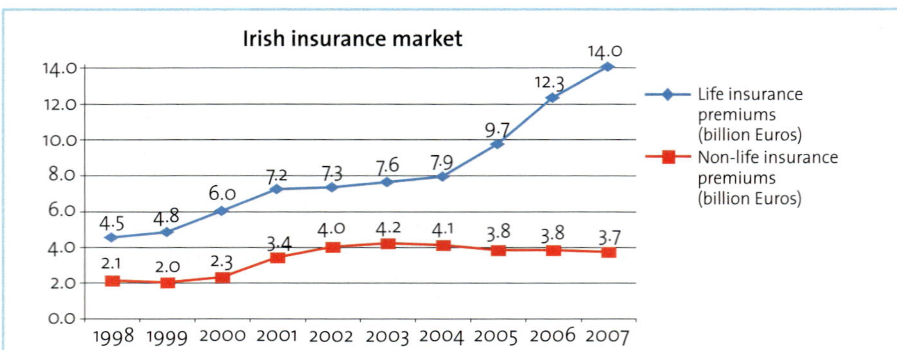

Source: CEA Statistics, *European Insurance in Figures*

5 Role-play: talking about a diagram

Frank Stahl, a colleague, is talking to John Fielding about the insurance study.

KMK Role-play their dialogue with a partner, using the information from the diagram below.

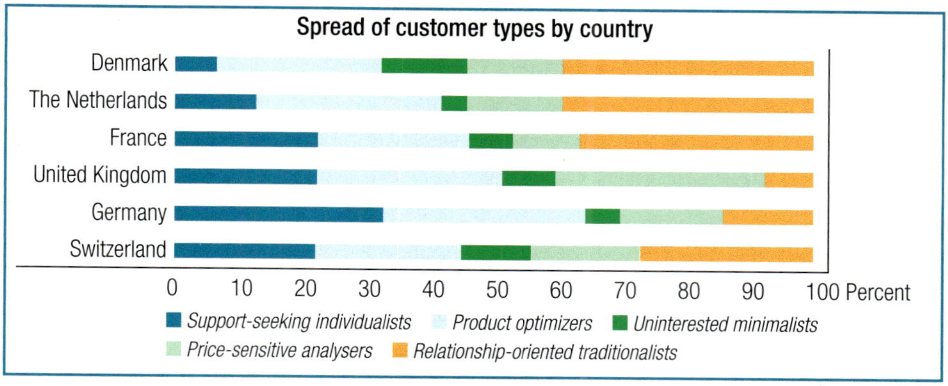

Source: IBM Institute for Business Value and I. VW University of St. Gallen 2007 Insurance Study

Frank Stahl

Begrüßen Sie Ihren Kollegen und fragen Sie, ob er einen Augenblick Zeit für Sie hat. Sie haben eine Frage zu der Studie, die sich mit verschiedenen Kundentypen beschäftigt.

John Fielding

Begrüßen Sie Ihren Kollegen und fragen Sie, was er wissen möchte.

Frank Stahl

Fragen Sie, ob die fünf Kundentypen in allen sechs Länder die gleiche Bedeutung haben.

John Fielding

Sagen Sie, dass die Verteilung der einzelnen Kundentypen in den sechs Ländern stark voneinander abweicht.

Frank Stahl

Bitten Sie ihn, ein Beispiel hierfür zu geben.

John Fielding

Erklären Sie ihm, dass in Frankreich der beziehungsorientierte Traditionalist das größte Kundensegment darstellt, während er im Vereinigten Königreich (UK) das kleinste Segment ist.

Frank Stahl

Fragen Sie, ob die Briten wohl mehr auf den Preis achten als die Franzosen.

John Fielding

Bejahen Sie und verweisen Sie darauf, dass der preissensitive Analyst dort die größte Kundengruppe darstellt. Auch Produktoptimierer gibt es dort viele.

Frank Stahl

Fragen Sie, welcher Kundentyp in Deutschland am häufigsten anzutreffen ist.

John Fielding

Sagen Sie ihm, dass es der unterstützungssuchende Individualist ist.

Frank Stahl

Sagen Sie, dass in Deutschland offenbar vielen Menschen die gute Beratung durch einen Experten wichtiger ist als niedrige Prämien. Verabschieden sie sich.

John Fielding

Stimmen Sie Ihrem Kollegen zu und verabschieden sich ebenfalls.

6 Language of presentations

The following list contains useful phrases for giving a presentation. Copy the table below and fill in the appropriate phrases from the list.

Welcoming the audience	Introducing your topic	Structuring the presentation	Moving to the next point	Describing visuals	Dealing with questions	Conclusion (summarizing points)
…	…	…	…	…	…	…

1 I'd like to finish my presentation with …
2 If you have any questions, please feel free to interrupt …
3 As you can see from the graph/chart/diagram/table …
4 If you have any questions, I'd prefer to take them at the end …
5 The purpose/objective/aim of my presentation is to …
6 This pie chart shows … You can see that the biggest segment indicates the …
7 Hello everyone. It's good to see you all here …
8 I have divided my talk into three main parts. Part one deals with …, part two …, part three …
9 To sum up, …
10 And now, let's move on to the next step/stage/point.
11 Ladies and gentlemen, I would like to welcome you to this presentation.
12 I'd prefer to answer any questions after finishing my presentation.
13 Let's now take a look at … / Now let's turn to …
14 Good morning/afternoon, ladies and gentlemen. It's nice to have you with us.
15 Today I'm going to talk about …
16 My presentation consists of three parts. I'll begin with …, then move on to … and after that I'll tell you …
17 And finally, … / In conclusion, …
18 I'd like to draw your attention to this organizational chart.

7 John's presentation

John Fielding is now giving his presentation to the Marketing Department.

4

A Listen to the presentation, choose the correct answers (1–3) and complete the notes (4).

1 What are the three parts of John Fielding's presentation?
  a personal experiences, success factors and conclusions
  b customer types, attitudes and customers' value perceptions
  c customer types, success factors and conclusions

2 What are the two most important customer groups in Germany?
  a product optimizers and price-sensitive analysers
  b product optimizers and support-seeking individualists
  c price-sensitive analysers and support-seeking individualists
  d relationship-oriented traditionalists and support-seeking individualists

3 What is the combined share of these two customer groups in Switzerland?
  a 65%
  b 45%
  c 35%

4 Complete the following notes.

- Success factors for the relationship are trust, transparency and ...[1]
- How to build up trust? Insurers need to be ...[2] in case of a claim.
- Transparency: Customers expect brief and ...[3] information about range of ...[4], exclusions and prices
- Technology: Insurers should use the Internet to ...[5] trust and transparency.
- Conclusions: Targeting a certain customer group in different European countries:
  - Which success factors are ...[6] for this customer group?
  - How can we ...[7] these factors effectively?
  - What are the ...[8]?

B Which phrases does John Fielding use for the following?

1 introducing the topic of his presentation
2 structuring his presentation
3 moving to the next point
4 describing visuals
5 dealing with questions

8 Tips for delivering a presentation

1 Practise your presentation. Practising builds your confidence and enables you to check your timing. Practise your presentation in front of friends or colleagues to get constructive feedback.

2 Watch your language. Keep it simple. Avoid jargon or, if not possible, define the new words and expressions. Check the pronunciation and spelling of difficult words beforehand.

3 Use your voice effectively. Speak clearly and loudly enough for everyone in the room to hear you. Do not speak too fast. If you vary the volume, pitch and pace of your voice, you will keep the audience interested.

4 Make eye contact with your audience. Don't talk to your prompt card, your feet or the back wall. Address the audience. When pointing out aspects of PowerPoint slides / OHP transparencies, be conscious of where you are standing: try to avoid turning your back on the audience.

5 Watch your body language. Use non-verbal signals like facial expressions and hand gestures to reinforce your message. Avoid negative body language such as crossed arms or clenched fists.

6 Use visual aids like graphs, flow charts and pictures to make your presentation more interesting. Take time to explain charts. Make sure that everyone in the room can read the text on your slides: Choose a font size that is sufficiently large, use contrasting colours for text and background and limit the number of words on the slides. Remember that you are the focus of the presentation. The slides are only meant to support you.

A Which of the tips do you find most useful? Can you add any other tips?

KMK **B** Übertragen Sie diese Tipps sinngemäß ins Deutsche.

9 Your presentation

Prepare a short presentation about one of the following topics:
- your training company
- a product of your company
- important factors for buying insurance

Use presentation phrases from exercise 6 and the tips from exercise 8.

10 Discussion

Form a group and discuss these comments on the insurance business.
- 'Insurance is something that you have to have and hopefully never have to use.'
- 'Agents sell the products with the highest profits for themselves and not what customers really need.'
- 'Insurance is, by nature, not a "sexy" product.'

USEFUL PHRASES How to express your opinion

In my opinion, ...	In my view, ...	I would say (that) ...
The way I see it, ...	From my point of view, ...	I believe (that) ...

11 Insurance fraud

Insurance fraud is a crime that costs Americans at least $80 billion a year, the Coalition Against Insurance Fraud estimates. 10 percent of all property and accident insurance claims are fraudulent, according to the National Insurance Crime Bureau (NICB).

Insurance fraud occurs when people deceive an insurance company to receive claim payments or to lower premiums. Insurance crimes vary in severity. Here are a few examples of common types of insurance fraud:

- Putting false information on an insurance application: A car owner understates how many miles he annually drives to lower his premium;
- Inflating a claim (also called 'padding'): A homeowner exaggerates the value of the stereo equipment that was stolen during a burglary.
- Faking a claim: An insured gets a disability pension because of an invented injury.
- Staging an automobile accident: Crime gangs cause intentional collisions with innocent drivers to get claim payments for non-existent passengers who they say suffered whiplash, loss of earnings, etc.

You might think insurance fraud is only committed by crooks and organized crime rings. Actually, many normally honest people tell 'little white lies' when they apply for insurance or make a claim. They may not even think this is real insurance fraud. Studies show that one in three Americans believe it is 'all right' to pad claims to make up for premiums paid in previous years when they had no claims.

A lot of people think insurance fraud is a victimless crime. It isn't. The real victims of insurance fraud are not insurance companies, but policyholders who have to pay higher premiums. In addition prices of consumer goods and services keep rising because businesses pass the higher costs of their employees' health insurance and business insurance on to their customers. NICB estimates that the average American household pays an additional $200 to $300 in insurance premiums every year to cover the cost of fraud. The 'hidden fraud tax' paid in the form of higher prices for goods and services may increase the cost to about $1,000 per year, per family.

Insurance fraud is widespread for various reasons:

- Insurers sometimes back off: Some companies encourage fraud by paying suspicious claims too easily. These companies believe it's cheaper to pay some smaller suspicious claims than fight them in court.
- Low-risk crime: Swindlers view insurance fraud as an easy crime with little risk of getting caught.
- Low legal priority: Prosecutors often give top priority to fighting drugs, violence and other high-profile crimes.
- People tolerate fraud: Too many consumers believe insurance fraud is justified. One in three Americans wouldn't report insurance fraud by someone they know, according to a study conducted by Progressive Insurance.

A Answer the questions on the text.

1 Explain the difference between 'inflating a claim' and 'faking a claim'.
2 Why do normally honest people commit insurance fraud?
3 Who pays for insurance fraud and how much do they pay?
4 What is the 'hidden fraud tax'?
5 The text mentions four reasons for insurance fraud. Which of them do you think is the most important? Give a reason.

B Form a group. Collect ideas on how insurers can fight insurance fraud and present them to the class.

Contents and buildings insurance

Anton Reiser works for a German retail chain with a network of branches in the UK. He is about to move from Nuremberg to Exeter, where his company has a branch office. He has rented a house in Exeter and now he is looking for contents insurance. He requests a quote from a local insurance broker.

1 An email from a broker

From: ian.redfield@sw-insurance-experts.co.uk
To: anton.reiser67@net-train.de
Subject: Request for a quote

Dear Mr Reiser

Thank you for your enquiry about contents insurance. We use a panel of over 30 top insurance companies to find you the best deal. In order for us to provide a quote we need further details of your home. Please complete the enclosed application form to the best of your knowledge and return it asap.

The second attachment is a table to help you to calculate the level of cover correctly.
Please work out, room by room, the replacement cost of your belongings at current prices and enter it in the space provided. Then add up the entries to calculate the sum insured.

It is very important that you take time to calculate the sum insured carefully. If the figure is too low, you will be under-insured – meaning that any claims you make will not be paid in full. If it is too high, you will be over-insured and pay too much for your contents insurance.

We look forward to welcoming you as a customer. If you have any questions, do not hesitate to contact us.

Best wishes
Ian Redfield
Southwest Insurance Experts

A Answer these questions on the email.

1 What is attached to the email?
2 What does Ian Redfield want Anton Reiser to do next?
3 Why is it important to calculate the sum insured correctly?
4 What does the abbreviation 'asap' mean?

B Work with a partner and answer these questions.

1 What information do you need to prepare a quote for contents insurance in Germany? Make a list.
2 How do German insurers calculate the sum insured for contents insurance (standard procedure)?

2 Email and website addresses

A How do you say each of these symbols?

1	@	2	.	3	/
4	\	5	-	6	_

dot | hyphen (dash) | slash | underscore | backslash | at

B Practise spelling Ian Redfield's and Anton Reiser's email addresses.

C Now work with a partner.
Partner A: Look at File 2 on page 130. **Partner B:** Look at File 11 on page 133.

D Read the information below. Which style does Ian Redfield use in his email? Why?

INFO Formal and informal emails

Business emails can have a *formal style* or an *informal style*. The formal style is similar to a standard business letter and is used in emails to somebody outside your company or whom you do not know very well. The informal style can be used for emails within your company and to people whom you know well. The style is much closer to spoken than to written English.

Salutation and close

Style	Salutation	Close
Formal	• Dear Mrs/Ms/Mr Smith • Dear Kathy *(after you have had contact)*	• Yours sincerely *(very formal in emails)* • (Best) Regards / Best wishes *(can be used in formal and informal emails)*
Informal	• Hi/Hello Peter • Peter *(recipient's name only)*	• Bye / All the best / Best regards • Anne *(sender's name only)*

Contractions
When writing formal emails, do not use contractions, such as *I'm, she hasn't, you'll, they've, etc.* Write them out in full (*I am, she has not, you will, they have ...*)

Abbreviations
Informal emails may contain abbreviations like *pls* (= *please*), *rgds* (= *regards*), *cu* (= *see you*). In a formal business email you should avoid too many abbreviations.

Emoticons
Emoticons, e.g. :-) for 'I'm happy (smiley face)', are only used in informal emails. They are written forms of body language or gestures.

Vocabulary
Informal emails sound more like spoken English than formal emails.

Formal	Informal
Thank you.	Thanks.
I am writing to inform you ...	Just a quick note to tell you ...
I would like to apologize for ...	Sorry for ...
I would appreciate it if you could ...	Can you ...
I am looking forward to your reply.	Hope to hear from you soon.

3 An email from a colleague

> Hi Ian
>
> Just a quick note to tell you that Mr Reiser called today. He's got some questions regarding his application for contents ins. which he'd like to discuss with you. Pls call him back on Tues. The number is 7456012. See you soon.
>
> Rgds
> Sally

A Which style does Sally use in her email? Why?

B What do the abbreviations in her email mean?

4 Over to you

Write an email for each of the following situations.

1 Your customer Alan Burton has mentioned in an email that he is going to move from Erlangen to Berlin. Write an email to Mr Burton based on the following prompts:
- address and size (m^2) of new flat?
- sum insured and premium of contents insurance need to be adjusted

2 Your customer Mrs Sloane wants to know whether her cat is covered by contents insurance. Write an email to answer this question based on the following prompts:
- cover only for injuries or death due to insured perils
- limit for veterinary expenses: replacement cost of a similar cat

3 Write an informal email to your colleague Thomas based on the following prompts:
- Sarah Fletcher called
- policy number: 3477592
- burst pipe caused water damage in her kitchen
- call her to arrange meeting for assessment of damage asap

INFO Writing emails

Subject line
Write a clear and concise title that describes the email's content.

Email body
Keep messages short and to the point. Include only one idea per paragraph and separate the paragraphs with breaks. The email body always starts with a capital letter.

Style
Don't mix styles in the same email. When you write to a customer for the first time, use the formal style. If the customer answers in the informal style, you can use the same register.

Signature
Include a professional signature with every business email. The signature should include:
- Your name
- Your company
- Your contact information

In Britain women often add *(Miss)* or *(Mrs)* in brackets after their name if they wish to be addressed in this way.

Attachment
Any kind of file that you send with an email is called an attachment.

5 Standard contents insurance policies

What is covered?

In insurance terms, home contents means anything that isn't a fixed feature of your home; or to put it another way – the contents of your home are the things you take with you when you move. Contents insurance protects you against damage or loss of these things, for example your clothing, furniture, carpets, curtains and domestic appliances. It also includes valuables like jewellery, pictures and other works of art, articles made from gold and silver, and money in the home up to a certain limit.

What you are covered for

Contents insurance provides cover against a long list of perils. The most common of these are loss or damage caused by ...

- fire, explosion, lightning, earthquake;
- storm or flood;
- burglary or attempted burglary;
- malicious damage;
- subsidence or heave;
- collision involving an aircraft or vehicles or animals;
- falling trees or television and radio aerials (including satellite dishes);
- water escaping from any fixed water or heating installation or domestic appliance;
- oil escaping from a tank or pipe.

Contents insurance also usually covers (up to certain limits):

- contents temporarily removed to another home (for example when your children are at university);
- accidental damage to stereo equipment, TVs, computers, DVD players and any fixed glass in furniture (e.g. a glass tabletop);
- your legal liability as occupier of the house, e.g. if a visitor has an accident and injures themselves;
- the cost of alternative accommodation if you can't live in your home because of damage (e.g. fire, flooding, etc);
- replacement door locks and keys if your keys are lost or stolen;
- contents in the garden, e.g. a lawn mower or a barbecue;
- loss of food if a freezer or fridge breaks down;
- contents in outbuildings like garden sheds and garages.

Some contents insurers offer a temporary increase of 10% in your contents sum insured for special occasions such as weddings and Christmas to make sure the gifts are protected.

Policy excesses

When you are considering a contents insurance policy, check the excesses that apply to the policy. The excess is the amount you pay towards a claim on your policy. Most insurers specify a compulsory amount, for example £25, but you can choose to pay an additional voluntary excess if you want to reduce the premium.

New-for-old cover versus indemnity cover

Many insurers offer contents insurance policies which provide new-for-old cover on most items, except for less durable things like clothes and linen. With new-for-old cover the insurer either pays the full cost of repairing damaged items or pays to replace them with equivalent new items if they're stolen or destroyed.

If you want to save money on your contents insurance, some insurers offer cover on an indemnity basis: that is, the policyholder is compensated for the actual value of the damaged item. This takes into account the cost of wear and tear when an item is replaced.

Premiums for indemnity cover are lower, but you only receive a portion of the cost of replacing damaged or lost items when a claim is paid.

A The words (1–12) are all from the text on page 31. Match them with their definitions (a–k). Define the word left over.

1 excess	**a** a machine that is used for a particular purpose in the home, e.g. fridge
2 compulsory	**b** a principle of insurance by which policyholders are put in the same financial position after a loss as they were before the loss occurred.
3 accidental	**c** a flash of very bright light in the sky caused by electricity
4 burglary	**d** sinking of the ground on which your house stands
5 peril	**e** a place to live or stay, e.g. a hotel room
6 wear and tear	**f** damage to your home or household goods that someone causes intentionally
7 domestic appliance	**g** the crime of breaking and entering into another person's building with the intent to steal
8 lightning	**h** happening unexpectedly, not planned by the insured
9 indemnity	**i** damage to things that is the result of normal use
10 accommodation	**j** when something must be done because of a law or a rule
11 malicious damage	**k** something that causes danger to your property, a risk
12 subsidence	**l** …

B Use words from exercise **A** to complete the following sentences.

1 Fire and storm are … which are covered by contents insurance.
2 When you claim on an indemnity policy you have to accept a reduction for … .
3 It is … for all motorcyclists to wear helmets.
4 The large cracks in the walls of our house are due to … .
5 The burglars used paint to cause a lot of … because they didn't find any money.
6 After the fire in my flat, the insurer paid for two weeks of alternative … in a hotel.
7 He died when he was struck by … .
8 Our company sells washing machines, freezers and other … .
9 I agreed to a voluntary … of £100 in my policy.

C Are the following statements about the text true or false? Correct the false ones.

1 Contents insurance does not provide new-for-old cover for clothing.
2 With indemnity policies the insured gets the full amount to replace a damaged item as new.
3 You can save insurance premiums by increasing the excess of your policy.
4 Standard contents policies cover you for water leaking from a dishwasher.
5 Your insurer doesn't pay for your temporary stay in a hotel if your home is destroyed by an earthquake.
6 Most standard contents policies cover you if gardening tools are stolen from your garden.
7 Your contents insurer only pays for replacement door locks if your keys are stolen but not if you lose them.

D Compare the elements of a British standard contents policy with a standard policy of your company. Make a list of the differences and exchange it with a partner.

6 Types of buildings

A

B

C

E

D

F

Match the definitions to the pictures.

1 A detached house is a building that is not joined to another house.
2 A semi-detached house is joined to another house.
3 A terraced house is a house that is one of a row of houses that are joined together on each side.
4 A flat (*AE* apartment) is a set of rooms for living in, including a kitchen, usually on one floor of a building.
5 A bungalow is a house built on one level, without stairs.
6 A block of flats (*AE* apartment building) is a tall building that contains flats.

INFO Different types of flats (*AE* apartments)

- A **maisonette** is a flat with rooms on two floors within a building (usually with its own entrance at street level).
- A **studio flat** consists of one main room for living, cooking, dining and sleeping. The bathroom is often in its own smaller room.
- A **loft** is a flat in a former factory or warehouse that has been made suitable for living in.
- A **penthouse** is an expensive and comfortable flat on the top floor of a tall building.

People may rent a flat from a landlord or buy it. If the flat is owned by the people living in it, it is called an **owner-occupied** flat (*AE* **condominium/condo**).

7 Cover for a new home

After a year in Britain Anton Reiser decides to buy a house. He rings his insurance broker for advice on buildings insurance.

5

A Listen to the phone call and answer these questions.

1 What type of insurance does Anton Reiser need?
2 What type of building is his new house?
3 What is his new address?
4 How many quotes will Ian Redfield get for him?
5 Give one example for each of the following:
- an outbuilding;
- a permanent fixture of the building.

6 How can you find out the rebuilding cost of your home?
7 What's the name and number of the chartered surveyor?

B Make a list of the questions you need to ask to get all the relevant information for a buildings insurance quote.

C Listen to the phone call again and complete these sentences from the dialogue.

1 Sally Wickham … . How can I … you?
2 Good morning. … is Anton Reiser. I'd like to … to Mr Redfield.
3 May I … what it's …?
4 … the line, please, I'll … you … to Mr Redfield.
5 Could you … the postcode, please? I didn't … it.
6 Could you … his surname for me, please?

8 Using telephone phrases

Use the box on telephoning on page 35 to find polite phrases for these situations.

Example You don't know the caller's name.
→ Could you give me your name, please?

1 The caller is speaking too quietly.
2 The caller is speaking too fast.
3 You didn't hear the caller's address clearly.
4 You don't know how to write the caller's name.
5 You want the caller's telephone number.
6 You aren't sure what the caller is phoning about.
7 You aren't sure if the caller wants to leave a message.

INFO Telephone numbers

When you give someone your telephone number, say each digit separately, except for double digits: e.g. 0911 74339 = oh (*AE* zero) nine double-one seven four double-three nine.
area code = *Vorwahl*
extension = *Durchwahl/Apparat*
mobile phone (*AE* cell phone) = *Mobiltelefon/Handy*
landline = *Festnetz(leitung)*

USEFUL PHRASES Telephoning

Making a call

Identifying yourself

(Hello,) this is Patricia Swan.
It's Bob Smith from GLS Insurance here.
(**Not:** Here is Bob Smith ...)

Explaining the reason for the call

I'm calling about ...
I have a question about ...
Could you give me some information about ...?

Asking for somebody

Could I speak to Mr/Ms Smith please?
Could you put me through to Mr/Ms Huber on extension 245 please?
Could you put me through to your claims department?

When the person is not available

What time will he/she be back?
When could I reach him/her?
I'll call back later.
Can I leave a message for him/her?
Can you ask him/her to call me back?

Giving your name and number

My name is Jane Cooper. I'm calling from Proximus and my number is 8439.
It's John Miller and I'm on 3124455.

Ending the call

Speak to you soon. Bye.
Goodbye. / Bye now.

Receiving a call

Identifying yourself and your company

Proximus Versicherung. Klaus Müller speaking.
How can I help you?
What can I do for you?
Could you tell me what it's about?

Asking for the caller's name

May I ask who's calling, please?
Could you give me your name, please?

Making the connection

Hold the line, please. I'll put you through.
I'm afraid his/her line is engaged/busy.
Shall I give you his/her extension number?
Would you like to hold/wait or shall I ask him/her to call you back?

When the person is not available

I'm afraid he/she is in a meeting / on a business trip / not in the office at the moment.
Can I give him/her a message?
Would you like to leave a message?
Shall I ask him/her to call you back?
Would you like to call back later?
I'll tell him/her you called.

Checking the message

Let me just read that back to you. That's 8439.
Let me just make sure that I got it right.

Ending the call

Goodbye Mr/Ms Smith. Thank you for calling.

Dealing with difficulties

Could you spell your name, please?
Could you speak a bit more slowly, please?
I think you must have dialled the wrong number.
I'm sorry, I must have the wrong number
Could you speak up a bit, please?
This is a really bad line. I can hardly understand you.
Sorry, I didn't catch (get) that. Could you repeat that, please?
Sorry, we got cut off. Where were we?

9 Making phone calls

A Put the sentences in the correct order.

a I see. Well, what time can I reach her?
b OK. Could you spell your surname, please?
c Southwest Insurance brokers, Sally Wickham speaking. Can I help you?
d Thank you for calling. Goodbye.
e I'm afraid she is out of the office at the moment.
f From about 4 p.m. in the afternoon. Would you like to leave a message?
g Goodbye.
h Yes. Could you just say that I called and that I'll call again later this afternoon?
i Good morning. This is Arthur Timperley of Rochester Consulting. Could I speak to Patricia Eden, please?
j Of course. It's T-I-M-P-E-R-L-E-Y.

KMK **B** Role-play this telephone conversation with a partner in English.

Southwest Insurance experts

- Melden Sie sich mit dem Namen der Firma sowie Ihrem eigenen und fragen Sie, was Sie für den Kunden tun können.
- Fragen Sie nach der Versicherungsscheinnummer des Kunden.
- Bitten Sie den Kunden, die Nummer zu wiederholen und dabei etwas langsamer zu sprechen.
- Fragen Sie, was der Kunde wissen möchte.
- Sagen Sie dem Kunden, dass Sie ihn nicht verstehen können und bitten Sie ihn, etwas lauter zu sprechen.
- Antworten Sie dem Kunden, dass er bei einem Selbstbehalt von £300 einen Beitragsrabatt von 20 % erhalten würde.
- Sagen Sie dem Kunden, dass Sie seinen Vertrag ändern und ihm eine neue Beitragsrechnung *(premium statement)* zuschicken werden.
- Verabschieden Sie sich.

Customer

- Melden Sie sich mit Ihrem Namen und sagen Sie, dass Sie eine Frage zu ihrer Wohngebäudeversicherung haben.
- Geben Sie (schnell) Ihre Versicherungsnummer an: 25693133 BI
- Wiederholen Sie die Nummer langsam und deutlich.
- Fragen Sie (ganz leise), welchen Rabatt Sie auf ihren Versicherungsbeitrag erhalten, wenn Sie einen Selbstbehalt vereinbaren.
- Wiederholen Sie Ihre Frage in ausreichender Lautstärke.
- Sagen Sie, dass Sie mit diesem Selbstbehalt einverstanden wären.
- Bedanken Sie sich und verabschieden Sie sich.

10 A policy summary

A Complete the policy summary of Anton Reiser's buildings insurance using words from the box. One word is used twice.

garden sheds | claim | subsidence | drilling | roofs | including | fixtures | accommodation | repairing

Buildings Insurance

Proximus UK

What is covered?

- Your home and its walls, …[1] drives, patios.
- Permanent …[2] such as kitchen units, bathroom fittings, fitted wardrobes.
- Outbuildings including …[3] and garages.

What you are covered for

- Fire
- Burglary
- Storm or flood
- …[4]
- Malicious damage
- Escape of water
- Your legal liability as a homeowner, up to £2 million

Additional benefits included as standard

- The cost of alternative …[5] while insured repairs are carried out. The most we will pay for a …[6] is £25,000.
- Emergency entries – The cost of …[7] damage caused by the emergency services if they have to break into your home as the result of a family emergency. The most we will pay for a …[8] is £1,000.

Accidental damage cover (optional extra)

- Accidental damage to your home, …[9] underground drains, pipes and cables.
- Accidental breakage of things like fixed glass and sanitary fittings as well as accidents like …[10] into a water pipe, or putting your foot through the loft floor.

B You work in the claims department of Proximus UK. Use the policy summary above to answer the customers' questions.

CALL 1: Mr Richard's small garden shed was destroyed by fire last night. He also lost two deck chairs which he kept in the garden shed. He would like to know whether his buildings insurance compensates him for the damage.

CALL 2: Ms Johnson has got a standard buildings insurance policy with your company. Yesterday her washbasin in the bathroom broke when she accidentally dropped a heavy vase. She wants to know whether her policy includes the breakage of the washbasin.

CALL 3: A flood has damaged Mr Ferguson's house so badly that he needs another place to stay until repairs have been made. He would like to know whether his standard policy covers him for the damage to the house and the cost of accommodation in a hotel. (If yes, is there a limit?)

Grammar review **Simple past and past continuous**

1 A vandal **broke** the patio door and **smashed** the mirror in the bathroom last night.
2 When I **entered** the room, the curtain **was burning**.
3 While Mr Miller **was filling** in the claims form, his wife **was estimating** the value of the stolen goods.

- Das **simple past** (einfache Vergangenheit) wird verwendet, um über Handlungen zu berichten, die in der Vergangenheit abgeschlossen wurden (1). Signalwörter: *yesterday, last month, in 1988, two years ago*, usw.
- Das **simple past** der regelmäßigen Verben setzt sich zusammen aus dem Infinitiv des Verbs + *-(e)d*. (Siehe Liste der unregelmäßigen Verben auf S. 167.)
- Mit dem **past continuous** (Verlaufsform der Vergangenheit) beschreibt man eine Handlung, die schon in Gang war, als eine andere gerade einsetzte (2). Es beschreibt auch zwei Handlungen, die gleichzeitig in der Vergangenheit abliefen (3).
- Das **past continuous** wird gebildet aus *was/were* + *ing*-Form des Verbs.

11 Practice

Put the verbs in brackets into the simple past or the past continuous.

1 Last night a thief … (get) into Mr Miller's house through an open window. He … (steal) some money from a drawer in the bedroom and … (leave) the house through the back door.
2 After the flooding of Mr Grey's house, the cleaning-up and restoration work … (take) three months. While the workmen … (repair) the damage he … (stay) at a hotel.
3 Mrs Cooper … (cook) a meal when a storm … (cause) a power cut.
4 When the fire brigade … (arrive), the policyholder and his wife … (try) to extinguish the fire in the kitchen.
5 What … (you/do) when the car … (crash) into your home?
6 The insurer … (not indemnify) Mr Heath for the spilled paint on the carpet because his policy … (not include) accidental damage cover.

12 A burglary

KMK *Aufgrund der stichwortartigen Vorgaben in Ihrer Rollenkarte sollen Sie ein möglichst freies Telefongespräch auf Englisch führen.*

Work with a partner.
Partner A: Look at this page.
Partner B: Look at File 8 on page 132.

Partner A:
Sie sind der Versicherungnehmer/in bei dem/der eingebrochen wurde. Sie waren über das Wochenende bei Freunden zu Besuch, bei der Rückkehr bemerkten Sie, dass in Ihr Haus eingebrochen worden ist. Sie melden der Proximus Versicherung den Schaden telefonisch. Wichtige Themen dieses Gespräches könnten sein: Was wurde gestohlen? Wie kamen die Täter ins Haus? Wurden Einrichtungsgegenstände oder Gebäudeteile beschädigt? Wurde die Polizei verständigt. Erfinden Sie erforderliche Daten wie z. B. Policennummern, Adressen und sonstige persönliche Daten.

13 Cutting costs on home insurance

When searching for the best home insurance cover, the quote you receive is dependent on your circumstances and the amount of cover you need. However, there are ways to reduce the cost of your policy without leaving yourself short of cover. Here are some possibilities.

Cutting the risk

One of the best ways to reduce your home insurance premium is to cut the risk of the insurer having to pay out. This can be done in a number of ways:

- Security measures to reduce theft risk – Fit a burglar alarm, change locks, install time-switch lights, join a neighbourhood watch scheme, install security lighting, etc. Standard alarms can get you up to a 7.5% discount.
- Reduce fire risk – Fit and maintain smoke alarms.
- Increase the standard policy excess – If you are willing to cover more of the cost of any claim then you will reduce your home insurance premium.
- No claims – The fewer the claims, the lower your premium. Also see which home insurance companies offer a no claims discount. This can save you up to 20% on your premiums.

Do your research

The best way to cut the cost of your home insurance is to get the best deal available. To do this, you will need to shop around. Using a price comparison website will save you time, effort and money.

This does not mean, however, that you should simply accept the cheapest quote you find. The reputation of an insurance provider is also very important, so you should be prepared to pay a bit more if an insurer is recommended by a friend or family member.

Another way to cut your home insurance premium might be to move house. A nationwide survey by the AA showed premiums could differ by 300% depending on where you live. Moving away from these postcode hotspots might be the best way to cut your premium.

Source: adapted from *www.moneysupermarket.com*

KMK **A** Give a summary in German of how you can reduce the cost of home insurance.

Life insurance

Julia Schmidt is a second-year trainee at Global Versicherungs-vermittlung GmbH. She is going on an exchange programme to a vocational school in London, but before she goes she has to write a paper on the following topic:

1 Why do people take out life insurance?

Julia has found the following case studies in an Internet survey.

1 **Simon Fitzpatrick, 42, self-employed carpenter**
My family depends on my income. My life insurance plan will replace that income if I die. As a father of two young children I think it is my responsibility to provide for my dependants. But not only for the children: my death would be a financial disaster for my wife, as she gave up her job when she got pregnant.

2 **Heather Nowack, 60, pensioner**
I don't want my children to pay for all those final expenses, like funeral and burial costs, legal expenses and so on. So I have death benefit insurance to cover them.

3 **Peter Hawkins, 52, teacher**
My daughter has two little boys aged 2 and 3. I want to save for their future. My house will go to my daughter, but I want to pass on some money to my grandsons. They are the beneficiaries of a cash value type life insurance plan. I think this is a good way of giving them an inheritance.

4 **John and Vivian Murray, new home-owners**
We've just bought a bigger house. The bank insisted on a term insurance policy for the duration of the mortgage. I think it is a good idea. If something happens to me, the insurance company will pay my mortgage and my wife will be able to keep the house.

5 **Deborah King, 32, shop assistant**
I decided to save money for retirement in a cash value type insurance policy. I can't get the money before I'm 60 years old but this type of insurance grants tax benefits. The money I pay into my plan is tax-free or, to be honest, tax deferred.

A Match the words and phrases on the left to the definitions on the right.

beneficiary | cash value | dependants | inheritance | mortgage | retirement | to take out | tax deferred

1 the time after you finish your working life
2 the person receiving the sum insured
3 a bank loan for a house or an apartment
4 the assets you receive from a person after his/her death
5 the amount of money you receive when you give up a policy or at the end of the term
6 people who are reliant on somebody
7 to buy insurance cover
8 something that is tax-free now, but liable to tax when you receive the money

INFO 'Insurance' or 'assurance'

On the British insurance market 'assurance' is used to describe cover for an event that is certain to happen. Nowadays it is only used with 'life'. For all other classes of business, the British use 'insurance', which refers to cover for an event that might happen (e.g. liability, fire, theft, etc.). Most other English-speaking countries, including the US, use 'insurance' for life business as well. In this unit we will refer to 'life insurance'.

B Are the following statements about the survey true or false? Correct the false statements.

1 Simon Fitzpatrick feels responsible for his company.
2 Banks nowadays insist on a protection policy when they lend you money.
3 Deborah King pays into a state pension.

C From what you know about life insurance, are the following statements true or false? Correct the false statements.

1 Life insurance policies are either protection policies or investment policies.
2 A death benefit insurance is a kind of investment policy.
3 Retirement plans are always tax-free.

D Most life insurance policies fall into one of these major categories: 1) protection policies, 2) investment policies or 3) a mixture of both.

Match the motivation of the five people from the survey with the categories 1–3. Explain your decision in a few sentences for each case.

Example: Simon Fitzpatrick wants to replace his income for his dependants. He takes out a …

2 Types of life insurance products

Simon Smith is British but lives and works in Nuremberg. He has just bought a flat and his bank has advised him to take out life insurance cover to protect his mortgage. He makes an appointment with Julia Schmidt to see her boss, Wolfgang Weber. In the meantime, Julia gives him a brochure about life insurance in English.

A Simon Smith makes some notes while reading the brochure (opposite). Read the brochure and say whether his notes are true or false. Correct the false statements.

1 Term insurance policies always run for the rest of the policyholder's life.
2 With endowment insurance the policyholder receives a regular income until he/she dies.
3 With unit-linked policies the investment risk is on the policyholder's side.
4 With a conversion option the policy term may be extended without providing additional health evidence.
5 A personal pension plan is a combination of savings scheme and life insurance policy.
6 An income protection plan is often sold as a rider to a life policy in Germany.

B Complete these sentences with terms from the box.

annuity | endowment insurance | income protection plan | personal pension plan | term insurance | terminal illness option | whole of life insurance

1 A/An ... provides a replacement income in case the policyholder can't work because of illness or a disability.
2 A/An ... has no life cover at all.
3 A/An ... pays the full amount insured in case of premature death or at the end of the term.
4 A/An ... only pays out the sum insured in case of death during the term of the insurance.
5 A/An ... secures a lump sum payment in case of diagnosis of a serious illness covered under the policy.
6 A/An ... is ideal for someone who wants to have an additional income, e.g. in case of retirement.
7 A/An ... runs for a long time, usually for the rest of the policyholder's life.

INFO Cultural differences

The British and the Germans have different attitudes to risk, which can be seen in the life policies on offer in each country. Whereas Germans tend to be risk avoiders, the British are generally more optimistic. Endowment insurance policies where the investment risk is with the insurance company still have a future in Germany, but they are not very popular in the UK. The average customer prefers a product with a more speculative element, such as some form of unit-linked policy.

Life Insurance Products

Term insurance

Term insurance is the simplest form of life insurance. It provides life insurance protection for the selected term (usually between one and 30 years) only. If the insured person dies during the term, the benefits are payable to the beneficiary named in the policy and if he/she survives till the end of the selected term, the policy expires without any benefit becoming payable. Term insurance may be regarded as a temporary insurance and there is no cash-in value at any time.

There are two basic types of term life insurance policies:

- *Level term* means that the death benefit stays the same throughout the duration of the policy.
- *Decreasing term* means that the death benefit drops, usually year by year over the term of the policy. This type of temporary life insurance is usually taken as a collateral to protect a bank loan or mortgage. The sum insured decreases over the years as the mortgage or loan is repaid.

Term life insurance policies are often sold with the following options for an additional premium:

- *Conversion option:* Without providing additional health evidence, the policy may be converted, for example, to a whole life or an endowment policy.
- *Renewal option:* Without providing additional health evidence, the policy may be extended at the end of the agreed term.
- *Terminal illness option:* Provides a lump sum if the policyholder is diagnosed as suffering from a terminal illness.

Whole of life insurance

Whole of life insurance (also called *permanent life insurance*) is intended to provide life insurance protection for a person's whole lifetime. It provides for payment of the sum insured upon the insured's death regardless of when it occurs. Under this type of policy, the payment of the sum insured is a certainty, only the time of payment of the sum insured is uncertain. Under some policies, the sum insured is paid out when the life insured dies or reaches the age of 85, whichever occurs first.

Endowment insurance

This is a long-term savings policy with life cover. The policy guarantees the sum insured at the end of the policy term. This lump sum payment may be increased by the addition of bonuses through the policy term. You can have endowment products with an annuity option, which means that the beneficiary receives a regular monthly or quarterly payment for a fixed term or for the rest of his/her life. In case of premature death the beneficiaries will receive at least the sum insured. The aims are to provide a lump sum payment at the end of the term or, for example in case of premature death, to pay back a mortgage.

Unit-linked insurance policies

Unit-linked insurance policies are investment-type policies with a flexible investment element. The investment part of the premium is invested in unit trusts selected by the customer and not by the insurance company. So the investment risk is on the customer's side. Even so, some companies offer a guaranteed sum in case of maturity. The policyholder will receive at least the value of his/her investment.

Annuities

An annuity provides a regular income either until death or for a fixed period. Payments can start when an initial payment in form of a lump sum is made or they can begin at a later date such as the date of retirement. Alternatively, the capital needed for the annuity can be saved over a longer period in monthly payments. Because of uncertainty about the future level of state pensions, annuities are very important.

Personal pension plan

This is a savings scheme to save for retirement. In most cases it is a unit-linked type of investment. It is usually sold by banks or other financial institutions such as building societies. There is no life cover at any time. Some employers use this type of investment as a kind of company pension plan. There may also be some tax benefits.

Income protection plan

This type of life insurance, also known as *disability benefit*, is designed to protect income if the policyholder becomes sick or disabled for more than six months during the term of the policy. The monthly payments are made until he/she returns to work, the plan term ends or the insured person dies. It aims to provide a replacement income. In some tariffs, this type is also called *occupational disability insurance*. In Germany it is usually sold as an additional benefit ('rider') to a life insurance policy.

C Decide on the most suitable life insurance product for the following customers and explain your choice in complete sentences.

1 A young couple, married for two years, a little boy (six months old); father self-employed sales person, mother part-time secretary, working for her husband; they are planning to buy a house with a mortgage (regular repayments).
2 A male CEO (chief executive officer), 54 years old, just divorced; is planning to invest €100,000 for his retirement.
3 A teacher, 42 years old, his wife, 38 years old, a bank clerk; two children, 17 and 19 years old, both children working; mortgage almost repaid; he wants to put some money away regularly for early retirement.
4 A widow, 55 years old; wants to make sure that the costs of her funeral will be paid.
5 A sales person, female, 30 years old; wants to keep her standard of living in case of long term sickness or disability.
6 A 28-year old computer technician; has just started his own business; needs life cover to protect his debts at the bank.

3 Mr Smith's life insurance needs

KMK *On the following Friday, Simon Smith arrives for his appointment with Wolfgang Weber.*

6 **A** Listen to the first part of their conversation. Copy the form and complete Wolfgang Weber's notes.

Global Versicherungsvermittlung GmbH

Versicherungsmakler
Allersberger Str. 13
90461 Nürnberg
Telefon 0911 440425

Beratungsprotokoll

Kunde: Simon Smith

Anschrift: Gudrunstr. 37, 90461 Nürnberg

Familienstand: ... Kinder (Anzahl/Alter): ...

Beruf: ... Beruf (Ehepartner): ...

Bestehende Versicherungen:

Privathaftpflichtversicherung

(5 Mio Deckungssumme)

1. Wünsche und Bedürfnisse des Kunden

1.1. Kundenwünsche / Anlass der Beratung

...

1.2. Kundenbedarf

...

B Discuss with your partner. What life insurance product would you recommend for Simon Smith? Give at least two reasons for your choice.

7 **C** Listen to the second part of their conversation and answer the following questions.

1 At the moment, what form of life cover does Simon Smith need most?
2 Does a conversion option make sense to him?
3 What would be a problem if he returned to Britain?
4 Why is it no problem to buy the insurance cover in Britain?
5 What has to be done to take out insurance cover in Britain?

USEFUL PHRASES Advice

Asking for advice	Giving advice
I've got a problem. Could you help me please?	If I were you, ...
What would you recommend/suggest in my situation?	I think you should ...
What would you advise me to do?	In your position, I would ...
	I recommend (that) you take out ...
	I suggest that you consider ...
	I'd (strongly) advise you to ...
	I'd advise against choosing ...

4 Counselling skills

Work with a partner and act out a role-play.
Student A is the insurance agent or broker. **Student B** is one of the customers from exercise 2C. Use the useful phrases to help you. Take turns at being the customer and the insurance agent.

You could start like this:

Kunde: Ich habe ein Problem, sprechen Sie Englisch?

Agent: Ja, ein wenig. Wie kann ich Ihnen helfen?

Kunde: Mein Name ist ... . Ich bin selbständige/r Grafikdesigner/in.

Agent: Darf ich Sie fragen, ob Sie Familie haben?

Kunde: Ich bin seit zwei Jahren verheiratet und wir haben einen 6 Monate alten Jungen. Wir möchten gerne ein Haus kaufen und benötigen zur Absicherung des Immobiliendarlehens eine Lebensversicherung.

Agent: In Ihrer Situation würde ich Ihnen folgendes empfehlen ...

Grammar review Since/for/ago

1 My wife has been at home **since last April**.
2 She has worked at the local hospital **for seven years**.
3 The apartment was renovated **three months ago**.

- **Since** *(= seit)* wird für einen Zeitpunkt verwendet, an dem etwas begann, das sich bis zum aktuellen Zeitpunkt fortsetzt. Das Verb steht im **present perfect** (1).
- **For** *(= seit)* wird für einen Zeitraum verwendet. Das Verb steht im **present perfect** (2).
- **Ago** *(= vor)* weist auf einen zurückliegenden Zeitpunkt hin und wird mit dem **simple past** verwendet (3).
- Bei **since** und **for** wird auch häufig das Verb im **present perfect continuous** verwendet: *She **has been working** for seven years.*

5 Practice

Complete the sentences with the correct tense of the verb in brackets and *since*, *for* or *ago*.

1 Riester pensions (be) … available on the German market … over five years.
2 … it was introduced in 2002 many customers (take) … advantage of this new product.
3 Proximus (sell) … life insurance products in Germany … over 50 years.
4 Proximus (start) … to sell the new tariff three months … .
5 Wolfgang Weber (work) … for Global … 2005.
6 Julia Schmidt (live) … in her new flat … only six months now.
7 Her training (start) … one year … .
8 I (have) … three appointments … 8 o'clock and it is only 10 o'clock now.
9 How long … (she/start) … her training?

6 Writing for a quotation

Simon Smith and Wolfgang Weber agree on a level term insurance policy with a conversion option. Wolfgang Weber asks Julia Schmidt to get at least four quotations to compare prices, with at least one of them being from a British life insurance company.

Von: Julia Schmidt <julia.schmidt@global.vv.de>
An: Colin Baker <colin@cia.co.uk>
Betreff: quote for life insurance

Hi Colin
Please quote for our customer Mr Simon Smith, 40 years old, for a level term insurance with conversion option during the first 10 years. Term should be 25 yrs. Sum assured 50,000 Euros or equivalent in GBP. Payment monthly. Occupation of customer: graphic designer. Non-smoker. No health problems so far.
Looking forward to your competitive quote asap.
Best wishes
Julia

A couple of days later Julia receives the following letter.

SOUTHWEST WIDOWS INSURANCE GROUP plc

Customer Service Department
7 Morven Drive
Exmouth
EX8 3LZ
Telephone 013952 333 258
Fax 013952 333 888

Global Versicherungsvermittlung GmbH
Allersberger Str 13
90461 Nuremberg
Germany

Your ref.:
Our ref.: DT/CS

Date: 10 February 20..

Dear Ms Schmidt

Quotation for Mr Simon Smith

Your partner in Great Britain, Countywide Independent Advisers Ltd, has informed us that your customer is interested in a level term assurance plan.

Please find enclosed a detailed illustration for your customer, a folder about our terms and conditions and an application form for your customer.

If you require any further assistance, do not hesitate to contact Colin Baker at Countywide Independent Advisers Ltd. Please send the filled-in proposal form directly to us.

We thank you for doing business with us.

Yours sincerely

Dennis Thornton

Dennis Thornton
Customer Services Department

Enclosures

Find out more about us on www.southwestwidows.co.uk

Compare Julia's email with the letter she received.

1 What differences can you find?
2 Give situations where you would write an email instead of a letter in your company.
3 Are there any situations in which you have to write a business letter?

INFO Business letters

Business letters have a lot in common with formal emails (cf. page 29).

Date

10 February 2011 *(BE)*
February 10, 2011 *(AE)*

> Be careful: *10.02.2011* means October 2nd, 2011 in America!

Addressee

For the attention of John Smith / Attn. John Smith	*zu Händen John Smith*
For the attention of the Managing Director	*An den Geschäftsführer*

Reference

Your reference (Your ref.) / Our reference (Our ref.)	*Ihre Zeichen / Unsere Zeichen*

Salutation	**Close**	
Dear Sir or Madam	Yours faithfully	*bei Firmen, Institutionen, Behörden*
Dear Sirs	Yours faithfully	*wie oben, eher konservative Schreibweise*
Dear Sir	Yours faithfully	*Ansprechpartner ist ein Mann, sein Name ist nicht bekannt*
Dear Madam	Yours faithfully	*Ansprechpartnerin ist eine Frau, ihr Name ist nicht bekannt*
Dear Mr/Ms Smith	Yours sincerely	*namentlich bekannte/r Ansprechpartner/in*
Dear John/Joanne	Best wishes / Regards / Kind regards	*gut bekannte/r Ansprechpartner/in oder Freund/in*

Mrs and *Miss* should be avoided, unless the woman prefers this form of address. If you use a comma after the salutation, you should also use one after the close.

Subject line

The subject line usually follows the salutation and may be centred or underlined.

Enclosures

Enclosure/Enclosures or *Enc(s)/Encl(s)*. If you enclose any items, this is stated after the signature.

7 Letter practice

Complete the salutations and closes.

a

The Manager
Hagamichi Insurance Group
Singapore
Dear …[1] …[2]

b

Mr Patrick Hail
60 Salterton Road
Bristol/GB
Dear …[3] …[4]

c

Hanson and Sons
The Broadway
Dublin
…[5] …[6]

d

Ms Johanna Scholl
Kaiserstr. 39
90402 Nuremberg
…[7] …[8]

USEFUL PHRASES Business letters

Introduction to an enquiry
We are writing to enquire about ...
We are interested in ...
We would like to know ...
We are writing in connection with ...

Introduction to a reply
Thank you for your letter/fax/email/enquiry of (date).
We were pleased to receive your letter/fax/email/enquiry of (date).
We would like to thank you for your letter/fax/email/enquiry of (date) asking if ... / enquiring about ... / concerning ...

Polite closing remarks
We look forward to receiving ... / hearing from you ... / seeing you ...
We hope to receive ... / to hear from you ... / see you ...
We hope to do business with you again.
I hope this information will help you.
If you require any further information/assistance, do not hesitate to contact us.
Please let me know / contact me if you need any further information.

8 Writing a business letter

KMK **A** Write Julia's email to Colin Baker (exercise 6) as a business letter. The address is Countywide Independent Advisers Ltd, Tyndall Avenue, Bristol, BS8 1TH, UK

B Julia has to answer a letter from a broker in Great Britain, Jack Major of West of England Insurance Services Ltd, 17 Haymarket, Exeter, EX3 7LL. She met him last December when he visited Global in Germany.

Jack Major wants information about an endowment insurance tariff. His customer is a 36-year old female sales person in normal health. She is looking for insurance cover for around €150,000 and a period of 25 years. The payment should be quarterly. How much is the payment at the end approximately?

Write a reply to Jack Major containing a quotation with all the necessary information and terms and conditions.

INFO Tips for writing good business letters

- Think carefully what you need to say before you write.
- Give your letter a subject line so that the person or company you are writing to can see immediately what the letter is about.
- Decide on the order of importance and give each point a separate paragraph.
- Make sure the letter is concise and delete anything that is irrelevant.
- Check your letter after you have written it. Will it create the right impression? Make sure there are no spelling, grammar or layout mistakes.

9 Filling in the proposal form

KMK *Simon Smith decides to take out his new life insurance policy with Proximus. As he is very busy at the moment, Julia Schmidt calls him at work and they fill in the proposal form over the phone.*

8 Your teacher will give you a copy of a proposal form. Listen to the telephone conversation and find out the missing information.

Rentenversicherung, Berufsunfähigkeits- und Risikoversicherung

☐ Antrag auf Abschluß eines Versicherungsvertrages
☐ Antrag auf Abgabe eines Vertragsangebots

Antrag auf Risikoversicherung (Privatversorgung	Tarif: 532	Versicherungssumme: €50.000	Versicherungsbeginn: ______	Versicherungsablauf: ______
	Endalter für die Versicherung: 65 Jahre Jahre	Endalter für die Beitragszahlung: 65 Jahre Jahre		
Überschussverwendung	Bonussystem			
Beitrag	Beitragszahlung ☐ 1/2	☐ 1/12 ☐ 1/1	☐ 1/4 ☐ einmalig	
	Beitrag gemäß Zahlungsweise ______ Euro			
Dynamikform	AV-Anpassung, mind. 5%		☐ ohne Dynamik	
Leistungsempfänger (bitte nur eine Verfügung treffen	Todesfall ☐ Versicherungsnehmer (für die Berufsunfähigkeit Versicherte) ☐ Ehegatte, mit dem der Versicherte im Zeitpunkt seines Todes verheiratet ist	☐ eheliche bzw. gesetzlich gleichgestellte Kinder des Versicherten ☐ Eltern des Versicherten; falls der Versicherte zum Zeitpunkt seines T[…] verheiratet ist, der Ehegatte	☐ eine andere Person Name und Anschrift	

Zeitlich befristete Fragen

1. Bestehen oder bestanden **in den letzten 5 Jahren** Krankheiten, Unfallfolgen, körperliche Schäden, Gesundheitsstörungen oder Beschwerden
1.1 der Atmungsorgane (auch Nasennebenhöhleninfektion, Heuschnupfeb, Kehlkopferkrankung)? ☐ nein ☐ ja
1.2 des Herzens oder der Kreislauforgane (auch Bluthochdruck, Krampfadern, Thrombose)? ☐ nein ☐ ja
1.3 der Nieren, der Harnwege oder der Geschlechtsorgane? ☐ nein ☐ ja

10 A project

Step 1: Get a copy of a proposal form from your training company and bring it to your next lesson.
Step 2: Find the English terms for the questions you have to ask your customer. Make a list of all the words you need.
Step 3: Act out a role-play with a partner. One of you is the insurance agent and the other plays the role of the customer. Translate the proposal form to your customer and fill in the information you receive.

11 Life insurance trends

The trend towards annuity insurance is continuing. This is due in part to the continued high amount of new business with Riester contracts. Furthermore, the final level of Riester tax breaks caused an increase in premiums – including existing contracts. Unit-linked life insurance contracts increased their share even further.

New business

In the first half of the year, life insurance, *Pensionskassen* and pension funds collectively saw approximately 3.2 million new contracts over an insured amount of 123.4 billion EUR. The number of new contracts therefore decreased by 8.6 per cent and the total insurance sum increased by 14.7 per cent.

In addition to immediate annuities, this is probably a result of more flexible products: many life insurance policies now have flexible payment options.

The structure of new business in life insurance shows clear differences between the insurance types. New business in the first half of the year showed a trend towards life insurance contracts with pension-like payouts: while endowment life insurance comprised only 15.3 per cent of total new business (previous year: 17.7 per cent) in number, the percentage of annuity insurance policies in total new business was 51.6 (previous year: 52.2) per cent.

Sales of Riester pensions decreased to 787,000 (down 14.0 per cent) for the first half of the year. A total of approximately 1.8 million Riester pensions are expected for the whole year. Most of the Riester pensions in the first half of the year were unit-linked Riester contracts (almost 58 per cent).

The number of new private endowment insurance contracts dropped to 255,700 (down 25.6 per cent), and the insured amount fell by 17.7 per cent to 5.0 billion EUR.

Source: adapted from *GDV Yearbook 2008*

A Are the following statements true or false? Correct the false statements.

1 Annuities increased their market share partly due to new Riester policies.
2 Premiums rose only due to new Riester policies.
3 The number of new contracts increased.
4 The percentage of annuities in new business increased.
5 Most of the new Riester policies are of the unit-linked type.

KMK **B** Finden Sie die fehlenden Informationen im Text.

1 Fondsgebundene Lebensversicherungen haben ihren Marktanteil … .
2 In der ersten Hälfte des Jahres wurden … Neuverträge abgeschlossen.
3 Die Gesamtversicherungssumme hat sich um … erhöht.
4 Der Verkauf an Riesterverträgen … um … %.
5 Für das ganze Jahr geht man von ungefähr … Riester-Neuverträgen aus.

Personal accident insurance

An accident can happen to anybody at any time. You are a very lucky person if you manage to go through your whole life without having an accident of some kind. Approximately nine million accidents occur in Germany every year.

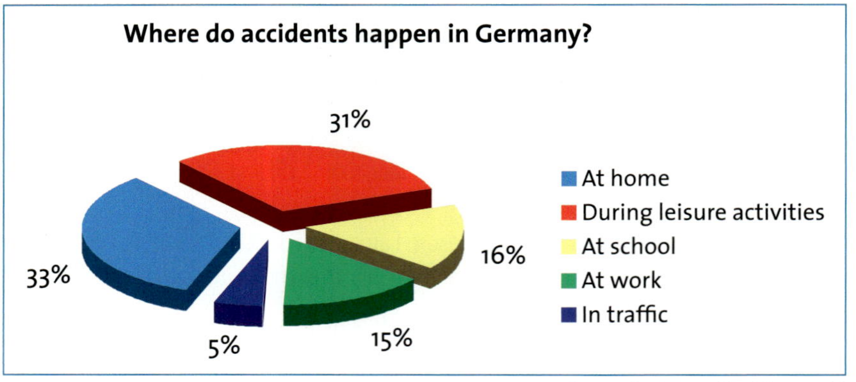

Source: Stuttgarter Versicherung AG

1 Accident statistics

Look at the pie chart and answer these questions.

1 Where do most accidents occur?
2 What percentage of the accidents do not happen at work?
3 Give an example of a possible accident for each area mentioned in the chart.
4 How could a serious accident affect your life and your financial needs?

2 Statutory accident insurance in Germany

Over 70 million individuals in Germany are insured with statutory accident insurance, which is financed by employers and public institutions. Most of the insured are employees, trainees, children and students.

Employees and trainees are covered for accidents at work, or on the way to and from work. Statutory accident insurance also protects them against occupational diseases. The benefits of statutory accident insurance include payment for full medical treatment, rehabilitation (for example, retraining) and cash benefits to the insured and their surviving dependants. The top priority of statutory accident insurance is to restore the health and ability to work of the insured. Pensions are paid to the insured only when it is not possible to fully restore their ability to work, i.e. for those whose earning capacity is reduced by at least 20 percent.

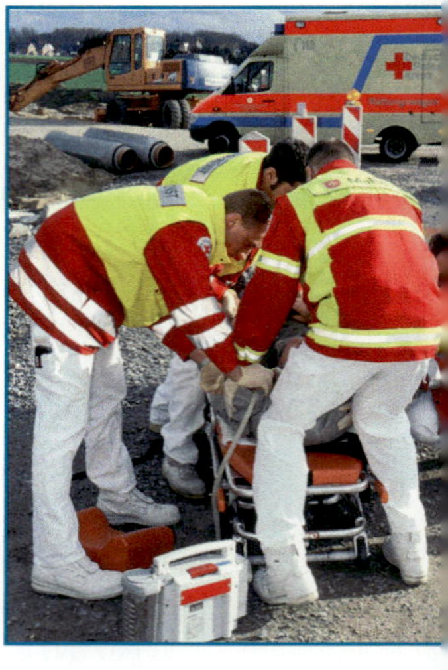

Children are covered for accidents that happen in school, nursery school or in after-school care centres and on the way to and from these institutions. Students are protected while they are at university and on the way to and from university.

The motto of statutory accident insurance is 'prevention before compensation'. For this reason, the statutory accident insurers use a wide range of measures and resources in order to prevent accidents and occupational diseases from occurring. They advise employers on how to avoid accidents and check that their advice is followed.

Most accidents happen at home and during leisure activities when people are not covered by statutory accident insurance. Therefore it is useful to buy personal accident insurance even if you are protected by statutory accident insurance. Some people are not covered by statutory accident insurance at all, e.g. housewives or most self-employed people.

Source: *www.dguv.de*

A Read the text and say if the following statements are true or false. Correct the false ones.

1 Statutory accident insurance covers employees for accidents occurring during their holidays.
2 Statutory accident insurance does not cover occupational diseases.
3 Statutory accident insurance is financed by employees, students and schoolchildren.
4 Statutory accident insurers take steps to improve safety in the workplace.
5 Statutory accident insurance provides cash benefits for the surviving dependants.

B Check the meaning of the word 'statutory' in a dictionary.

C Are these people covered by statutory accident insurance? Why (not)?

1 A worker in a factory who accidentally cuts off his thumb when operating a saw.
2 A five-year-old boy who breaks his arm when playing football with his friends at home.
3 A freelance journalist who breaks his ankle while on a business trip to Chicago.

3 Arranging a meeting

9

Susan Thompson, a language teacher and single parent from Manchester, moved to Munich with her son Roger four months ago to teach in-company language courses. Today she is phoning her German insurance agency, Versicherungsagentur Hagen.

KMK **A** Copy this table and complete it while you listen to the phone call.

1	Why does Susan Thompson need a new accident plan?	…
2	Day and time of appointment:	…
3	Susan Thompson's address:	…
4	What is Susan Thompson going to fax?	…
5	Claudia Zeller's fax number:	…

B Listen again and complete the following sentences from the phone call.

1. When would … you?
2. What … Wednesday 19 June … 5 p.m. … my place?
3. I'm sorry, I'm … all day on 19 June.
4. Would Thursday be … for you?
5. I'm … 5 p.m. is a bit too … for me.
6. Are you … at 5.30?
7. That's … with me.

USEFUL PHRASES Making appointments

Suggesting a time
When would suit you?
Would Thursday be convenient for you?
Can we fix a meeting for Wednesday 25 March, at 6 p.m.?
Are you free at 11 a.m.?

Replying to a suggestion
Any time tomorrow morning.
Yes, that's fine/OK with me.
I'm sorry. I'm not free / I'm tied up / I'm busy then. Could we arrange something else?
I'm afraid that's too early / too late. I'd prefer 11.30 a.m. / 10 a.m.

4 Role-play: making appointments

KMK Work with a partner. **Partner A:** Look at this page. **Partner B:** Look at File 4 on page 131.

Partner A:
You are John/Jane Wells and have just started a new job in Munich. You would like some information about personal accident insurance and would like to arrange for an adviser to visit you at home. Your address is Mozartstraße 31.
You have these dates in your diary for the following week:

Date	AM	PM
Monday 26 June	*Marketing meeting (all day + dinner!)*	
Tuesday 27 June		*Dentist 16.30*
Wednesday 28 June		*Tennis 17.00*
Thursday 29 June	*Department meeting –> 15.30*	
Friday 30 June		

5 Parts of the body

Label the diagram using words from the box below.

ankle | arm | chest | chin | ear | elbow | eye | fingers | foot | hand | head | heel | hip | knee | leg | mouth | nose | neck | shin | shoulder | thigh | thumb | toes | waist | wrist

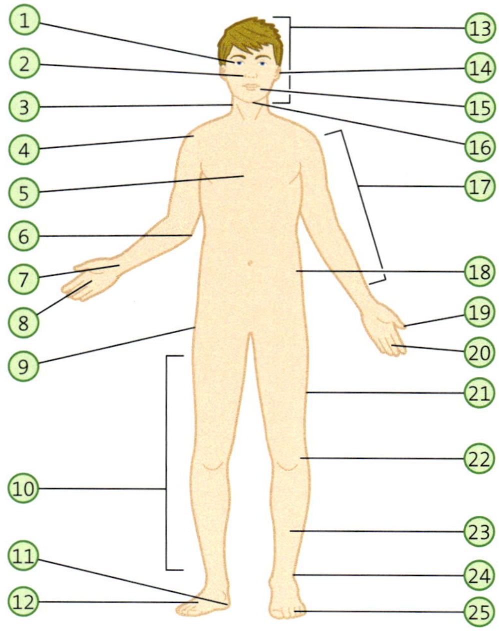

6 Types of injuries

A Match the English words (1–7) with their German equivalents (a–g).

1 to burn
2 to cut
3 to fracture
4 to hit
5 to paralyse
6 to scald
7 to sprain

a verbrühen
b lähmen
c verstauchen
d schneiden
e brechen
f stoßen
g verbrennen

B Now use the words from exercise A to complete these sentences.

1 Mr Lewis is confined to a wheelchair, because both his legs were … in an accident two years ago.
2 The X-ray showed that I had … my left thigh in the accident.
3 I … my hand when I touched the hot pan.
4 Paul landed awkwardly after the high jump and … his ankle. He is lucky it is not broken.
5 Jane … her arm with hot water.
6 My finger started bleeding when I … it on a piece of glass.
7 He suffered from concussion when he … his head against the wall.

7 A German personal accident plan

With a Proximus personal accident plan you can insure the following benefits ...

Benefit	What is it?
1 Disability or disablement benefit	Lump sum payment in case of permanent body injury resulting from an accident
2 Accidental death benefit	Lump sum payment in case of accidental death of the insured person
3 Bridging benefit	Lump sum payment you receive if the degree of disability has permanently been at least 50% for a period of six months following the accident
4 Plastic surgery	Cost of medical operations to repair injury to the insured's skin resulting from an accident
5 Cost of rescue operations	Cost of searching for and taking the casualty to a nearby hospital, including expenses for transport of a dead body to the insured's hometown.
6 Hospital daily benefit (hospitalization benefit)	Sum you receive for each day you have to stay in hospital because of an accident
7 Daily accident benefit	Sum you receive for each day you are temporarily unable to work because of an accident
8 Accident annuity	Regular monthly income you receive if the degree of permanent disability that is due to an accident is at least 50%. The income doubles if the degree of disability is 90% or even more.

What progressive disability benefits provide ...

		If the sum insured of your disability benefit amounts to €100,000, you will receive the following cash payments:			
Loss of ...	Degree of disability as percentage	Disability benefit without progression	225% with progression	350% with progression	500% with progression
one thumb	20%	20,000	20,000	20,000	20,000
hearing in one ear	30%	30,000	35,000	40,000	50,000
one eye	50%	50,000	75,000	100,000	150,000
one leg	70%	70,000	135,000	200,000	290,000
both eyes	100%	100,000	225,000	350,000	500,000

A Look at the brochures carefully. Which benefits cover the following expenses?

1 If you die in an accident, this benefit may be used for paying your funeral costs and supporting your surviving dependants.
2 If you are temporarily unable to work, this replacement income enables you to pay rent, groceries and clothes.
3 It covers the cost of a rescue helicopter from the scene of an accident to a nearby hospital.
4 It covers medical treatment to remove any scars on your face due to serious burns.
5 It enables you to cover extra costs while you stay in hospital, e.g. expenses for renting a TV set or telephone, and employing a housekeeper.

6 It helps to finance expensive medical treatment and rehabilitation measures.
7 It provides the money for adapting your house or flat if you are confined to a wheelchair because of an accident.
8 If you are unable to work for the rest of your life, this replacement income will help you to pay your daily living expenses.

B Match the English expressions from the brochure with their German equivalents in the box.

Invaliditätsleistung | kosmetische Operationen | Krankenhaustagegeld | Rettungskosten | Todesfallleistung | Übergangsleistung | Unfallrente | Unfalltagegeld

C Explain the advantage of having a progressive disability benefit.

D What details do you need to know about Susan Thompson and her son to prepare a quotation for them? (e.g. her income, their ages, …)

Grammar review Future tenses

1 My current accident policy **is going to terminate** in two months.
2 Tom **is going to have** an operation soon.
3 I **will** probably **return** to the UK in about five years.
4 I suppose Mary **won't be able to** work again because of her serious injuries.
5 Mr Finch is not available at the moment so I'**ll put** you **through** to Ms Brown.

Es gibt im Englischen mehrere Möglichkeiten, die Zukunft auszudrücken; zwei davon werden hier besprochen:

- *to be going to* + Infinitiv wird verwendet, wenn man sich sicher ist, dass etwas tatsächlich eintreten wird. **(1, 2)**
- *will* + Infinitiv wird verwendet, wenn lediglich Annahmen oder Vermutungen über die Zukunft ausgesprochen werden **(3, 4)**. Typische Signalwörter sind *maybe, probably* oder Verben, wie *think, hope, suppose,* etc.
- *will* + Infinitiv wird auch für spontane Entscheidungen auf eine gegebene Situation verwendet. **(5)**

8 Practice

After finishing my vocational training I …[1] work as an insurance agent. Maybe I …[2] start my own little company. Some of the students here …[3] stay in their training company. Most of them …[4] probably work in the field. A few other trainees tell me that they …[5] start an academic career at university. Maybe they …[6] join an insurance company after finishing university.

Next month my sister …[7] buy a new computer. She thinks the price for computers …[8] drop even more. Maybe she …[9] buy a new monitor as well. But she probably …[10] buy a printer as her old one still works well.

9 A British accident plan

This is Susan Thompson's current accident plan that she faxes to Claudia Zeller.

Woodford

Personal Accident Plan

If **you** have an **accident** which results in any of items 1–9 in the benefits table, you will be entitled to the following benefits:

TABLE OF BENEFITS			
Items	**Susan Thompson**	**Roger Thompson**	**Definition of terms used in the policy**
1. Permanent total disability	£140,000	£7,000	'Permanent total disability' means a total and permanent disability which medical evidence confirms will last for the rest of your life and which stops you doing any paid job.
2. Loss of use of: i) one limb ii) two limbs	 £70,000 £140,000	 £3,500 £7,000	'Loss of use of a limb' means total and permanent loss of use or loss by physical and permanent separation at or above the wrist or ankle.
3. Loss of sight in: i) one eye ii) both eyes	 £70,000 £140,000	 £3,500 £7,000	'Loss of sight' means total and permanent loss of sight in either one or both eyes.
4. Loss of hearing in: i) one ear ii) both ear	 £28,000 £140,000	 £1,400 £7,000	'Loss of hearing' means total and permanent loss of hearing in either one or both ears.
5. Loss of use of a: i) shoulder ii) hip, knee, ankle, wrist	 £17,500 £14,000	 £875 £700	'Loss of use' means total and permanent loss of use of a shoulder, hip, knee, ankle or wrist.
6. Loss of use of: i) one thumb ii) one forefinger iii) any other finger	 £10,500 £7,000 £7,000	 £525 £350 £350	'Loss of use of a finger, thumb or toe' means total and permanent loss of use or loss by physical and permanent separation of the entire finger, thumb or toe.
7. Loss of use of: i) one big toe ii) any other toe	 £7,000 £3,500	 £350 £175	
8. Daily hospitalization (up to a maximum of 180 days for each accident)	£70 per day (24 h)	£3.50 per day	'Hospitalization' means staying in a hospital on the advice of a doctor because of an accident.
9. Accidental death	£75,000	£3,750	'Accidental death' means death due to an accident.

The benefits will go up by 5% of their starting amounts on each anniversary of the start date.

A Look at the benefits and amounts insured under this British accident plan and answer these questions.

1. What are the differences compared to a German accident policy (e.g. Proximus)?
2. Are there any benefits you think are missing in this plan?
3. Compare Roger's amounts insured to those of his mother. Do they provide sufficient cover?

B Calculate the benefits that the insured would receive in the following cases:

1. Ms Thompson loses the thumb of her right hand and the hearing in one ear in an accident. She has to stay in hospital for 16 days.
2. Roger Thompson loses his right arm and his left big toe in an accident. He has to stay in hospital for 14 days.

C Read the terms and conditions on the right. Use the accident plan on page 58 to calculate the compensation for Charles Wilcox and his daughter Daisy.

1. Daisy Wilcox (aged 8) loses her left arm in an accident. The forefinger of her left hand was lost in a previous accident.
2. Mr Charles Wilcox (aged 36) suffers a total paralysis of both legs in an accident. According to a medical report 40% of the impairment is due to blood circulation problems which existed before the accident happened.

Where it is proven that the effects of an **accident** on **you** are made worse because **you** already had a condition, sickness, disease or injury then the **insurer** will assess the effects that **your** condition, sickness, disease or injury has on **your bodily injury** and the **insurer** will reduce **your** benefit by an appropriate amount to take this into account. Example of an existing medical condition:
You were partially blind in your left eye and you then had a car accident which left you totally blind in both eyes. We ask an independent ophthalmic surgeon to assess the difference between the amount of vision you had before and after the accident. He assesses the pre-accident vision in your left eye at 50%, so we pay 50% for the loss of vision in that eye (£35,000). The vision in your right eye was normal before the accident, so we pay 100% of the loss of eye benefit (£70,000).

INFO Doing calculations

4 + 7 = 11	Four and seven is eleven.
	Four plus seven equals eleven.
65 – 22 = 43	Twenty-two from sixty-five is forty-three
	Sixty-five minus twenty-two equals forty-three.
9 x 6 = 54	Nine times six is fifty-four.
	Nine multiplied by six is fifty-four.
36 : 12 = 3	Thirty-six divided by twelve is/equals three.

D Work with a partner to act out a meeting or phone call with the insured from B and C (or one of their close relatives) where you explain how you made your calculations. Remember to express sympathy. Use the useful phrases.

USEFUL PHRASES Expressing sympathy

Injuries and illnesses

I'm sorry to hear that.
That sounds bad. It must be very painful.
I hope your wife/child/... gets better soon.
Please give him/her my best wishes for a quick recovery.

Death

I'm sorry to hear about your loss.
Please accept my condolences on your husband's/wife's/... death.

INFO **Occupational risk**

Personal accident insurance premiums vary with the policyholder's occupation. In Germany there are two classes of occupational risk:
Class A: People engaged in mainly sedentary (desk-bound) work or in non-manual work in non-hazardous places, such as office clerks and teachers.
Class B: People engaged in manual work not of a particularly hazardous nature but involving the use of tools or machinery, such as bakers, plumbers and technicians.
There are also some occupations that are uninsurable because of their hazardous nature, e.g. professional sportsmen/sportswomen, divers.

10 Role-play: changing your occupation

KMK Work with a partner and role-play the following telephone conversation.

Proximus

- Melden Sie sich am Telefon und fragen Sie, wie Sie dem Anrufer helfen können.
- Fragen Sie nach der Policenummer.
- Fragen Sie, was der Kunde zu seiner Unfallversicherung wissen möchte.
- Sagen Sie dem Kunden, dass die neue Tätigkeit ein geringes Risiko darstellt und er nun zwei Möglichkeiten hat:
  1. Option: Er zahlt weiterhin den bisherigen Beitrag, dann erhöhen sich seine Versicherungssummen.
  2. Option: Er behält die bisherigen Versicherungssummen, dann sinkt sein Beitrag.
- Sagen Sie, dass der Beitrag um ca. ein Drittel sinkt.
- Sagen Sie, dass Sie den Vertrag ändern und neue Dokumente zusenden werden.
- Verabschieden Sie sich.

Kunde

- Stellen Sie sich vor und sagen Sie, dass Sie eine Frage zu Ihrer Unfallversicherung haben.
- Sagen Sie Ihre Nr.: PAI 2-2-7-6-4-3-2
- Sagen Sie, dass sich Ihre berufliche Tätigkeit geändert hat. Sie haben Ihre Tätigkeit als Tierpfleger (*zoo keeper*) aufgegeben und arbeiten nun im Callcenter eines Tierfutterhändlers (*pet food dealer*). Fragen Sie, ob dies Auswirkungen auf Ihre Unfallversicherung hat.
- Fragen Sie, um wie viel der Beitrag sinkt, wenn Sie die bisherigen Versicherungssummen behalten.
- Sagen Sie, dass Sie dann die 2. Option möchten.
- Bedanken Sie sich und verabschieden Sie sich.

11 Writing a claims report

Make up an accident and report it to Proximus Versicherung. Your teacher will give you a suitable claims report form. Use the vocabulary of exercise 5 and 6 to describe the accident and the injuries it caused.

12 Is accident cover just a waste of money?

Personal accident insurance is usually already packaged into other existing policies for travel, car and even household insurance, and it is often given away free with credit cards. For example, Barclays already sells personal accident insurance in other policies – up to £30,000 in its travel policy, and up to £2,500 with its car insurance, as well as up to £500,000 on its stand-alone policy.

'Given that this insurance is [often] given away as a freebie, I don't see why consumers should pay for it at all,' says Richard Mason, a director of price comparison website Moneysupermarket.com. 'In terms of insurance policies, I would put it right at the back of the queue – it's absolutely useless. ...'

The cover is designed to pay out if you are severely injured or die in an accident. Policyholders receive a tax-free lump sum if they are involved in an accident resulting in the loss of one or more limbs, one or both eyes, the loss of use of any of the above, or some other form of permanent disability …

Policies vary between insurers but, for example, Nationwide won't pay out if you suffer an accident as a result of riding or being a passenger on a motorcycle, or mountaineering, rock climbing or parachuting. And despite steady annual accidental death figures – 240 in the workplace; 4,000 in the home; about 3,200 deaths on roads – the Royal Society for the Prevention of Accidents points out that it's mainly the elderly and the very young who are most vulnerable.

Simon Burgess at broker British Insurance says that, on top of life cover, money spent on personal accident cover premiums 'can be better used elsewhere to buy proper cover such as income protection' that pays out a regular monthly premium until you return to work or retire. Income protection covers occupational disability as well as accidents.

Earlier this year, a FSA (Financial Services Authority) review of the way consumers buy general insurance policies included a number of warnings on personal accident insurance. 'There may be a risk that customers buying [it] may not understand the limitations ... compared with full private medical insurance,' the report said.

…

The regulator also emphasized its anxiety over the low claims ratio (the total annual claims as a percentage of total premium value), suggesting that it could be down to 'excessive prices' and a 'lack of competition'.

Source: *The Guardian*, 17 November 2007

A Read the text and answer these questions.

1 What other insurance policies already include some sort of personal accident cover?
2 What is a 'freebie'?
3 What is Richard Mason's view on personal accident insurance?
4 What age groups are mostly involved in accidents?
5 What should consumers buy instead of personal accident insurance according to Simon Burgess?
6 Why is the FSA concerned about personal accident insurance?

B From what you know about German accident insurance, do you agree with Sam Dunn's point of view?

C Work with a partner and discuss the pros and cons of buying a German stand-alone private accident plan. Present your results to the class.

D Mediation: A colleague asks you to summarize the last two paragraphs of the article in German.

Private health insurance

With the exception of the United States, most westernized countries have a form of universal health insurance coverage for all their citizens. However, due to increasing health care costs and rising life expectancy, the state system of health care is under enormous pressure. Private forms of health insurance are becoming more and more popular.

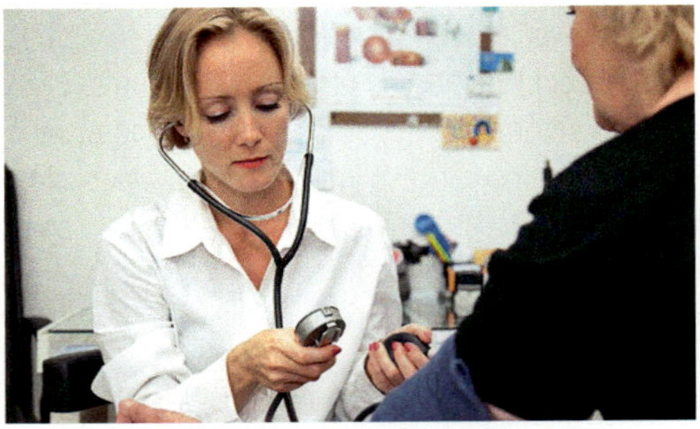

1 What do you know about health insurance?

George Arnold, a health insurance expert, is talking about private health insurance.

A Before you listen, discuss these questions with a partner.

1 What types of policy do private health insurers sell in Germany?
2 Can anyone buy a private health policy in Germany?
3 What are the advantages of private health insurance?
4 What have you heard in the news recently about health insurance in Germany?

10

B Now listen to the CD. From what George Arnold says, are the following statements true, false or not mentioned? Correct the false statements.

1 The comprehensive covers of private health insurers are long-term covers.
2 Top-up benefits are additional benefits for people in the statutory system.
3 Top-up policies are strictly underwritten.
4 Top-up benefits include an ageing reserve.
5 Anyone can take out comprehensive health insurance with a private health insurer.
6 All self-employed people can take out comprehensive health policies.

INFO Top-up benefits

Additional benefits provided by German private health insurers to those with statutory health cover are known as **supplementary benefits/covers** or **top-up benefits**.

2 Letters to a newspaper

Read the three letters on page 63 and answer these questions.

1 Which letter writers are in favour of comprehensive private health policies?
2 Why is private health insurance better than the statutory cover?
3 What disadvantages are mentioned?
4 What was one of the legal changes in 2008 in connection with health insurance?
5 Compare why premiums for statutory and private health insurers increase.

1

Dear Sir,
In your recent article entitled 'Living in Germany: what Brits should know', you hardly mentioned health insurance, yet this is very different to what we are used to in the UK. In Germany you can opt out of the statutory health system, which is the equivalent of our NHS, so that private health insurers will cover you for everything. Such comprehensive policies must provide benefits that are at least as good as those provided by statutory insurers, and in all cases they are actually much better. They pay much more for dental treatment and alternative medicine is covered, which is excluded in almost all statutory schemes.
For those who choose to stay with a statutory provider, private health insurers offer a wide range of top-up benefits, such as the guarantee of a single or double room for in-patient treatment and the security that any operation will be performed by a consultant. Health insurers also provide travel insurance. It is much cheaper to buy this cover on an annual basis rather than for each journey. The benefits include emergency evacuation and there are also useful services if a policyholder has to be hospitalized in a foreign country.
Yours faithfully,
Eleanor Beatty, (Stuttgart, 17 March)

2

Dear Sir,
Ms Beatty [Letters, 17/03] paints a rather rosy picture of German health insurance in my view. She fails to mention that allthough statutory health insurers require only one premium for a family, each person must pay a premium in a private scheme. Consequently, private health insurance may be cheaper for single people, but it is quite definitely more expensive for large families.
Furthermore, some elderly people who are privately insured have difficulty in paying their health premiums. And what makes matters even worse, they cannot get back into the statutory system! Those who are thinking of taking out a comprehensive policy with a private health insurer should be sure they will have a good pension when they retire. If the statutory system isn't good enough for them, it is better to buy a top-up benefit. At least you can always cancel that later if you wish to.
Yours faithfully,
Bill Walker (London, 19 March)

3

Dear Sir,
Mr Walker's letter [19/03] is misleading, because it is based on out-of-date information. New laws about health insurance were passed in 2008 that improve the situation of the sort of people he describes: pensioners on small incomes.
If their private health premiums rise to a level they cannot afford, they have two options. They can approach their insurer and request to be transferred to a basic tariff. This provides the same benefits as the statutory system, and it is cheaper. Alternatively, they can transfer to another private health insurer that provides a cheaper tariff. In the past that did not make much sense, because they would not have been able to take their ageing reserve with them, but now they can at least take part of it.
Consequently, there is now no reason for anyone to be afraid of his or her private health insurer raising its premiums to a level they cannot afford.
I would also like to point out that the increases in private health insurance are not due to errors in the premium calculation but are mainly due to new types of treatment. Statutory health providers are also affected by this development and their premiums rise even more rapidly because they do not have an ageing reserve.
Jamie Ferguson (Ludwigshafen, 21 March)

3 Health insurance definitions

A Use the following syllables to make words for the definitions below. You will find all the words in the three letters you have just read.

> af | be | com | con | der | ex | fer | fit | ford | hen | ing | lead | ma | ment | mis | ne | nent | pen | per | pre | pro | quest | re | ry | sive | sive | sta | sul | to | tant | trans | treat | tu | vi

1. What you get when you go to a doctor or a hospital.
2. If you can pay for something, you can … it.
3. Set up by the state, not owned privately.
4. Your insurance policy gives you this.
5. Gives you the wrong idea.
6. A polite way of asking for something.
7. To send money from one bank account to another.
8. Costing a lot of money.
9. An insurance company is sometimes called a … because it gives cover.
10. Not temporary. It is always there.
11. Covering many things. In the context of health insurance it is not a top-up cover.
12. The head doctor in a hospital. He is the person you want to treat you.

B Use 11 of the words from A to complete these sentences. Which word is missing?

1. If you are an in-patient, you stay in hospital for … . If you did not have health insurance, you might not be able to … this, because it is very … .
2. A private health … offers two types of policy: … covers and top-up policies. The former type of policy has many … that … companies do not provide, such as alternative medicine and treatment by a … in the event of an operation.
3. Although a private health policy should be a … policy, the policyholder can … to be … to the basic tariff.

4 Comparisons of health insurance in Germany and the UK

Tom Hobson, a financial journalist, and Florian Hartmann, who works for a German health insurer are discussing a reform of the British health insurance system. They are talking about whether the British system could learn anything from the German one.

INFO

An **acute condition** occurs relatively suddenly and does not last long: influenza, appendicitis, broken bones.
Chronic conditions last a long time or are permanent: diabetes, asthma, osteoporosis.

11

A Listen to the conversation and answer these questions.

1. What is the dual system of health insurance in Germany?
2. Which chronic conditions does Florian Hartmann mention?
3. Who is responsible for treating chronic conditions in Britain?
4. What is the principle of being able to transfer part of the ageing reserve called?
5. What does the ageing reserve in German private health insurance cover?
6. Do private health policies in the UK have an ageing reserve?
7. What is the main problem with private health insurance in Britain?
8. Why doesn't Tom Hobson think that an ageing reserve would be a good idea?
9. What does Florian Hartmann suggest to solve that problem?
10. Why might the Minister of Health disagree with Florian Hartmann's suggestion?

B Listen again and answer these questions.

1. What are the arguments in favour of German private health insurance?
2. Why would comprehensive plans on the German model not work in Britain?
3. What are the questions of principle raised by the discussion?

C Discuss these questions with a partner.

1. In what ways does statutory health insurance not follow insurance principles?
2. Is it in the public interest to encourage or restrict private health insurance?

5 Odd one out

A Which word is the 'odd one out'? Explain why.

Example a switch b work c exchange
→ *'Work' is the odd one out. To 'switch' something means to 'exchange' something.*

1	a subsidize	b explain	c support	
2	a indicate	b refuse	c show	d suggest
3	a retiree	b patient	c pensioner	
4	a laughable	b amusing	c ridiculous	d absurd
5	a permit	b allow	c approve	d dispute
6	a advise	b consider	c think about	
7	a provide	b give	c receive	d supply
8	a claim	b discuss	c talk about	

B Use the odd ones out in the following sentences. (You may have to change the tense.)

When I was a …[1] in hospital the doctor …[2] me to have an operation. I …[3], however, because I had not …[4] enough information about the risks involved. I asked the doctor to …[5] what these were, but he …[6] that there was no risk. I …[7] this, and he did not find this very …[8] and said I should leave the hospital if I did not want him to operate.

6 Role-play: an enquiry about reimbursement

In contrast to statutory insurers, private health insurers expect their policyholders to pay doctors' bills and prescriptions themselves. These payments are later reimbursed by the health provider. Stanley Lu from Taiwan has just taken out a comprehensive health policy with Proximus Health. This is a special contract for foreign residents in Germany. He now wants some information about the payment of claims under his policy.

KMK Role-play the telephone conversation with a partner, using the information below and the useful phrases.

USEFUL PHRASES **Mildly disagreeing**

But this could ..., couldn't it?
But what happens if ... ?
But don't you think ... ?
Really? Isn't that ... ?

Proximus receptionist

Melden Sie sich mit Namen und Firma und fragen Sie den Anrufer / die Anruferin, wie Sie behilflich sein können.

Stanley Lu

Stellen Sie sich vor und fragen Sie, ob man manche Ausgaben vorstrecken muss?

Proximus receptionist

Bejahen Sie und sagen Sie, dass das für Arztbesuche und für Medikamente zutrifft.

Stanley Lu

Sagen Sie, dass diese Regelung für den Versicherungsnehmer teuer sein kann.

Proximus receptionist

Teilen Sie ihm mit, dass die Obergrenze €100 ist. Krankenhäuser werden direkt bezahlt. Rückerstattung erfolgt am Monatsende, vorausgesetzt, dass die Rechnung vor dem 20. des Monats ausgestellt wurde.

Stanley Lu

Fragen Sie, ob die Regelung flexibel ist, falls Sie in finanzielle Schwierigkeiten geraten.

Proximus receptionist

Antworten Sie, dass er in einem solchen Fall, Kontakt mit der Proximus Kranken-versicherung aufnehmen sollte.

Stanley Lu

Fragen Sie, wie lange es bis zur Zahlung dauert, nachdem Sie die Rechnung eingereicht haben.

Proximus receptionist

Antworten Sie, dass es etwa zwei Wochen dauert.

Stanley Lu

Fragen Sie, was Sie genau zuschicken müssen.

Proximus receptionist

Teilen Sie ihm mit, dass er nur die Rechnung zu schicken braucht. Fragen Sie etwas überrascht, ob er die entsprechenden Informationen nicht erhalten habe.

Stanley Lu

Antworten Sie, dass Sie zweifelsohne die Information bekommen haben, aber Sie haben sie gleich irgendwo hingelegt und dann verloren.

Proximus receptionist

Teilen Sie Herrn Lu mit, dass Sie das Zeug noch einmal schicken werden. Fragen Sie ihn, ob Sie sonst noch etwas für ihn tun können.

Stanley Lu

Sagen Sie, dass alles in Ordnung ist. Bedanken Sie sich. Verabschieden Sie sich.

Proximus receptionist

Verabschieden Sie sich ebenfalls.

7 An email enquiry

KMK Work with a partner.
Partner A: Look at this page. **Partner B:** Look at File 5 on page 131.

Partner A:
You are a claims manager at Proximus Health. You have received the following bill from policyholder Stanley Lu. This is his first claim since taking out the comprehensive policy a year ago.
You have some questions about the items on the bill. You believe Stanley Lu does not speak German well, so write him an email in English asking him for details for all the items. Use the notes you made while you were reading the bill (below) as the basis for your inquiry:

Proximus
KV
18.05.

Dr. Angelika Pernt
Fachärztin für Allgemeinmedizin
Rosenweg 115 • 20095 …

zu 1 Warum zwei Telefonberatungen? Was wurde diskutiert? Wie ist der Unfall passiert?
zu 7 Was genau wurde vom Arzt untersucht?
zu 375 War die Impfung eine Erneuerung oder eine neue Impfung?

Liquidation Ref 989787667

Für ärztliche Leistungen erlaube ich mir, gemäß untenstehender Aufstellung, zu berechnen:

Rechnungsbetrag: € 71,22

Diagnose(n):
Wunde im Gesicht, Td-Auffrischung, V.a. Ganglion am Steißbein

Datum	GOÄ-Nr	Text	Mult Faktor	Eur
19.04.	1	Beratung – auch mittels Fernsprecher	2,3	10,72
	7	Vollst. körperl. Unters. mind. e. Organsystem	2,3	21,45
	375	Schutzimpfung (intramuskulär, subkutan)-	2,3	10,72
		Td		15,11
		Impfpaß		2,50
20.04.	1	Beratung – auch mittels Fernsprecher	2,3	10,72

Summe: € 71,22

Bitte überweisen Sie den Rechnungsbetrag mit Angabe der Rechnungsnummer auf mein o. g. Bankkonto.

Grammar review Phrasal verbs

1 The health insurer **sent out** many flyers and used advertisements on TV. As a result many people wanted to **take out** a policy with the company.
2 So they **filled in** the proposal forms and the agents **handed** them **in** to the insurance company.
3 The underwriters **looked** them **over** to see that all questions had been answered. Then they **read** them **through** carefully. They either accepted the risks or **turned** them **down**.
4 After a risk has been accepted, the policy administration department issues a policy and **sends** it **off** to the proposer, who is now the policyholder.
5 A policyholder with monthly premiums must **pay in** enough to cover the monthly payments.

- *Phrasal verbs* bestehen aus Verb + Adverb oder Präposition (z. B. *in, through, out*). Die oben stehenden *phrasal verbs* werden häufig im Versicherungswesen verwendet.
- Wenn das Objekt eines *phrasal verbs* ein Substantiv ist, so kann es entweder direkt hinter dem Adverb oder zwischen Verb und Adverb stehen. Ein Pronom (z. B. *it, them*) dagegen muss zwischen Verb und Adverb stehen.

8 Practice

Complete the text below using phrasal verbs from the box.

cross out | open up | plug in | read out | read through | send in | send off | sort out | switch off | switch on | take off | think through | type in | type out | work out | work through | write out

I usually get to work at about eight o'clock. The first thing I do is to …[1] my electric kettle to make myself some tea. When the water has boiled, I …[2] the kettle and pour the water into the teapot. Then I …[3] the list of things I have to do today. I …[4] my computer and …[5] my password. I get into the system and …[6] my emails. I …[7] my emails into the more important and less important ones, and then I …[8] and reply to the most important ones. If my line manager has asked me a question, I have to …[9] a reply as soon as possible. Sometimes I am asked to calculate a premium and I …[10] [this] using a program we use. In the evening I …[11] the computer and …[12] the light before I leave the office.

9 Top-up benefits

The brochure below shows the top-up benefits offered by a German health insurer.

Copy the word spider on the right. Start by adding the words in the offer of the German health insurer below and then add as many other words as you know.

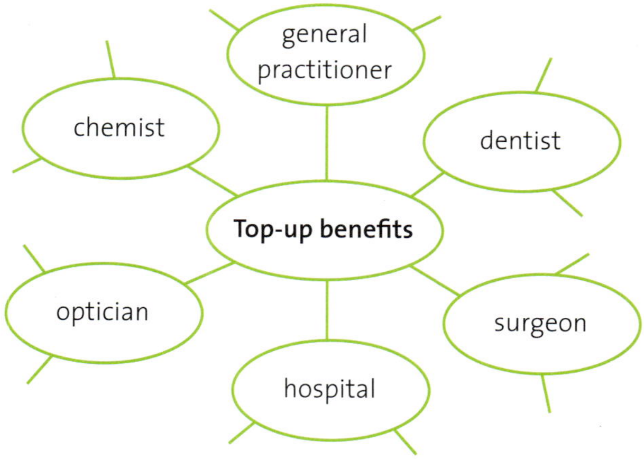

Benefits	Private Health Insurance
Contact lenses & glasses	80% costs up to € 200 within 2 yrs
Medication, treatment, aids	Up to €500 p. a.
Naturopathy	80% costs of naturopath
Hospital accommodation	1 or 2 bed room with telephone; Consultant; Special treatment
Payments in hospital	Nothing
False teeth, implants	65–80% paid for
Sickness benefit	70% income limit for assessment of contributions
Foreign travel	Worldwide for up to 6 weeks per journey; Emergency evacuation included.

10 Role-play: top-up benefits

Mr Osaka Kuromito is discussing the benefits of a top-up policy with an agent from Proximus Versicherung.

Work with a partner.
Partner A: Look at this page.
Partner B: Look at File 7 on page 132.

When you have completed the role-play, exchange roles and do it again.

Partner A: You are Osaka Kuromito.
You are Japanese, but you are now permanently resident in Germany. You want to take out a top-up policy with benefits similar to those described in the table above. You do not want to leave the statutory system of health care. You are 48 and married with three children, aged 19, 14 and 7. Your wife is German and you intend to stay in Germany. You want to know how the benefits compare with the statutory health insurers. You want as much information as possible. Look at the table in exercise 9 and ask questions.

11 Travel insurance

Axa Travel Insurance

Cancellation or curtailment cover up to £3,000 per person
Our travel insurance covers you for cancellation or curtailment if, for example, you fall ill or are made redundant and have to cancel or cut short your holiday.

Medical expenses cover up to £5,000,000 per person
With our travel insurance we cover you for the costs of emergency medical expenses and other necessary expenses such as transport and accommodation for a friend or close relative to come out to you from the United Kingdom if medically necessary.

Daily hospital benefit up to £500 per person
We give up to £500 (£30 per day) of hospital benefit per person with our travel insurance. This payment is meant to cover your costs incurred through being in hospital, such as phone calls and taxi fares.

Personal accident up to £25,000 per person
Our travel insurance includes up to £25,000 of personal accident cover per person (subject to age). This covers you for death, loss of limb(s) or sight, and permanent total disablement.

Baggage up to £1,500 per person
Our travel insurance includes up to £1,500 of baggage cover per person. This travel insurance cover can be removed if you do not require it. (You may already have your personal belongings covered under your home insurance policy.)

Personal money and documents up to £150 per person (up to a maximum of £300)
With our travel insurance you get up to £150 of cover per person for cash and £150 of cover per person for other documents such as passports and visas. Cover for cash is limited to £50 for travellers under the age of 16.

Loss of passport expenses up to £300 per person
Our travel insurance includes cover for up to £300 of additional travel and accommodation expenses per person if your passport is lost or stolen outside the United Kingdom.

Personal liability up to £2,000,000 per person
Up to £2,000,000 of personal liability cover per person is included in our travel insurance policy. This covers you for compensation you become legally liable to pay for – bodily injury to another person or for loss or damage to another person's property.

Delayed departure up to £200 per person
Our travel insurance includes cover for delayed departures of up to £200 per person (£25 after 5 hours and £25 per 12 hours delay after that). After five hours of delay you can claim up to £3,000 per person for unused travel and accommodation costs if you cancel your trip before departure from the United Kingdom.

Missed departure up to £500 per person
We include cover in our travel insurance for missed departures of up to £500 per person to cover additional travel and accommodation costs to reach your overseas destination.

Legal expenses and assistance up to £25,000 per person
Our travel insurance includes up to £25,000 of cover per person for legal expenses. This is limited to a total of £50,000 if there are two or more people insured on the travel insurance policy.

20% online discount
Buying our travel insurance online will get you a 20% discount on the premium you'd get over the phone.

Source: *www.axa.co.uk*

A Read the description of a travel insurance plan for a single journey and then answer these questions.

1 What is the maximum benefit paid in the event of an accident? Is the sum insured paid if you lose an arm on your holiday?
2 How many of the eleven benefits are concerned with the policyholder's physical well-being?
3 How many benefits are concerned with the travelling aspect of the journey?
4 How many classes of insurance cover the policyholder's possible carelessness?
5 If the holiday was a disaster and everything went wrong and a policyholder made a valid maximum claim for every benefit in this policy, how much would the insurer have to pay?

B Discuss the following questions.

1 From an insurer's point of view, the risk lies in the frequency or severity of loss, i.e. that there are too many claims or that single large claims make the business lose money. Which benefits, in your view, are the most subject to frequency or severity of loss?
2 What, in your view, are the three most important and the three least important benefits?
3 From the insurer's point of view, which benefits provide the greatest opportunities for fraud or moral hazard?
4 Compare the benefits described here with German travel policies. Is there any benefit missing that you would have expected or would like to have seen?
5 Have you or anyone you know ever made a claim under a travel insurance policy? Tell the story.

C Find words in the text that mean the same as the following:

1 shortening
2 place where you stay
3 unemployed
4 reduction in price
5 things that you own (two possibilities)
6 private
7 does not change, the opposite of temporary
8 help
9 dangerous situation when you need help quickly
10 costs

Liability

1 Personal liability

Wolfgang Beck, an insurance journalist, is talking about liability insurance to an English liability expert, Paul Avery.

A Before you read the first part of their conversation, discuss the following questions with a partner:

1. Why is liability insurance important?
2. Who are the beneficiaries?
3. Who are the three parties involved in a liability claim?
4. Which of these parties have a contractual relationship with each other?
5. What steps does an insurer take when a claim is made?

B Now read the conversation and answer the questions below.

BECK Mr Avery, you recently suggested that personal liability insurance should be made compulsory. Can you explain why?

AVERY Just imagine that you're walking along the street. Without thinking, you step off the pavement into the road and a car swerves to avoid you. As a result, it crashes into a lorry that is carrying a load of gas cylinders. These fall off the lorry and explode with loss of life and enormous property damage. You would be liable for everything. Not having a personal liability policy is like playing negative lotto.

BECK OK, I take your point. But what you've described is rather unlikely, isn't it?

AVERY Well, I could think of many far more likely situations that would still cost a lot of money. And we shouldn't forget that liability policies exist not only to protect the first party, the insured, but also to provide compensation for the third party, the victim of carelessness, or negligence as insurers call it. And can you explain why we are forced to have third-party liability cover if we have a car, but not for our daily lives? We're all human. No one is perfect, and we can all be careless. In both Germany and the UK the penetration rate of personal liability is only about seventy percent.

BECK But if it is so important, why doesn't everyone have this kind of policy?

AVERY Ignorance? Lack of imagination? You tell me. Those are probably the main reasons, but I also think a big problem is that agents and brokers don't have much interest in selling it. It's not always easy to explain how the policy works in the event of a claim: the process involving the first, second and third parties – the insured, the insurer and the claimant. And, of course, many people don't understand why you only get the money if you've done something stupid!

BECK Could the problem be that policies are quite cheap and the commission is low?

AVERY No, I don't think that's important. It doesn't mean much work for a broker to sell a personal liability policy. For an insurance company, however, there can be a lot of hassle over claims. For instance, there is often a conflict of interest between the insurer and the claimant, who wants the claim to be paid even though the insurer can show there is no liability. This is often the case when the third party is a neighbour or friend of the claimant. Members of the family are naturally excluded.

BECK Would moral hazard be a problem if liability cover was compulsory?

AVERY Not really. As a matter of fact, there's far more moral hazard with a household policy than with personal liability. It's the policyholder himself who benefits from a buildings or contents policy, but in the case of liability, it's the third party. No, the main objection to compulsory liability is the administration involved. How would you check that everyone was covered? That would be difficult and cost a lot of money.

1. Why does Wolfgang Beck think Paul Avery has given an unlikely example of a liability claim?
2. Who benefits from a liability policy?
3. Why does Paul Avery compare not having a liability policy to playing 'negative lotto'? In your view is that a helpful idea?
4. You have probably never seen the word 'hassle' before. Can you guess its meaning from the context?
5. How many reasons does Paul Avery give for the fact that not more liability policies are sold? What, for him, are the main reasons and what is the least likely reason for this? What about you? What do you think?

C Explain the process of a liability claim by putting these steps in the correct order. Say which of the three parties is responsible for each step.

- first party: the insured
- second party: the insurer
- third party: the injured party

Process steps
asks for full details of incident from 1st & 3rd party
settles or rejects claim or asks for more information
reports the incident to insurer
injures 3rd party or damages his property
decides who was responsible for the incident
responds and sends account of incident to insurer
checks whether claimant is insured & premium paid
demands compensation from 1st party

D If an insured person injures a neighbour or damages his property and the insurer rejects the claim, there may be conflict between the first and second party. Why? Discuss with a partner.

2 Working with words

A Match the words or phrases with their definitions. Define the word left over.

1 negligence	a the money a court awards against a first party
2 voluntary	b having no choice, being forced to do something
3 moral hazard	c the number of actual customers as a percentage of those in the population who could be customers
4 commission	d indemnity, the money paid in settlement of a claim
5 compulsory	e harm done to someone's property
6 damages	f responsibility for bodily injury, property damage or financial loss
7 third party	g the injured person
8 damage	h the danger that people's behaviour changes for the worse when they are insured: e. g. they become more careless
9 compensation	i carelessness
10 liability	j money that an agent or broker receives for bringing business to an insurance company
11 penetration rate	

B Use words and phrases from A to complete the following sentences.

1 The court ordered Mr Jones to pay … of £20,000 for the … to Mr Smith's reputation after he had told a damaging story about Mr Smith that was untrue.
2 If you are careless, the court will make you pay for your …, and for this reason it is important that you have a … policy.
3 Motor insurance is … in all European companies. If it were … , an accident victim (the …) would not receive … if the driver who was liable could not pay.
4 … is a greater problem for property insurers than liability insurers, because whoever causes an accident does not get the money.
5 Wolfgang Beck thinks if agents received more … for selling liability policies, the … might be higher.

INFO 'Damage' and 'damages'

Damage refers to things, such as damage to property.
Damages (*plural noun*) refers to the money given to a claimant by a law court in a liability case.
Compensation (also: **indemnification**) is a general term for money paid in return for something: 'The damages awarded to the claimant were compensation for the bodily injury and property damage he suffered.'

USEFUL PHRASES

Asking for repetition
I'm sorry. I didn't quite catch that.
Excuse me, could you repeat that, please?
Would you mind repeating that please?

Asking someone to speak more slowly or loudly
Sorry, could you speak (a bit) more slowly.
You're speaking rather quickly. Could you please slow down a bit/little?
I'm afraid I can't hear you very well. Could you speak up a bit/little?
Could you please speak (a bit) more loudly?

3 Role-play: a liability claim

Harold Prince was travelling on a crowded bus when he accidently hurt a small boy. As he was getting off the bus, his briefcase hit the boy on the forehead. He left his card with the child's mother when he saw the boy was quite badly hurt. Harold Prince has just received a solicitor's letter stating that the boy was concussed and was treated in a private clinic, for which he should pay the medical expenses. He phones Proximus, his personal liability insurer, to report this. He has difficulty understanding his telephone partner.

KMK Work with a partner. Role-play the conversation below using the useful phrases from page 74.

Proximus receptionist

Melden Sie sich mit dem Namen der Firma sowie Ihrem eigenen.

Harold Prince

Sagen Sie, dass Sie einen Haftpflichtschaden anmelden möchten.

Proximus receptionist

Bitten Sie den Anrufer um seine Policenummer.

Harold Prince

Bitten Sie Ihre Gesprächspartnerin / ihren Gesprächspartner höflich etwas langsamer und lauter zu sprechen.

Proximus receptionist

Entschuldigen Sie sich und wiederholen, dass Sie die Policenummer des Anrufers brauchen.

Harold Prince

Lesen Sie Ihre Policenummer vor, und zwar: 3000658/201.

Proximus receptionist

Sagen Sie, dass Sie in Ihrem Computer nachgeschaut haben, und fragen Sie, ob er Harold Prince heißt.

Harold Prince

Bestätigen Sie (*confirm*) dies.

Proximus receptionist

Bitten Sie Herrn Prince, seine Geschichte ganz kurz zu erzählen.

Harold Prince

Beschreiben Sie das Ereignis. Betonen Sie wie viele Leute im Bus standen: es war nämlich die Stoßzeit (*rush hour*) und die Busse nehmen viel zu viele stehende Passagiere mit.

Proximus receptionist

Unterbrechen Sie Herrn Prince höflich und fragen Sie, was dann passiert ist.

Harold Prince

Beschreiben Sie, was auf dem Gehsteig passierte. Das Kind übergab sich. Sie mussten ins Fitness Studio weiterfahren und gaben der Mutter Ihre Karte. Heute haben Sie einen Brief von einem Rechtsanwalt erhalten. Das Kind liegt nun in einer Privatklinik und Sie sollten für den Aufenthalt (*stay*) bezahlen.

Proximus receptionist

Sagen Sie Herrn Prince, Sie haben seinen Fall notiert und werden die Informationen an die Schadenabteilung weiterleiten. Bitten Sie ihn aber, einen kurzen Bericht (*report*) darüber an die Schadenabteilung zu schicken. Die E-Mail Adresse lautet: flanders@proximus.com

Harold Prince

Wiederholen Sie die E-Mail Adresse. Fragen Sie sie/ihn, wie detailliert (*detailed*) der Bericht sein sollte.

Proximus receptionist

Kurz und bündig. Wenn mehr Information benötigt wird, wird man sich mit ihm sofort in Verbindung setzen.

Harold Prince

Beenden Sie das Gespräch.

Proximus receptionist

Bedanken Sie sich kurz für das Gespräch und beenden Sie es höflich.

4 A policy query

Jessica Raver is British and works as a dresser in a small theatre in Bavaria. She often works late and is sometimes the last person to leave the theatre in the evening. If she locks the theatre up at night, she has to take the keys home with her. She has just received the following memo from the director of the theatre.

LECHTALER OPERETTENBÜHNE

An alle Mitarbeiterinnen und Mitarbeiter

Aus aktuellem Anlass möchte Sie die Direktion darauf aufmerksam machen, dass der Verlust eines Dienstschlüssels für Sie sehr kostspielig sein könnte.

Die Kosten, um einen Schlüssel zu ersetzen, sind ca. €30, für einen Schließzylinder ca. €100. Wesentlich problematischer ist jedoch, dass die Schlüssel in der Regel alle Türen schließen und somit müssten im Falle des Falles alle Schließzylinder im Theater ersetzt werden. Bei Verlust eines Schlüssels kann daher ohne weiteres eine Schadensumme entstehen, die in den vier- bis fünfstelligen Bereich gehen könnte.

Diejenigen, die Verantwortung für Theaterschlüssel haben, sollten deshalb Ihren Versicherungsschutz dahingehend überprüfen!

Mit freundlichen Grüßen
Karl-Heinz Kaspar
Direktor

A Read the letter and do the following tasks.

1 Describe in a few short sentences what the message of this memo is.
2 Although Jessica has a personal liability policy, why is she worried about the letter?

Jessica's father took out a personal liability policy in her name and he pays the premium, because she earns so little. So she sends him an email. Unfortunately, her written English is much worse than her spoken English and she is not very good at typing.

B Help her to correct the email on the next page before she sends it off.

From: Jessrav99@gmx.de
To: Peter.Raver1@gmx.de
Cc:
Subject: Key problem

Hi Daddy,

How you are? I have a big broplem. The theater director sent a round writing about key loss. it says if we the keys lose we must much money pay. Sometimes I close theater, and what if I loose the keys?

Do you remind, you took a personal liberty for me with that broker fiend you play golf with him. But does it cover key loss? That's where the bunny's lying in the pepper! Could you please find this without for me? If it doesn't, would the insurer make wider cover so as to this risk? (I scan doc from theater and enclose).

I discuss the matter with some fiends and they think theater should cover this risk with their pubic policy. But place is almost plighter, so perhaps no cash. Anyway, it would be good if you can bring the cow off the ice.

Love,
Jessie

C Answer the following questions on the email.

1 Who should Peter Raver speak to?
2 What does Jessica want her father to do?
3 Why does she think that loss of keys may not be covered by a personal liability policy?
4 Who has the same opinion as Jessica?
5 What does she send with the email?

5 Role-play: a telephone conversation

Peter Raver contacts his broker, Christian Stamm, who rings up the insurance underwriter, Anke Müller, in Hamburg. They know each other well and always speak English on Fridays. Role-play their conversation.

KMK Work with a partner. **Partner A:** Look at this page. **Partner B:** Look at File 9 on page 133.

Partner A:
Sie sind Christian Stamm.
Sie schildern das Problem von Frau Raver und möchten wissen, ob ihre private Haftpflichtversicherung den Verlust von Schlüsseln deckt.
Sie schätzen, dass eine Deckungssumme von EUR 25.000 ausreichend wäre.
Sie halten eine Selbstbeteilung für unnötig, da es kein subjektives Risiko gibt.

6 An email

On Monday Christian Stamm sends the following email to Peter Raver. Complete the email with the missing words.

assist | best regards | confirm | excess | further | indemnifies | indemnification | third

Inbox - Outlook Express

From | Subject | Received

Dear Mr Raver

I am glad to ...[1] that Jessica's personal liability policy (No. 202401 56111) ...[2] her for lost keys belonging to ...[3] parties according to the special conditions. Please note the limit of ...[4] for such cases is EUR 25,000 with an ...[5] of EUR 150 per claim.

If you have any ...[6] questions, we would be glad to ...[7] you.

...[8]

Christian Stamm

7 The nature of liability

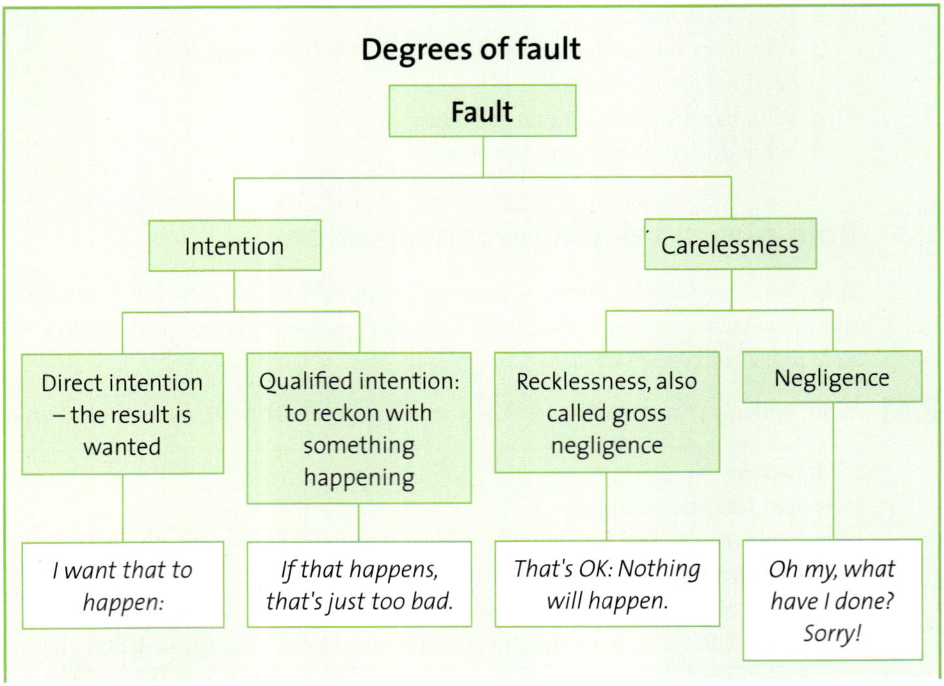

1 **Direct intention** means deliberate action. The result of the action is known and wanted. Not covered by a personal liability policy.

2 **Qualified intention** occurs if someone knows that his actions could cause injury or damage but he does not care. This might be the case if someone drives much too fast past a school in the lunch hour. He may not care whether he kills or injures a child. Not covered.

3 **Recklessness / Gross negligence** is the term used if the result was foreseeable but not wanted. This might be the case if someone drove much too fast past a school in the lunch hour. He thought nothing could happen, because he was a good driver and could avoid any children. Covered.

4 **Negligence** means carelessness or thoughtlessness, possibly due to a lack of concentration. Covered.

There are two other possibilities that involve either partial fault only or no fault:

5 **Contributory negligence** is when the third party is partly responsible for bodily injury or property damage that arises from the first party's actions.

6 **Fortuity** means pure chance. If an event is fortuitous, there is no fault. The insurer will fight the case for the insured.

A Look at the diagram and read the text and then decide which of the six categories listed above the following cases fall into. If you cannot decide, think of questions you would need to ask in order to be able to make a decision.

1 The lead of the coffee machine in Robert Streit's kitchen was frayed and a guest got a fatal electric shock when he turned it on.
2 While having a drink with a friend, Bill Sykes said that Joe Smith had been bribed. A reporter overheard him and wrote a story in the local paper. It turned out that the story was not true.
3 Fanny Green fell down the stairs while attending a party in your home. She had an alcohol level of 1.5 per mille in her blood.
4 A mentally ill person ran into the road, causing two cars to collide.
5 Bill Clumsy was painting the upper bedroom window of his terraced house. The pavement was next to it, because there was no garden. He dropped a tin of paint which fell on Nancy Peabody's new fur coat.
6 The wind blew away Nancy Peabody's wig, which landed on a cyclist's face. He could not see where he was going and crashed into Bill Clumsy, who broke a leg and was off work for three weeks as a result.

B Make up a liability claim or describe a real claim to your partner. See if he/she can recognize which of the six categories above it belongs to.

Grammar review Modal verbs

1 The injured driver **couldn't** identify the driver of the other car.
2 You **might** come across drivers who do not have third-party motor liability cover.
3 Everyone **should** have third-party motor liability cover.
4 In Germany you **needn't** have a personal liability policy.
5 Maybe in the future everybody **will have to** have the cover.

Modalverben (und ihre Ersatzverben) drücken u.a. aus, welcher Grad an Fähigkeit (*ability* – 1), Möglichkeit (*possibility* – 2) oder Pflicht (*necessity* – 3, 4, 5) besteht. Modalverben haben eine Gegenwartsform (2–4), manche auch eine eigene Vergangenheitsform (1). Ersatzverben werden benutzt, um andere Zeiten zu bilden (5).

Modalverb	Ersatzverb oder Ersatzausdruck	Entsprechung
can*	be able to	*können*
could*	was able to	*konnten/könnten*
may*		*könnten*
may*	be allowed to	*dürfen*
might*		*könnten*
must not	not be allowed to	*nicht dürfen*
should		*sollten*
must	have to	*müssen*
need not	not have to	*nicht müssen / nicht brauchen*

**may/might/can/could* können auch eine Möglichkeit (= *possibility*) ausdrücken.

8 Practice

A Complete the gaps below with a modal verb.

If an incident involving a third party occurs for which you …[1] be made liable, you …[2] (not) admit liability. You …[3] report the matter to your insurer so that it …[4] be dealt with. The insurer will contact the third party so that it …[5] learn its version of the incident. In this way the insurer …[6] get a good idea of what actually happened.

Harold Prince told Proximus that he …[7] (not) see the child in the crowded bus. Even though the bus was crowded, however, he …[8] have seen him because the boy was wearing a yellow pullover. For this reason the company …[9] (not) claim that the mother was partly to blame. They …[10] (not) claim contributory negligence.

B Work with a partner. For each of the situations (1–4) think of at least two sentences:

- What must you do?
- What needn't you do?
- What can you do if you want to?
- What mustn't you do?

1 Your liability insurer wants to know why you took so long to report a claim.
2 You have changed your bank account.
3 You have received a third warning that a bill payment is overdue.
4 Proximus have rejected your liability claim. You believe they have made a mistake.

9 Types of liability insurance

12

Wolfgang Beck and Paul Avery are now talking about the different types of liability.

A Copy the chart and fill in the boxes as you listen.

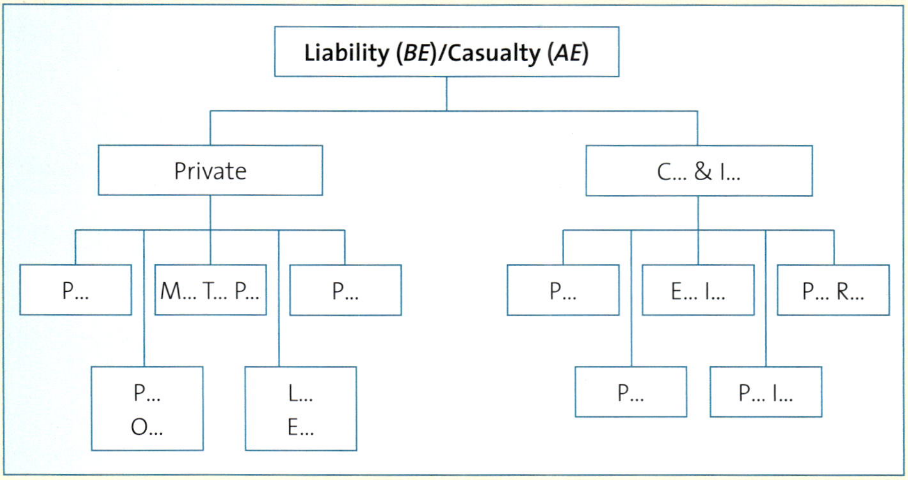

B Decide which kind of liability insurance would be needed for the following situations.

1. Someone drinks a glass of lemonade that is contaminated with oil.
2. Your dog bites the postman.
3. You trip someone up in the street and he or she breaks a leg.
4. You are a factory owner. Oil has been leaking from a tank on your property and polluting the ground water.
5. Trend Engineering Plc design a new bridge. It collapses three years after it has been built.
6. The plumber breaks a lamp when he visits your home to repair a broken pipe.
7. The plumber slips on your highly polished staircase.
8. A manufacturer of laptops informs customers who bought laptops made in June to return them to the retailer. There is a danger that they could catch fire.

C If you had to decide whether the first party was liable in the above cases, what additional information would you need in each case?

D Discuss the following question: What other types of commercial and industrial covers can you think of?

Motor insurance

Andrew Fox from Newcastle is surfing the Internet for information about car insurance in Germany. He is starting a job in Hamburg soon and wants to insure his car there. He finds the following car insurance guide in English.

http://www.insurance-faqs.org/auto/what-insurance-do-i-ne

Motor insurance

Europe | Germany

What kind of car insurance do you need?

When you take out a car insurance policy in Germany, you will be offered a choice of three main levels of cover.

Third-party cover

The minimum type of motor insurance you can take out is 'third-party', which is compulsory in Germany. This covers liability for …

- injuries to other people, including passengers;
- damage to other people's property;
- accidents caused by passengers;
- damage caused by the use of a caravan or trailer towed by the car.

TIP: This level of cover makes sense for an older vehicle where almost any repair would cost more than the car is worth, or where replacing the vehicle might only cost a few hundred Euros.

Third-party, fire and theft cover

The next step up is 'third-party, fire and theft' (sometimes written as TPFT) or partial cover. This provides the above cover, plus cover for fire damage or theft of the vehicle. In Germany, explosion, hail, storm, lightning and breakage of glass are also included. If you are at fault in the event of an accident, partial cover will not pay for repairs to your car unless the collision was with an animal.

TIP: Partial cover is useful for vehicles of average or minimum value. It can also be useful for younger drivers who find comprehensive policies too expensive, for occasional drivers and for drivers with minimal no claims discounts. It is generally unsuitable for regular drivers or drivers with expensive cars.

Comprehensive cover

This is the most complete form of car insurance and protects against the above, plus …

- accidental damage to the vehicle;
- malicious damage to the vehicle.

TIP: Not all comprehensive policies are the same. All insurers cover the basics, but many also offer additional benefits, such as courtesy cars in the event of theft, breakdown or accident, or protected no claims discounts. If you agree to use an approved repairer in case of accidental damage, some insurers will offer you a discount or extra benefits.

Source: adapted from *www.moneysupermarket.com*

1 Shopping for motor insurance

A Match these words from the website to the definitions below.

approved repairer | at fault | comprehensive cover | compulsory | courtesy car | no claims discount | partial cover | third-party cover

1 a discount for not claiming on your policy
2 the minimum cover available in motor insurance
3 required by law
4 a replacement car while your car is being repaired
5 cover that includes accidental damage to your own car
6 a garage that is licensed by your insurance company
7 If you cause an accident, you are …
8 fire and theft of the insured vehicle is covered

INFO No claims discount

A **no claims discount** (also: **no claim discount**) is the same as the German *Bonus-Malus* system. In Britain and Australia it may also be called a **no claim bonus**.

B Are the following statements about the website true or false? Correct the false statements.

1 Third-party, fire and theft cover is required by law.
2 Damage caused by a towed trailer is covered by the towing car's liability insurance.
3 Malicious damage to your car is covered under partial cover.
4 Comprehensive cover also includes cover against hail and storm damage.
5 Passengers who cause an accident while using your car need a private liability policy.
6 Comprehensive cover is most suitable for expensive cars.

2 What covers what?

Copy the table below and put the following perils under the correct type of insurance cover.

accidental damage to one's own car | bodily injury to third parties | breakage of glass | collision with animals | damage caused by martens | damage to the property of third parties | explosion | fire | flood | hail | lightning | storm | theft | vandalism

Third-party liability	Partial cover	Comprehensive cover

3 Types of vehicles

A Match the types of vehicles with the pictures.

camper van | convertible | coupé | crossover | estate | four-wheel-drive | hatchback | limousine | motorhome | pick-up | people carrier | saloon | van

B Find an American expression (AE) or a synonym (S) from the box below for each type of vehicle (1–7).

liftback | MPV (multi-purpose vehicle) | off-road vehicle | roadster | RV (recreational vehicle) | sedan | station wagon | SUV (sports utility vehicle)

1 estate car (AE)
2 saloon (AE)
3 motorhome (AE)
4 four-wheel-drive (AE + S)
5 people carrier family van (AE)
6 hatchback (S)
7 convertible (S)

4 What cover do I need?

Discuss the following profiles with a partner and find the most suitable motor insurance cover.

1 The Argentine football star Javier Piñeta has signed a contract with a German first division football team and wants to insure his brand new Porsche Cayenne.

2 Adrian Banks is working in Germany for six months. He has a company car, but only for company use. He purchases a scooter worth €500 for shopping trips.

3 Peter Fuchs wants to lease a new car on a three-year leasing contract.

4 Jennifer Heinz drives a ten-year-old Smart; she has just passed her driving test.

5 Manfred Hofer drives a 6-year-old family van. He bought it a year ago for €8,000.

5 What factors influence the premium?

13

Andrew Fox is listening to a radio programme on car insurance in Germany.

KMK

A Listen to the programme and take notes on the following questions.

1 What is the first factor of premium mentioned?
2 In Germany there are categories from group … to group … .
3 Is it always the same group for third-party, partial and comprehensive cover?
4 Name three groups of 'high-risk' drivers.
5 What is the maximum period for a no claims discount?
6 How many years do you typically lose in case of an own-fault accident?
7 What is the bonus for more than one insured car called?
8 What is the typical starting percentage for first-time motorists?
9 How does the use of the car influence the premium?
10 What is the typical excess agreed on in partial cover?

B Make a list of factors that determine the cost of motor insurance with your company. Compare it with your partner's answers and discuss any differences.

Grammar review *If*-sentences

1 If you **accept** an approved repairer, some insurers **will offer** a discount.
2 Third-party cover **may make** sense if you **drive** an older car.
3 If you **had** a claim, it **would cost** you a fortune.
4 If I **had followed** your advice, I **wouldn't have paid** so much money.
5 Motoring **becomes** more expensive if petrol prices **rise**.

- *If*-Sätze vom Typ 1 drücken eine erfüllbare Bedingung aus (1–2). Der *if*-Nebensatz steht im **simple present** und im Hauptsatz wird das *will-future* (1) oder ein Modalverb wie *may, can, must* oder *need* + Infinitiv verwendet. (2)
- *If*-Sätze vom Typ 2 drücken eine Bedingung aus, die eher unwahrscheinlich ist (3). Der *if*-Nebensatz steht im **simple past** und im Hauptsatz wird *would/could/might/should* + Infinitiv verwendet.
- *If*-Sätze vom Typ 3 drücken eine Bedingung aus, die nicht mehr erfüllbar ist (4). Der *if*-Nebensatz steht im **past perfect** und im Hauptsatz wird *would/could/might/should* + *have* + Partizip Perfekt verwendet.
- Bei grundlegenden Erkenntnissen, die sich nie ändern, stehen beide Satzteile im **simple present**. (5)
- Steht der *if*-Nebensatz an erster Stelle, wird der Hauptsatz durch ein Komma getrennt. (1, 3, 4)

6 Practice

A Match the beginnings (1–5) with the endings (a–e) to make complete sentences.

1 If the car is destroyed or stolen,
2 If the car was damaged,
3 If the stolen car is recovered within a month,
4 If the stolen car wasn't recovered within a month,
5 If the repair is more expensive than the car's value,

a the insurer would indemnify the policyholder for the costs of restoring it to its previous condition.
b the insurer only indemnifies the car's value.
c the policyholder must take it back.
d the car would become the property of the insurer and they would pay the claim.
e the policyholder receives the replacement value of an equivalent car, with the agreed excess deducted.

B Complete the following sentences with your own ideas.

1 If you damaged other people's property, …
2 If you park your car in the street, …
3 If you are added to your parents' policy, …
4 If you drive an older car, …
5 If you were at fault in case of an accident, …
6 If you accepted an approved repairer in case of accidental damage, …

7 Role-play: making a motor insurance quote

Andrew Fox has now moved to Germany. He has a company car for himself but has bought a car for his wife, Tess. He is phoning his insurance agent.

Work with a partner. **Partner A:** Look at this page. **Partner B:** Look at File 10 on page 133.

> **Partner A:** You are an insurance agent.
> Make a list of questions you need to ask Mr Fox to make a motor insurance quote.
> Ask your partner for all the information you need.

8 Contacting an insurer abroad

KMK Send a letter to Mr Fox's former insurance company in Britain. Ask them to confirm his 5 years no claims discount. Take the necessary information from his last cover note.

Westhill
Direct

25 Bath Road
BRISTOL
BS32 4AW
Fax: 01454 611722
Email: service@westhilldirect.co.uk

Your Personal Details

Date: 10th November 20..
Your reference number: 29308560
Policy Period: 10/11/20.. to 09/11/20..

Policyholder details
Name: Andrew Fox
Address: 7 Reeves Road, Aldershot, Hampshire, GU12 4NT
Telephone: 01234 567890
Date of Birth: 01/01/1958
No. of years No Claims Discount entitlement: 5 years
Do you wish to protect your No Claims Discount? Yes

9 A motor insurance claim

14

A Six months later you have the following message on your answering machine. Prepare a note/memo for your boss in German.

B Match the parts of a car to the illustration below.

bonnet (BE) / hood (AE) | boot (BE) / trunk (AE) | door | front bumper | front wing (BE) / front fender (AE) | headlight | hub-cap | indicator | rear bumper | rear-view mirror | roof | steering wheel | tyre (BE) / tire (AE) | windscreen wipers | wheel | windscreen (BE) / windshield (AE)

10 Helping a customer over the phone

Andrew Fox is now talking to Petra Müller, his agent, about his accident claim.

15

Your teacher will give you a copy of a claim report. Listen to the telephone conversation and complete the claim report.

11 Ever had an accident?

Think of an accident you were involved in or have heard about. Explain to your partner what happened or write a report about the accident.

USEFUL PHRASES Describing a car accident

to (not) be able to stop the car
to ignore someone's right of way
to skid on a slippery road
to crash into another car
to move forward/backwards
to back into a parking space
to overtake another car
a dent
a scratch
a crack in the windscreen

12 What drives the cost of car insurance?

People often grumble about rising car insurance costs. Why do prices go up? Clearly, there are many factors that influence the quote you will be given. Some are personal to you and will be discussed in another section of this guide. Others depend on the level of benefits you want from your motor insurance policy. Details of these – which you can pick and choose between and thereby influence the price you pay – are also listed elsewhere.

But there are other factors that you have little or no control over and depend on outside circumstances. Here are some factors that influence how much you pay for your motor insurance.

1) **The soaring cost of litigation:** Drivers are more likely nowadays to claim for personal injury, like a serious case of whiplash, and the amounts paid out for injuries are much higher than they used to be.
   Insurers have attempted to intervene to control these costs. But courts that rule in favour of claimants still make very significant awards in cases of serious injury or death. And from the point of view of claimants, this is a positive thing.
2) **Medical costs:** Accident and emergency departments can claim for cost of treatment from the insurance company. This also includes ambulance costs.
   If you are the blameless victim of an accident, the bill will be paid by the opposite party's insurer. If you are to blame, your insurer will have to pick up the bill. Medical costs can be very expensive.
3) **Uninsured drivers:** Official statistics say that one in 20 drivers is uninsured. But recent research carried out by Pollsters Insurance specialists suggests that this figure is more like one in 10 drivers, although the uninsured period in many cases may run to just a few days or a few weeks.

This is cold comfort to someone who is involved in an accident with an uninsured driver. This adds around £30 to the average annual premium.

Ironically, this can produce a Catch-22 situation: as premiums get higher it becomes even more tempting for some people not to take out car insurance.

Source: adapted from *www.moneysupermarket.com*

A Answer these questions on the text.

1 What factors for the price of motor insurance are discussed in detail somewhere else?
2 Can you think of examples of these factors?

KMK **B** Summarize the most important facts from topics 1) to 3) for your boss in German.

Financial products

Tina Haupt is going to work in Britain for a year. Therefore she needs to open a bank account to receive her salary. The company she will be working for has sent her the following brochure about bank accounts.

Basic bank accounts in Britain

There are two types of bank accounts for managing everyday money: a basic bank account and a current account. Banks also offer a range of accounts designed for medium or longer-term savings. Savings or 'term' accounts usually pay more interest than basic and current accounts.

Basic bank accounts

Basic bank accounts offer a convenient place to keep the money you need for everyday use. You can arrange to have your salary, state pension payments and benefits or tax credits paid into one. You can also pay in cheques or cash free of charge and set up direct debits, which pay regular bills automatically from your account.

With a basic bank account you get a cash card which you can use at a bank machine to withdraw cash. Some also offer a debit card that you can use to pay for items and get 'cash back'; but with a basic account these will only work if there's enough money in your account.

You don't get a cheque book with a basic bank account and you can't take out more money than is in the account, which means that you can't 'go overdrawn'. For this reason basic bank accounts are useful for anyone worried about overspending.

Current accounts

Current accounts have more features than basic bank accounts. For example, they usually offer:

- a cheque book
- a cheque guarantee card (acts as a 'guarantee' so makes cheques more widely acceptable)
- a debit card (some allow payments without checking your account)
- a credit card
- direct debits (automatic bill payments direct from your account)
- standing orders (regular set payments from your account to someone of your choice)
- BACS (Bankers' Automated Clearing Service) – the facility to accept payments directly into your account (e. g. from your employer), or for you to make one-off payments to someone else out of the account
- overdraft facility – the bank may allow you to go overdrawn up to a certain amount; but you need to arrange this in advance and charges apply (you pay extra charges if you go overdrawn without an agreement)

Some current accounts pay interest on money you leave in the account, but the rate is usually low.

Savings accounts

Banks offer a wide range of savings accounts. The main differences between them are how quickly you can get at your money, the minimum amount required to keep the account open and the type and rate of interest paid.

Source: adapted from *www.direct.gov.uk*

1 Bank accounts in Britain

A Are the following statements true or false according to the brochure on page 90?

1 Savings or term accounts are ideal for everyday banking.
2 Your wage or state pension can be paid into your basic bank account.
3 You get a cheque book with all types of accounts.
4 With a basic bank account you can take out more money than you have in your account.
5 You get interest on the money you have in your current account.

B Choose the most suitable type of account for these situations/needs.

1 You want to make sure you don't go overdrawn.
2 You travel a lot and need a credit card.
3 You want to put money aside for a purchase or expense (for example, a holiday, a car or a deposit on your home).
4 You might not get through the bank's credit check to open a current account.
5 You want to get extra benefits like a debit card.

C Make a list of the additional benefits you get with a current account.

2 Inside a British bank

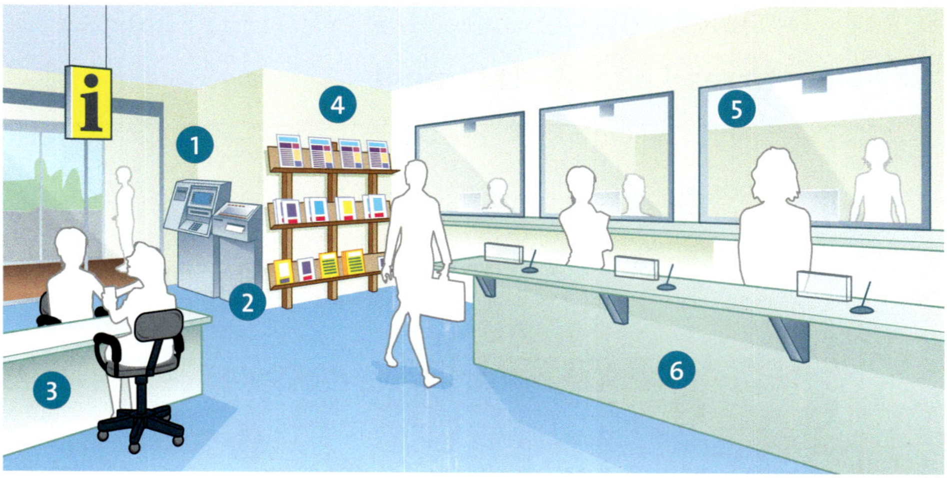

A Match the words from the box to the parts of the interior of a typical branch of a British bank.

> ATM / cash dispenser | information desk | leaflet/flyer rack | self-service desk | service tills/counters | statement printer

B Are there any differences to the German bank branch you usually use? What advantages or disadvantages can you see?

3 How to pay?

A Read the brochure on page 90 again. Copy the table below and complete it with the methods of payment mentioned in the brochure.

Means of payment	
Cash payments	Non-cash payments
...	...

B Complete the table with any other means of payment you know.

C What do (or would) you use for the following payments? Explain why.

1 Paying your insurance premium.
2 Paying the rent for your flat.
3 Paying a doctor's bill.
4 Paying for your groceries.
5 Paying for items ordered on the Internet.
6 Paying a parking fine.
7 Paying your mobile phone bill.
8 Paying the membership fee for your sports club.

4 How to read a bank statement

Sort Code (1)
Account
Account Type

(2)
Opening Balance: **£432.76**
Closing Balance: **£1289.26**

Date	Type	Description	Paid Out	Paid In	Balance
(3)	(4)				(6)
01 Aug	CR	A Smith	(5)	330.00	762.76
02 Aug	TFR	IBM	(5)	1300.00	2062.76
03 Aug (8)	DD	Orange	45.00		2017.76
04 Aug	SO (9)		632.00		1385.76
05 Aug	ATM	ABC Bank (10)	31.50		1354.26
06 Aug	ATM	Bank Inc	30.00 (11)		1324.26
07 Aug	CH	B Smith	35.00	(7)	1289.26

Match these descriptions to the items (1–11) on the statement.

a the balance at the beginning of the statement period
b denotes a regular payment from your account to another account by standing order
c the date of transaction
d the amount of transaction
e the running balance after each transaction
f the balance at the end of the statement period
g denotes a regular payment from your account by direct debit
h the type of transaction
i shows an ATM withdrawal of £30 at an extra cost of £1.50
j bank account details and sort code
k shows an ATM withdrawal of £30 at no extra cost

USEFUL PHRASES **Bank accounts**

pay (cash) into / make a deposit to / credit sth to a/your account
take (cash) out of / make a (cash) withdrawal from / debit sth to a/your account
be overdrawn / in the red

5 A German bank statement

Proximus

Girokonto	12345678	BLZ 700 333 88		Kontoauszug 7
Proximus Privatbank München		Steuer-Nr. 280/123/45678		Blatt 1
Datum	Erläuterungen	Wert		Betrag
Kontostand in EUR, 11.05.20.., Auszug 6				188,40+
30.05.20..	LASTSCHRIFT ALDIDL MITTE SAGT DANKE EC 1020304050 29.05 11.37 CE3 EUR01234567890123456789O	30.05	28,44-	
01.06.20..	LOHN/GEHALT 05/20.. FIRMA MÜLLER & Co			1.107,59+
Kontostand in EUR, 01.06.20.., 19:34 Uhr				1.267,55+

Herr
Manfred Schmidt
Schillerstr. 12
80333 München

IBAN:
DE44 7003 3388 0000 1234 56
SWIFT-BIC.: PPBMUC10001

A Find the following information in the statement.

1 the bank sort code
2 the balance at the end of the statement period
3 the international bank code
4 the account holder's name
5 a direct debit beneficiary
6 the account number

B What type of bank account do you have? Explain why. (80 words)

C Make a list of entries to your account, sorted into incoming and outgoing payments.

6 Saving money

There are many different ways of saving your money, including very safe and stable investments. These are important for money that you are going to need in the near future, e.g. for a new computer. This category includes bank savings accounts and money market investment funds, which are some of the safest short-term investments. When placing your money with a bank or money market fund, you earn interest, or yield, which may vary, depending on the rates of interest.

TYPES OF SAVINGS ACCOUNTS:

Bank savings accounts:
When you are beginning to save, you should place your money in investments that are as safe as possible. In addition, you should have at least some of your money in short-term investments. Bank savings accounts are such an investment.
The most popular type today is the **instant access** savings account. It is ideal for money you may need in a hurry. Your emergency fund should be in this type of account so that you can immediately meet any unexpected costs. Some instant access accounts come with a cash machine card so you can get your money 24 hours a day. There will probably be a limit on how much you can take out but it should be enough to cope with financial emergencies. Some savings accounts are designed as **notice accounts**. Traditionally, your savings earn a better rate of interest if you agree not to touch them for some time. With **notice accounts**, you can only get your cash by giving prior notice of your intention to withdraw it. For example, with a **90-day notice account** you would have to wait three months to get your money or you have to pay a penalty fee to get it earlier.

Money market accounts:
These are accounts offered by banks and building societies. The interest rate of these accounts is higher than that of a savings account. You are able to transfer your money on a daily basis and therefore this type is also called cash account.

CD or certificate of deposit:
The bank holds your money for a set period of time, usually one to six months, or one to five years. Unlike an instant access savings account, you may not withdraw your money at any time. If you do, the withdrawal will carry a penalty fee.

Money market funds:
Money market funds are available from investment fund companies. They are similar to a money market account, but you usually get a better return with money market funds, because they invest in very short-term bonds, which tend to be less risky than longer-term bonds and they also invest in safe government papers and other related investments. Money market funds that invest exclusively in government securities have very little risk, while giving you better rates of return than typical bank savings accounts.

National savings accounts:
The Government-run National Savings & Investments department offers a range of accounts and bonds. National Savings might not offer a solution to all your savings problems but there are few safer places for your money. All products are capital secure – investors will get their money back whatever happens.

Source: adapted from *www.moneyinstructor.com*

A Match these words from the text to the definitions.

certificate of deposit | money market account | money market fund | national savings account | notice account | penalty fee | yield

1 The return you get on your investment.
2 Investment in short-term and secure papers, like corporate commercial papers.
3 You are able to withdraw money without prior notice.
4 Money you have to pay because you withdraw your savings before maturity.
5 An investment with the maximum security.
6 Your investment is fixed for a certain period like 1 to 5 years.
7 You have to tell the bank that you want to withdraw money from your savings account.

B Find the best investment for these situations. Explain your choice.

1 Peter Banks has received £15,000 from his insurance company for his stolen car. He is looking for a replacement on the Internet but hasn't found the right car yet.
2 Fiona Hull wants to put some money away for 4–5 years. She is very concerned about the financial crisis and is safety-conscious.
3 Marion Richardson is looking for a medium-term investment which should be safe but should also earn some interest.
4 Ten-year-old Tim Blake wants to save part of his pocket money each month.

7 Borrowing money in the UK

Susan Peterson is a 23-year-old shop assistant from Honiton. She has found a new job in Exeter, 20 miles away from the place where she lives. So she needs to buy a car.

16 Listen to the CD and then copy and complete the table below.

KMK

1	Einfachste Form der Kreditaufnahme		...
2	Voraussetzung hierfür ist		...
3	Wer bietet Kredite an?		...
4	Welche Finanzierungsgründe werden genannt?		...
5	Wie verdient die Bank an Krediten?		...
6	Was ist in die APR eingerechnet?		...
	Angebot der Hausbank:		
	7	Zinssatz	...
	8	Laufzeit	...
	9	Monatliche Rate	...
10	Folge von verspäteter Zahlung		...
11	Empfehlung bei Aufnahme eines Kredites		...

8 Borrowing money in Germany

A Summarize the text below for an English-speaking customer.

Der Kredit, der nur Vorteile kennt

Unsere Vorteile im Überblick:

- ✓ Wunschbetrag von 1.000 bis 75.000 Euro
- ✓ Ratenhöhe individuell bestimmbar
- ✓ Laufzeit wählbar von 12 bis 84 Monate
- ✓ direkte Online-Sofortzusage
- ✓ 1 Monat Rückgaberecht
- ✓ Sondertilgungen und Ablösung jederzeit einfach möglich
- ✓ mit Best-Preis-Garantie
- ✓ Ermittlung des persönlichen Maximal-Kreditbetrages und Zinssatzes
- ✓ keine zweckgebundene Kreditbestellung
- ✓ Hinterlegung von Gegenständen zur Kreditabsicherung ist nicht erforderlich
- ✓ TÜV-geprüfte und -zertifizierte Online-Bestellung
- ✓ partnerschaftliche Begleitung in allen Finanzlagen
- ✓ Restkreditversicherung jederzeit kündbar

Source: *www.easycredit.de*

B Work with a partner. Discuss the best solution for the following people. Explain why you have chosen your solution.

1 Andrew Wolfe bought a new car for £27,000. He got £10,000 from selling his old car. He would like to pay back the money over a period of three years.
2 Nicole Bright is going to finish university in three months time. She has a part-time job, but has to stop working for her final exams. She needs £1,500 for her daily living expenses.
3 John and Patricia Svenson are planning to buy a house for £275,000. They have a deposit of £50,000.

Grammar review **Verb + infinitive or verb + ing-form?**

1 The bank clerk **suggested investing** in unit trusts.
2 Don't **risk losing** your money.
3 You can **arrange to have** wages transferred to your account.
4 She can't **afford to buy** a new car.
5 I **prefer to save/saving** part of my salary on a regular basis.
6 I **stopped smoking**. *(= Ich hörte auf zu rauchen.)*
7 I **stopped to smoke**. *(= Ich hielt an um zu rauchen.)*

- Im Englischen folgen oft zwei Verben aufeinander. Das zweite Verb kann in der *ing*-Form (*gerund*) **(1–2)** oder im Infinitiv **(3–4)** stehen.
- Verben + Infinitiv wird verwendet u.a. bei: *afford, agree, decide, expect, learn, manage, offer, plan, promise, seem, tend, want, wish.*
- Verben + *ing*-Form wird verwendet u.a. bei: *admit, appreciate, avoid, carry, consider, dislike, enjoy, finish, insist, miss, risk, suggest, think of, talk about, worry about.*
- Nach einigen Verben können beide Formen ohne wesentliche Bedeutungsunterschiede stehen. **(5)**
- Andere Verben haben jedoch unterschiedliche Bedeutungen, je nachdem, welche Form verwendet wird, z. B. *forget, remember, stop*. **(6–7)**

9 Practice

Complete the following sentences with the correct form of the verb in brackets by using the infinitive or the gerund.

I wish (speak) …[1] to the manager. He offered (send) …[2] me some brochures. After I have finished (read) …[3] the brochures, I will probably want (invest) …[4] in government bonds. They seem (be) …[5] a secure investment. I dislike (invest) …[6] in risky papers. I don't want (risk) …[7] (lose) …[8] my money.
Robert always wants (read) …[9] the paper first thing in the morning. He particularly enjoys (read) …[10] the newspaper on Sunday mornings. He never worries about (be) …[11] late for college. His teacher expects him (learn) …[12] for the final test. She talked about (do) …[13] a test next week. Robert's colleague offered (help) …[14] him with a motor insurance claim. He told him (start) …[15] with the claim report first. Robert has just stopped (smoke) …[16] for health reasons.

10 The way Britons pay

Chris Stuart is an economics student who has to write a paper about trends and changes in the ways people prefer to pay for goods and services. Listen to the dialogue between him and John Hawkes, a specialist from the Payments Council. The Payments Council is an organization that has been established to ensure that the UK payment systems and services meet the needs of users, payment service providers and the whole economy.

17

KMK

A Listen to the CD. Copy the table and fill in the missing information.

1	Percentage of cash payments in 1998	...
2	Percentage of cash payments last year	...
3	Number of cash machines in the UK	...
4	Most of the cash was withdrawn from	...
5	Cash withdrawals per second	...
6	Total amount of cash withdrawals in 2008	...
7	The use of 'cash back' ... over the last three years.	

B Are the following statements true or false? Correct the false statements.

1 The share of cash payments increased to 66% last year.
2 Cash payments will fall by 30% next year.
3 More than half of the cash payments were for payments of £5 or less.
4 The use of debit card cash backs dropped from £7.2 billion to £6.7 billion.
5 Almost 10,000 statements were printed at each bank branch.

INFO Writing and saying numbers

Fractions

1/2	a/one half
1/3	a/one third
2/3	two thirds
3/4	three quarters (also three fourths)
4 5/8	four and five eighths

Decimals

0.738	nought (zero/oh) point seven three eight
13.9	thirteen point nine
63.916	sixty-three point nine one six
63,916	sixty-three thousand nine hundred (and) sixteen

Large numbers

1,000,000	one million
1,000,000,000	one billion
1,000,000,000,000	one trillion

C Now listen to the text again and write down all the numbers mentioned in the text.

11 How we will pay in the future

Prepare for the day that we transfer money as easily as sending a text message, pay for products by placing a card next to a sensor and only see cheques in a museum.

That's the future suggested in the UK Payments Council's first annual plan.

Unlike the cheque book, cash will survive – but will become less fashionable than card or automatic payments. Payments themselves will become faster, with consumers and businesses able to access up-to-the-minute information about their finances. Just don't expect the changes overnight.

First plan

The UK Payments Council was set up in March 2007 and immediately set about formulating its first annual plan. The Council is partly an industry body, with 11 directors drawn from its members, but it also has an independent chairman, four independent directors and a mantra of transparency. It operates where co-operation is needed within the payments industry but says it will not intervene when competition delivers the best outcome. The most striking subject in its first plan is the end of the cheque.

'Our diagnosis that use of the cheque is in irreversible decline went almost unchallenged,' says chairman Brian Pomeroy.

Cheques have been part of life since 1659, having been developed from a system of notes written by merchants and goldsmiths. But the Payments Council predicts that by 2016 only one payment in 50 – some 840 million transactions – will be made by cheque.

Many High Street stores are already refusing to accept them, claiming they are slow, easy to fake and unpopular with consumers. These retailers include Tesco, Asda, Argos, Boots, Next, Sainsbury's, WH Smith and Marks & Spencer. So, it is a case of when, not if, cheques will be phased out.

Finding an alternative

The Payments Council suggested that cheques should go by 2018, but the date has been dropped from the final plan owing to concern over viable alternatives. This will now be looked at during an 18-month review, with consumers having generally been against setting a closure date and the industry promoting it.

This step was welcomed by consumer group *Which?* which suggested in a survey last year that 57% of people continue to find cheques 'really useful', while 31% disagreed.

Instead of writing cheques, consumers will increasingly use contactless or prepaid cards – similar to the Oyster card system seen on London's public transport system.

Meanwhile, the Council says it will decide whether to work on a collaborative bank account to bank account mobile payment service. New technology is also making it more likely that a mobile phone number could be a proxy for a bank account number, making transferring money as easy as sending a text message.

Source: *news.bbc.co.uk*

A Are the following statements true, false or not mentioned in the text?

1 Cheque books and cash will disappear in the future.
2 Transferring money will be as easy as sending a text message.
3 The changes will happen very quickly.
4 The UK Payments Council is a government body.
5 Cheques developed from notes written by merchants and goldsmiths.
6 Some High Street stores like WH Smith and Marks & Spencer refuse to accept cheques.
7 31% of consumers find cheques really useful.

B Write a text (80 words) about the future trends mentioned in the article.

KMK **C** Summarize the section headed 'Finding an alternative' in German.

Business insurance

There is no separate class of insurance called 'business insurance'. By 'business insurance' we mean the complete programme of insurance that is designed to minimize a company's risk of ruin. That programme will depend on the risks arising from the nature of the business of each specific company as well as its financial resources. For smaller shops, offices and companies there are standard insurance programmes, but large manufacturers need customized insurance programmes that are put together by experienced brokers.

1 How a business insurance programme is created

Step 1: Risk analysis
A broker visits the company to get to know its business at first hand. There is usually a meeting with the Commercial Manager, who explains the company's business and how it works. After a tour of the plant/factory, the broker writes an internal report, describing the risks and sums insured for the various classes of business the company needs.

Step 2: Tender and submissions
The broker sends an outline of the company's business and a list of the covers needed to a number of insurance companies. The tender may include the broker's own assessment of the approximate premium for each class of business. Those insurers that want to quote for the business then submit their quotations. The broker then selects the best submission for each class of business.

Step 3: Presentation by the broker to the company
The broker returns to the company and explains the insurance programme to the Commercial Manager and perhaps the Finance Director as well. They may have questions about the scope of cover, the price, policy conditions and the insurance companies selected, as well as other matters. After this discussion, changes may need to be made to the broker's concept.

Step 4: Completion
After agreement has been reached, a broker agreement is signed. The company is now the broker's client (called the principal in the London market). This means the broker now has the authority to arrange the insurance programme with the agreement of the insurance company. This arrangement is usually reviewed every two or three years.

A Answer the following questions on the introduction and text.

1 What is the purpose of business insurance?
2 What would be a better name than 'business insurance'?
3 What do you understand by 'customized'?
4 Is the four-step process outlined above more suitable for a corner shop or for a company that manufactures goods?

B Discuss the following questions with a partner.

1 Why might a broker want to visit a company's plant personally rather than relying on information from the current insurance programme?
2 What aspects of a company and its business (e.g. location, turnover) is an insurance broker interested in?
3 If brokers were not used to set up a business insurance programme, what would be the alternative? Why do you think brokers are often preferred?
4 Why is the broker agreement important?

2 Classes of insurance

A Match the classes of insurance with their definitions.

Class of insurance	Definition
1 life	a Covers loss of gross profit (turnover minus variable costs) as a result of loss of production due to property damage.
2 kidnap and ransom	b Covers the insured against a sudden and unexpected event, not under the control of the insured, that results in death, bodily injury or property damage.
3 employers' liability (only in the UK, not in Germany)	c Pays for the costs incurred in having a product returned that could cause bodily injury or property damage.
4 public liability	d Covers losses during transport, not only as cargo on ships, but also by other means of transport.
5 credit	e Indemnifies manufacturers who are the victims of deliberate damage to foodstuffs or the threat of such damage.
6 marine	f Pays a specified sum on death or upon the insured surviving a given term of years. Key man insurance: death or disability cover for companies or partnerships.
7 business interruption	g Indemnifies company managers and the companies themselves for claims due to the wrongful acts of managers – e.g. giving misleading information about the company.
8 fidelity	h Covers the liability for bodily injury or property damage caused by objects manufactured or supplied by the insured.
9 personal accident (PA)	i Covers a business against bad debts: failure to pay bills due to insolvency or delay in paying bills.
10 product recall	j Covers the legal liability to third parties for bodily injury or property damage caused by gradual pollution.
11 product liability	k Indemnifies the insured for legal liability with respect to third-party bodily injury and property damage arising from the business.
12 product tamper	l Protects employers against financial loss due to the dishonesty of employees.
13 directors and officers (D&O)	m Covers the insured's legal liability for bodily injury or disease to employees if caused at work.
14 environmental impairment	n Indemnifies the insured for the money paid to pirates and others who capture employees and/or their relatives and only release them when money is paid.

B Which cover is needed in each of the following situations?

1 An accounting clerk transfers company money into his own bank account.
2 A customer does not pay its bills.
3 Someone is injured by a machine that a company manufactures.
4 A motor manufacturer discovers that the brakes on some of its models do not work properly. These models must be taken to a workshop to be repaired.
5 A company loses money because a manager ignores internal guidelines.
6 Oil from a manufacturing plant seeps into the ground and poisons the groundwater. As a result of this a farmer cannot grow crops and suffers financial loss.
7 There is a fire in a factory so that no goods can be produced for several weeks.
8 Two partners are concerned about the future of their business if one of them dies.

3 The broker visit (part 1)

Cut & Trim is a manufacturer of lawnmowers. Alison Kent, the Finance Manager, has invited a broker, Roger Bell from Ultima, to propose a new business insurance programme.

KENT Good morning, Mr Bell, welcome to Cut & Trim.

BELL Good morning, Ms Kent, nice to meet you. This is my colleague, Jane Roberts, who will be working with me.

KENT Fine. So, let's get down to business. In the past we simply renewed our policies every year with our only insurer. However, our new Managing Director now wants a broker to take a critical look at our insurance programme, and your company has a good reputation in the market … so here we are. Please ask any questions you like.

BELL Thank you, Ms Kent. We're glad to have the chance to do business with you. The main purpose of our visit today is to make a risk analysis. I understand that you manufacture lawnmowers. We'd like claims experience for property, liability and electronic insurance and anything else that is relevant.

KENT I've prepared detailed statistics for you, but our loss experience is pretty good: only a few small claims in the last five years. In that period we've had only one storm claim in property and no business interruption or liability claims. Our Production Manager will take you round the factory later, so that you can see the plant for yourselves.

ROBERTS Fine. Then let me ask you a few questions about the business. Do you use forklift trucks?

KENT Not as far as I know.

ROBERTS What about paint and varnish for the lawnmowers? Are they stored here on site?

KENT Yes, they are. But quite far away from buildings, in tanks.

BELL Does the company own its own buildings?

KENT Yes, we do.

BELL And what's the value of the buildings and their contents?

KENT At the last valuation – only six months ago – their value was estimated at £10 million and the contents at £3 million. They are insured against fire, water and windstorm on a reinstatement basis. The contents are also insured against theft.

BELL And what's the value of stock?

KENT By stock do you mean raw materials, products being manufactured and finished products?

BELL Yes, all three.

KENT Well, that's roughly £16 million. That figure is based on a one-day estimate and can vary both upwards and downwards. Stock is insured against the same perils as the buildings, and also against theft.

BELL The sum insured for business interruption is £13 million, I believe. We usually calculate the sum insured for business interruption by subtracting the figure for stocks – that's £16 million – from turnover.

KENT I see. Well turnover is £30 million.

BELL OK, so turnover (£30 million) minus stock (£16 million) gives £14 million sum insured for business interruption, and until now you've had £13 million, you tell me. That's not so far off. A little low perhaps. Do you intend to raise the sum insured?

KENT No, and we've never had a claim, by the way.

BELL And what about the indemnity period?

KENT Sorry, what's that?

BELL If you had a business interruption claim, what is the maximum period of time that your insurer would pay?

KENT That's one year, but we have to pay the first three days of any claim.

BELL OK, I see: an indemnity period of one year with a time deductible of three days. Jane, would you like to take over now?

ROBERTS Sure. Ms Kent, I suppose you have public and products liability insurance. Do you export to North America – the United States and Canada?

KENT Occasionally, and our current products liability policy includes that region.

ROBERTS Good, OK. And I imagine you have product recall cost cover?

KENT Do you mean to pay for our costs if we have to ask customers to return faulty lawnmowers?

ROBERTS Yes, that's what I mean.

KENT Yes, we do, with a cover limit of £500,000. We've never had to recall a product, I'm glad to say.

ROBERTS And D&O?

KENT D&O?

ROBERTS Directors and Officers, to protect people like you – managers – if you are sued for any mistakes you make.

KENT We're a privately-owned company. We don't have any shareholders and so we don't need this cover.

ROBERTS Well, we could discuss that. You also have electronic insurance, I believe. What's the sum insured?

KENT £2 million.

BELL Fine. So if it's all right with you, Ms Kent, I'd suggest that we take a stroll around the plant with your Production Manager.

KENT Right. I'll give him a ring.

A Answer the following questions on the dialogue.

1. Why has Cut & Trim contacted Ultima?
2. What is the main purpose of the visit from Ultima's point of view?
3. How has the responsibility for informing the brokers been split between Alison Kent (the Finance Manager) and the Production Manager?
4. Why does Jane Roberts ask about the storage of paint and varnish?
5. How do we know that Alison Kent understands why she has asked that question?
6. Why does Roger Bell think the sum insured for business interruption is a little low?
7. What liability covers does Cut & Trim have and which cover does it not want?

B Discuss the following questions with a partner.

1. What do you understand by the 'indemnity period' and the 'time deductible' for business interruption insurance?
2. Alison Kent explains why Cut & Trim does not have D&O. Do you agree with her?

4 The broker visit (part 2)

Roger Bell and Jane Roberts have been shown round the plant by the Production Manager and they are now back in Alison Kent's office to discuss the findings.

18

A Listen to the CD once and answer these questions.

1 What aspects of the business have the two brokers focused on?
2 Are they prepared to place the risks in the market?
3 What will the next steps be?

B Listen to the discussion again and answer the following questions.

1 What is problematic about the storage of paint and varnish? What do the brokers want Cut & Trim to do about this?
2 What is the fire hazard that the brokers discover?
3 How do the brokers propose to use the site plan?
4 Why does Jane Roberts want more information on the claims against Cut & Trim's electronic insurance policy?
5 Why is Alison Kent worried about having several insurers covering the insurance programme?
6 What is the compromise that Roger Bell suggests?
7 In your view, was the visit a success?

5 The tender

Below is an outline of the tender that Ultima sent to its panel of insurers.

Policyholder	Cut & Trim Lawnmowers Ltd 17 Commercial Road, Blackburn BB1 7HH		
Tender of	01.09.	**Submission by**	30.11.
Insurance classes	Property Electronic Liability, including product recall Transport, including baggage Legal expenses Accident		
Broker	Ultima Brokers Plc 200 Ring Road North, Manchester M12 4XY		
Documents enclosed	1. General customer information 2. Submission requirements • Premium modality 3. Underwriting information • Relevant risk factors • Sums insured / perils • Loss experience • Conditions / policy articles 4. Suggestion about premium volume		

A Answer the following questions on the tender on page 104.

1 What is the address of Cut & Trim's head office?
2 How long has Ultima given the insurance companies to send in their submissions?
3 Which classes of insurance are required that were not discussed during the visit?
4 What are the four supporting documents that the broker sends to each insurer?

B Discuss the following questions with a partner.

1 Why is the premium modality important?
2 How will the loss experience be expressed?
3 What conditions would you expect to see?
4 Why does the broker make a suggestion about the premium volume?

USEFUL PHRASES

to submit a proposal = to send a proposal
a submission = the sending of a proposal
a proposal = an offer
premium modality = how the premium is paid, e.g. monthly, quarterly or annually

6 Role-play: rearranging a meeting

Ultima inform Cut & Trim that they have received all the submissions from their panel of insurers and suggest a meeting for Friday, 16th October at 9.30 a.m.

KMK **A** Work with a partner. **Partner A:** Look at this page. **Partner B:** Look at File 6 on page 131.

Partner A:
You are Alison Kent's secretary. She gives you the following instructions:
"Give Roger Bell a ring please, and tell him I can't make it. Arrange a time the following week. Look in my diary and pick a reasonable time when I won't be playing golf. Oh, and you'd better let him know that the boss* wants to join us. You'll have to find out when he's free, of course. Thanks a lot."
Ring Roger Bell and re-arrange the meeting.

*Dr Clement Lear, the Managing Director

B Write an email to Roger Bell at Ultima confirming the arrangements you have made. In the meantime, Dr Lear has said that he wants to invite the brokers for lunch. Mention this in your email.

USEFUL PHRASES Changing an appointment

I'm calling/writing about our meeting appointment on ...
I'm afraid I can't make it. Something unexpected has cropped up.
I'm sorry, but I can't keep / have to cancel our appointment for next Wednesday.
Would you mind postponing/rearranging our meeting on Thursday?
Could we fix another time?
Would ... suit you?
Could I suggest Monday the 20th instead?
Would Monday the 20th at 9 o'clock be convenient for you?

7 A summary of insurance cover

Roger Bell and his colleagues at Ultima select the best submissions and summarize these covers in preparation for their presentation to Cut & Trim. This is the part of their summary that deals with property and liability. At the end you will find a number of important clauses they intend to mention in their discussion.

Property including business interruption

Contract parameters	Subject/perils	EUR
Insured perils for property	fire, piped water, storm, hail, natural perils and burglary	
Insured perils for business interruption	fire	
Sums insured	Value of buildings in 2011 Value of contents in 2011 Stocks (one day random sample) Clean-up expenses Business interruption	10,000,000 3,000,000 16,000,000 400,000 13,000,000
Retentions	Fire Piped water Storm/hail Flood, earthquake Subsidence, landslip, snow pressure	None 1,000 500 15,000 5,000
Terms and conditions	Usual conditions and articles – see table below	
Annual net premium	Including 100% stocks	**30,700**

Liability

Contract parameters	Subject	EUR
Basic sums insured	Public & product liability: Bodily injury Property damage Financial loss Environmental impairment: Personal injury, property damage, financial loss	 3,000,000 1,000,000 100,000 3,000,000
Retention	Basically none, except for personal injury in Canada and the USA	between 250 & 1,000
Terms and conditions	Usual conditions and articles	
Annual net premium for a turnover of 30,000,000 EUR	Public & product liability	**9,000**
Basic sums insured	Product recall	500,000
Retention	At least 10% of claim	10,000
Terms and conditions	Usual conditions and articles	
Annual net premium for a turnover of 30,000,000 EUR	Only product recall	**6,000**

Selected property clauses from property and business interruption policies

Class of insurance	Article / clause / basis of cover	Meaning
Property material damage	average clause	If the sum insured is less than the value of the property, claims payments are reduced pro rata.
Property material damage	escalator clause	Sums insured increase automatically p.a. This helps avoid underinsurance due to inflation.
Business interruption [BI]	indemnity period	This is how long the insurer has to pay for a loss due to a break in production.
Business interruption [BI]	time deductible	This is how long the insured pays for a loss in production before the insurer begins to pay.
Business interruption [BI]	contingent BI	This covers the insured for the financial effects of an interruption in its suppliers' or customers' production.

INFO

A policy of *indemnity* compensates the policyholder for an insured loss on the basis of the market value of the object at the time of loss.
A policy of *reinstatement* provides the replacement value at the time of loss. For this reason this type of cover is sometimes called *new for old*.

A Are the following sentences about the policy summary true or false? Correct the false statements.

1 The insurer pays for a business interruption loss from the first day.
2 Cut & Trim has cover against arson.
3 Financial loss is only covered by the liability policies.
4 The property policy is a policy of indemnity.
5 The premium for liability insurance depends on the volume of business written.
6 Cut & Trim holds a retention for all property perils.
7 The business interruption policy taken out by Cut & Trim does not have contingency cover.

B Discuss with a partner: A factory owner wishes to insure his machines, some of which are quite old, against fire. Which is better for him – a policy of indemnity or a policy of reinstatement?

8 The broker presentation

Dr Clement Lear, Managing Director of Cut & Trim, and his Finance Manager, Alison Kent, meet Roger Bell and Jane Roberts of Ultima Brokers in order to consider their business insurance proposal. The meeting has already started.

19

A Listen to the CD and answer the following questions.

1 Are Dr Lear and Alison Kent satisfied with the broker's presentation?
2 What is Dr Lear's fear about arson and how does Roger Bell answer?
3 Why does Dr Lear want to know whether Proximus knows about Cut & Trim's risk management weaknesses?
4 Why does Alison Kent think that Cut & Trim may need contingent interruption loss for suppliers but not for customers?
5 What arguments does Jane Roberts use to persuade Dr Lear that Cut & Trim needs product recall insurance?

B Discuss the following questions with a partner.

1 Is Dr Lear's fear about the behaviour of a new insurer justified?
2 Is the broker's answer convincing?

9 Working with words

A Copy the table and complete it with words from the dialogue.

Verb	Noun
administer	...
...	interruption
recommend	...
...	reduction

Verb	Noun
...	avoidance
...	extension
supply	...
...	proposal

B Use the correct form of the words from the table to complete these sentences. Some nouns may be in the plural.

1 If Cut & Trim accept Ultima's … , they will improve their risk management and … many losses in the future.
2 An … in business production can ruin a company in quite a short time.
3 Covering a company for the losses arising from an interruption in the production of its … or customers is a natural … of business interruption insurance.
4 Normally a business … has a time limit and if it has not been accepted by that date, it is no longer valid.
5 If Ultima succeeds in … Cut & Trim's insurance premiums, they may be asked to … their whole business insurance programme in future.

Grammar review **Relative clauses**

1 Brokers **who/that** can provide risk management expertise are often used to put together such programmes.
2 Ultima Plc, **which** has been in business for over 40 years, is prepared to place our risks in the market.

- In Beispielsatz 1 definiert ein **defining relative clause** das vorhergehende Substantiv (= *Brokers*) genauer. Man braucht diese Information, um zu wissen, welche *brokers* gemeint sind.
- In Beispielsatz 2 liefert ein **non-defining relative clause** zusätzliche Informationen über das vorhergehende Substantiv (= *Ultima Plc*). Ohne diesen Relativsatz würden wir den Sinn genauso gut verstehen können. Solche Relativsätze werden mit einem Komma eingeleitet.
- Man verwendet immer ***who/that*** für Personen oder ***which/that*** für Sachen. In einem *non-defining relative clause* kann man *that* aber nicht verwenden.

10 Practice

Join the following sentences using defining or non-defining relative clauses. Label the sentences *defining* or *non-defining*.

Example Robert Smith works for Proximus. He complains about the long hours.
→ Robert Smith, **who** works for Proximus, complains about the long hours. (*non-defining*)
1,000 people work for Proximus. They complain about the long hours.
→ The 1,000 people **who** work for Proximus complain about the long hours. (*defining*)

1 Some companies have poor results. They should improve their work processes.
2 Proximus is a German insurer. It has just appointed a new CEO.
3 Uwe and Willi work in Nuremberg. They are great Frankonian guys.
4 No-one is perfect. Nevertheless, everyone can do a good job. (Begin: *Even someone …*)
5 The head office of the DVA is located in Munich. It has a wonderful view of the Alps.
6 Personal liability insurance is a cheap form of cover. Everyone should have it.
7 Roger Bell is an experienced broker. He has worked for Ultima for 15 years.
8 Dr Lear is the new Managing Director. Cut & Trim has just appointed him.

11 Role-play: a presentation

The Ultima brokers did not give a formal presentation to their business partners at Cut & Trim, because Dr Lear and Alison Kent had read their documents beforehand and simply asked questions. This sometimes happens. But just as often the business partners do not see anything before the meeting and then the broker must give a formal presentation.

Imagine that this had been the case with Ultima. Work in a group of four. Prepare and deliver a broker presentation, using the facts from this unit. Two of you are the brokers and two of you are Dr Lear and Alison Kent.

12 Named perils and all risks property policies

Ultima's property policy was a named perils policy. This type of policy is given this name, because the perils – fire, piped water, storm, and so on – are listed up front. Perils which are not mentioned are not covered. This is the traditional way of providing property cover.

All risks policies, on the other hand, do not list the perils that are insured. This does not mean, however, that the insurance company will pay all claims whatever has happened. Instead, excluded perils are listed at the end of the policy and limit the range of cover.

Isn't it misleading to speak of 'all risks' when many perils are in fact excluded? In practice, isn't it a case of swings and roundabouts as to whether a policyholder has the one type of policy or the other? Not quite. Under a named perils policy the insured must prove that property damage was caused by an insured peril. All risks policies reverse the burden of proof: a claim will only be rejected if the insurance company can demonstrate that it was excluded by the policy. All risks policies are therefore, by nature, more consumer-friendly, and an insurance company offering this type of cover will have to define its list of exclusions very carefully and clearly.

Defining perils to be excluded means that all risks policies generally give rather wider cover than named perils policies and that they are more flexible. As a result they can more easily meet the policyholder's specific requirements, and this is their secret of success in the market.

So is a policyholder better off with an all risks policy than one based on named perils? It all depends. Why didn't Ultima offer to obtain property cover for Cut & Trim on an all risks instead of a named perils basis? Possibly because it may have been more expensive, especially if the insurance market was in a hard market phase, when demand exceeds supply. In such a market all risk cover may not even be available.

A Read the text then answer these questions.

1 My house has been damaged by subsidence and I make a claim under my buildings policy. If my insurer does not want to pay the claim, it will have to prove 1) that subsidence is excluded, and 2) if it is not excluded, that the loss was not caused by subsidence. What type of property policy do I have?
2 If I had the other kind of property policy, what would I have to do to make a claim?
3 Why is the burden of proof an important issue? Refer to questions 1 & 2 in your answer.
4 Why are all risks policies more flexible than named perils policies? Name some types of business that may not need this flexibility.

B Work with a partner. The last two sentences of the text refer to the market cycle.

1 What is it?
2 How does it work?
3 Are all classes of insurance equally affected by it?

13 Just for fun

INFO Idioms

It's swings and roundabouts. = *gehüpft wie gesprungen*
A bird in the hand is worth two in the bush. = *Lieber den Spatz in der Hand als die Taube auf dem Dach.*
He who pays the piper calls the tune. = *Wes Brot ich ess, des Lied ich sing.*
The British are fond of such expressions, which they very often shorten (**bold** type), making them even more difficult for foreigners to understand.

A What do you think the following idioms mean?

1 **Don't cross your bridges** before you come to them.
2 Empty vessels make most noise.
3 It's an ill wind that blows no-one any good.
4 One man's meat is another man's poison.
5 Don't teach your grandmother to suck eggs.
6 **When the cat's away**, the mice will play.
7 **A stitch in time** saves nine.
8 **It takes all sorts** to make a world.
9 It's like water off a duck's back.
10 **Don't count your chickens** before they are hatched.

After the meeting with Cut & Trim, Roger Bell and Jane Roberts are talking at the bar of their hotel. For everything Jane Roberts says, Bell has a comment.

B Complete the dialogue, using the short form of the idiom if there is one.

20

ROBERTS Poor old Alison Kent does whatever Dr Lear tells her, doesn't she?
BELL Well, he who pays the piper …
ROBERTS Yes, I know, I can't stand people like that.
BELL …[1]
ROBERTS Yes, I suppose you're right. It's better to have someone like Kent than someone who has too much to say.
BELL …[2]
ROBERTS Yes, like that guy in our department, what's his name – Fortesque. He's always telling other people how to do their jobs, even the experienced colleagues.
BELL …[3]
ROBERTS And if you try to point out something to him, he just doesn't listen.
BELL …[4]
ROBERTS Right! But to change the subject, I really am a little worried that if we get this business, Proximus will insist on Cut & Trim spending a lot of money on risk management, and then we as brokers could have a problem.
BELL …[5]
ROBERTS Yes, I suppose you're right. And even if Cut & Trim and Proximus have problems with each other, that's a chance for us, the brokers, to show how diplomatic we are.
BELL …[6]

Reinsurance

1 How reinsurance works

Belinda Whitehead, a business consultant, wants to know more about reinsurance. She is speaking to a reinsurance manager from Unterhaching Re, Uwe Döring.

21

WHITEHEAD Uwe, you've been in reinsurance for many years, but it's quite a mysterious business for many people. What do reinsurers actually do?

DÖRING It's very simple really. We insure insurance companies, and in reinsuring themselves with us, they reduce their risk of going bankrupt.

WHITEHEAD But why should insurance companies need reinsurance? If their underwriting is good and they are well capitalized, why should they lay off part of their business to reinsurers?

DÖRING That's a good question, and this time the answer is not so simple. Perhaps I can try to explain using the example of an insurance company with a large property portfolio that has been conservatively underwritten.

WHITEHEAD 'Conservatively underwritten' – you mean the premiums are quite high.

DÖRING Let's say the rates are adequate, the claims are under control and the insurer understands its business. If everything runs according to plan, the insurer expects to make a profit.

WHITEHEAD So where's the problem?

DÖRING Well, let me ask you a question: What could go wrong? How could an insurer with a fairly rated book of business fail to make a profit and even make a severe loss?

WHITEHEAD Hm.

DÖRING Imagine that the portfolio contains one thousand buildings and that the average value is €500,000. However, a few of them are very expensive, costing well over €1 million, with one even costing €20 million.

WHITEHEAD Yes, I see. If one of the most expensive buildings burns down …

DÖRING Exactly, that's what we call the risk of random loss. In plain English, bad luck. And so reinsurance is often bought to pay for the large claims. But tell me, what else could happen?

WHITEHEAD Well, let me see. Let's imagine the insurer believes that its risks were adequately rated, but perhaps it made a mistake, and they weren't. Or perhaps there was a lot of competition in the market so that the rates were too low. It might make sense to reinsure then.

DÖRING Yes, the risk of error. That happens, too. But of course a reinsurer will generally not accept a share of risks that are underrated. Reinsurers, too, must have a fair chance of profit. They also have shareholders. And there are two other unpleasant possibilities for our property insurer, however. The rates may have been OK when the risks were priced, but what if something happened in the market later making them no longer sufficient?

WHITEHEAD The risk of change, you mean.

DÖRING Exactly. And finally there is one other thing that could happen. The worst thing of all.

WHITEHEAD A catastrophe, you mean. A huge loss.

DÖRING Yes, that's right. By the way, a catastrophe for reinsurers means an accumulation of losses due to one event. For example, many yachts destroyed in a harbour by one windstorm would be a catastrophe. So let's sum up. There are four good reasons for transferring risk to reinsurers: the risk of random loss, the risk of error, the risk of change and the accumulation or catastrophe risk.

A Answer the following questions on the dialogue.

1 What is the purpose of reinsurance?
2 Even if an insurer underwrites its risks conservatively, how could it still suffer heavy losses if it did not have reinsurance?
3 What does the 'risk of random loss' mean?
4 When might a reinsurer not want to accept risks from an insurance company?
5 How does a reinsurer define a catastrophe?

B Insurers need reinsurance because of the threat of 1) random loss, 2) error, 3) change or 4) catastrophe. Which is the main threat in each of the following situations?

1 In the 1970s and early 1980s many life insurance companies wrote term insurance policies at cheap rates. Then a new disease, AIDS, became a significant factor.
2 An insurance company has a book of marine business. There is a storm in the North Sea and three of its ships sink.
3 A jumbo jet with three hundred passengers on board crashes on landing. There are no survivors.
4 Until the year 2000 all life companies in Ruritania offered the same rates for smokers and non-smokers. Then some companies offered lower rates for non-smokers and higher rates for smokers. Consider now what the situation of the companies will be that still offer the same rates.
5 An insurance company offers a new product on the market. This type of policy has been sold in other European countries for a number of years, but this is the first time in Germany.
6 The coach carrying a top Bundesliga football team crashes and falls off a bridge into a river.

2 Balanced and unbalanced portfolios

22

Belinda Whitehead and Uwe Döring are now talking about two types of portfolio and how each portfolio is endangered by different threats. As you listen, look at the diagram, starting at the left-hand side with the portfolio profile.

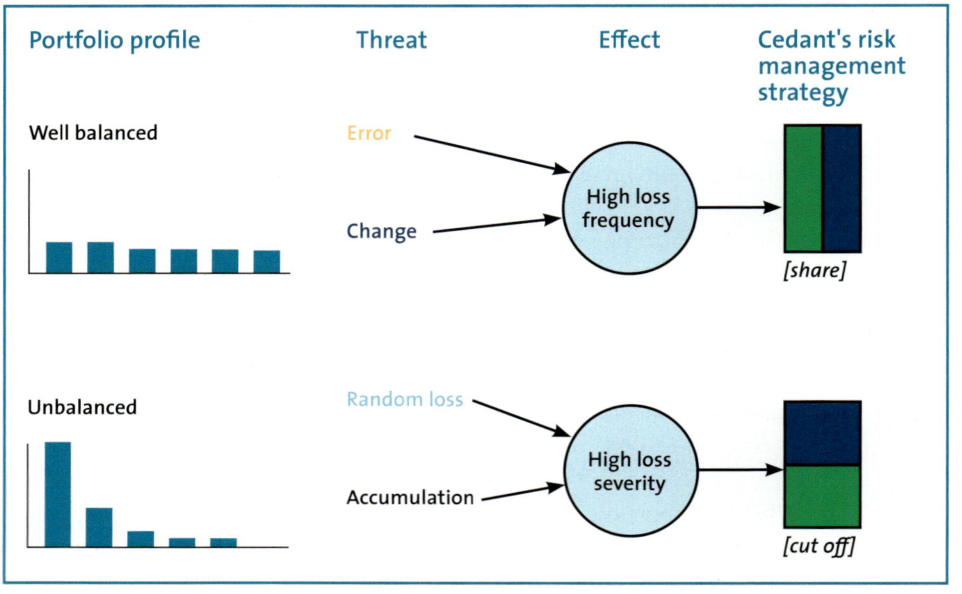

Listen to the CD and answer these questions.

1 What is the difference between a balanced and an unbalanced portfolio of risks?
2 What are the main threats to a balanced and an unbalanced portfolio of risks?
3 What do you understand by the catastrophe risk? How does an insurer reinsure itself against it?
4 Use the words *cedant* (noun), *cede* (verb) and *cession* (noun) in one or two sentences of your own.

3 Non-proportional reinsurance

Belinda Whitehead and Uwe Döring are now discussing reinsuring an unbalanced portfolio.

WHITEHEAD So you've just told me that an insurer that wants to reinsure a balanced portfolio tends to share the risks with its reinsurer. In the case of an unbalanced portfolio, however, the insurer is more likely to use reinsurance in order to cap its claims. I still don't really see how that works. Can you give me a practical example?

DÖRING Let's think first of all about an unbalanced portfolio of risks. The cedant – the insurance company – will keep a deductible and the reinsurer will pay for all claims above this amount up to a certain limit, as in this diagram.

WHITEHEAD And how is the premium calculated?

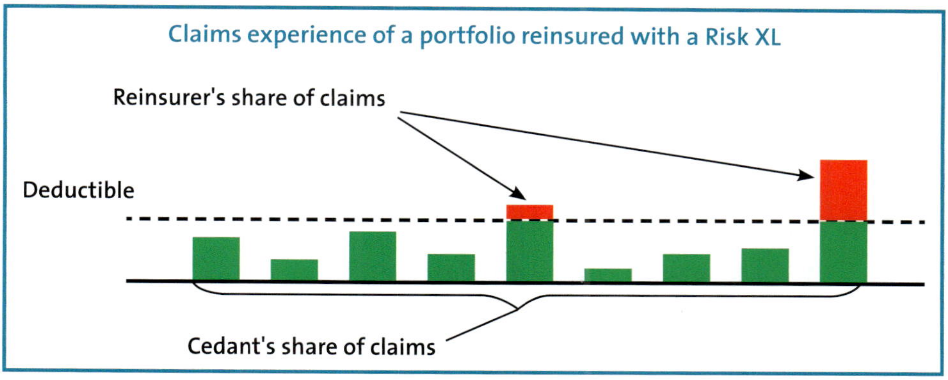

DÖRING On the basis of past experience. The reinsurer will want to know the loss experience over at least the last five years for the share of claims it should pay for in the future. On the basis of these statistics, it calculates a net premium for the book of business in order to cover expected claims. This net premium may need to be modified in view of market developments. Then it adds a loading to cover its expenses, profit and tax, and the net premium plus the loading is the reinsurance premium. The really important thing to understand is that the reinsurer calculates its own premium. It does not base its premium on the cedant's original premiums from its policyholders. That's why this form of reinsurance is called non-proportional reinsurance.

WHITEHEAD You mean because it has no relationship to the cedant's original premium?

DÖRING That's right.

WHITEHEAD And this type of reinsurance covers single risks, is that right?

DÖRING Yes, that's right.

WHITEHEAD And does it have a name?

DÖRING Yes, it does. It's called risk excess of loss – or Risk XL for short.

A Answer the following questions on the dialogue.

1 When an insurer wants to use reinsurance to limit its liability for claims, what is the part of the claim called that the insurer keeps for its own account?
2 Why is reinsurance that is based on a calculation of past claims called non-proportional reinsurance?
3 What sort of portfolio is suitable for non-proportional reinsurance?
4 How does a reinsurer calculate the premium it needs to cover the claims from a portfolio of non-proportional risks?
5 What kind of risks does Risk XL cover?

B Discuss these questions with a partner.

1 Why is risk excess of loss a good name for this type of reinsurance?
2 Bearing the premium calculation in mind, would you expect a risk excess of loss treaty to be 1) a long-term arrangement that is automatically renewable at the end of a year or 2) a short-term arrangement that has to be renegotiated at the end of the year?

4 Working with words

A Match the words or phrases on the left with their definitions on the right. One word is left over for you to define yourself.

1 underwriting	a cannot do business because there is no money
2 well capitalized	b risk portfolio
3 bankrupt	c risk assessment
4 accumulation	d sufficient
5 book of business	e enough money or funds to keep the business solvent
6 random loss	f bad luck, it is the big risk that causes a large loss
7 survivor	g mistake
8 error	h several losses happen at the same time
9 adequate	i …

B Copy the table and fill in the missing spaces.

Verb	Noun	Adjective
exist	…	…
compete	[2 words]	…
…	reinsurance	…
vary	[2 words]	…
…	…	threatening
…	expectation	…
differ	…	…
protect	[2 words]	…
…	summary	
retain	[2 words]	…
destroy	…	…
…	[2 words]	simple

5 Negotiating the terms of a Risk XL

The following day Jan Lubbers from the Dutch insurer KKV visits Uwe Döring at Unterhaching Re to review their reinsurance agreement.

	Last year	Year before last
Deductible	200,000	200,000
Lines	2	2
Reinsurance capacity	400,000	400,000
Reinsurance premiums	700,000	680,000
Reinsurance claims	670,000	580,000
Reinsurance results	30,000	100,000
Reinsurance rate	1.1‰	…
Highest claim for the reinsurer	…	
Number of claims for the reinsurer	…	…

A Find the missing information from the table while you are reading their discussion.

23

DÖRING Nice to see you again, Mr Lubbers.

LUBBERS Good morning, Mr Döring. Nice to see you again, too.

DÖRING Well, first of all, before we begin, please help yourself to tea or coffee.

LUBBERS Thank you.

DÖRING Now, looking at the figures for last year's business, I see that it was only marginally profitable. Reinsurance premiums were €700,000 against reinsurance claims of €670,000. The respective figures for the previous year were €680,000 and €580,000. So profit for us has fallen from €100,000 to only €30,000. For this year we reduced the rate from 1.25‰ to 1.1‰ I believe. Your deductible remains at €200,000 with a two line capacity of €400,000. Do you have any further information for me?

LUBBERS Well, as you point out, Mr Döring, the results are slightly worse this year. This is because there have been rather more claims – eleven in comparison to eight last year. The highest claim was for €550,000, so that after our deductible of €200,000, you paid €350,000 on that one.

DÖRING Mm. In future we'd like not only to have details of claims above your deductible, but also of larger claims within it: claims above €100,000 for each of the last five years, so that we can assess the trend more accurately. The trend seems to be negative, and if we are taking on the risk for next year, too, we don't want any surprises.

LUBBERS I have those figures here. I think you will agree that there is no upward trend.

DÖRING Well, of course, I see it a bit differently, but we'll study them in the next few days and be in touch with you. But I can say now that we will need a higher rate. We suggest that we return to the previous rate of 1.25‰.

LUBBERS That's rather difficult, Mr Döring. As I am sure you know, other reinsurers are also interested in our business and perhaps some of them could offer lower rates than yours. You have been our reinsurer for the last three years and we want to keep it that way. However, you must make it possible for us.

DÖRING Well, we'll study the figures you have given us, and then we'll see. Can you now tell us a little more about developments in the Dutch property market? Have there been any significant changes?

B Answer the following questions on the negotiation.

1 Why is Uwe Döring not happy with the development of this reinsurance account?
2 Why does he want information about claims within KKV's deductible?
3 What does Jan Lubbers want from the negotiation and what is Uwe Döring's aim?
4 The market cycle plays a background role in this discussion. Does it appear to be a hard or soft market?
5 What could the result of the negotiation be?

C Lubbers will find it difficult to keep the rate at 1.1‰. What do you think of his negotiating technique? Find language in his speeches to back up your opinion.

USEFUL PHRASES Negotiating

Making a concession
Well, as you point out, ...
I agree that the losses are slightly worse ...
Admittedly the losses are slightly worse ...
I take your point, Mr Döring. The losses are slightly worse this year ...
Well, of course, the losses are slightly worse this year. There's no point in denying that.

Persuading someone to make a concession
I think you will agree that there is no upward trend.
You must admit, there's no upward trend.
I think we can agree that there's no upward trend.

Disagreeing
Well, of course, I see it a bit differently.
Well, that's not quite how I see it.
That's one way of looking at it. However, ...
Really? I'm afraid I have a rather different opinion.

Playing for time
Well, we'll study the figures you've given us, and then we'll see.
We'll have to consider how we go forward.
We need to do our homework before making a final decision.
Let's look at it more closely.

6 Role-play: negotiating a renewal

Role-play another renewal negotiation, in pairs (Döring from Unterhaching Re and Lubbers from KKV) or in groups of four, in which case both Döring and Lubbers are accompanied by a colleague.

This time last year's business results are much better than the previous year and Uwe Döring is under pressure to renew the treaty at much better rates. Below are the statistics you need:

	Last year	Year before last
Deductible	200,000	200,000
Lines	2	2
Reinsurance capacity	400,000	400,000
Reinsurance premiums	700,000	680,000
Reinsurance claims	370,000	580,000
Reinsurance results	330,000	100,000
Reinsurance rate	1.20‰	1.25‰
Highest claim for the reinsurer	110,000	150,000
Number of claims for the reinsurer	10	10

Grammar review Reported speech

We can report what someone says using reported speech.

1 Döring: 'Please help yourself to tea, coffee or whatever else you would like to drink.'
Döring **invited** Lubbers to help himself to tea, coffee or whatever else he wanted to drink.

2 Döring: 'I'll study your statistics in the next few days and be in touch with you.'
Döring **told** Lubbers he would study the figures in the coming days and would then be in touch with him.

3 Lubbers: 'I have those figures here. I think you will agree that there is no upward trend.'
Lubbers **replied** that he had the figures with him. He **claimed** that there was no upward trend.

4 Lubbers: 'You have been our reinsurer for the last three years and we want to keep it that way.'
Lubbers **pointed out** that Unterhaching Re had been KKB's reinsurer for the previous three years and that they wanted to keep it that way.

- Bei der indirekte Rede wird ein einleitendes Verb wie *say*, *report*, *reply*, *claim*, usw. benutzt, um zu verdeutlichen, dass etwas berichtet wird.
- Steht das einleitende Verb in der Vergangenheit, verschieben sich die Zeiten folgendermaßen:

direkte Rede	indirekte Rede
simple present	simple past
present continuous	past continuous
simple past	past perfect (simple past *auch möglich*)
present perfect	past perfect
will	would
past perfect	*keine Verschiebung*

7 Practice

Rewrite what Jan Lubbers said at the negotiation in reported speech.

'Our business is still profitable despite more claims last year. We have taken steps to improve our underwriting, so that the quality of the risks will be better in the future. I advise you not to raise your rates, because there are other reinsurance companies we can turn to if Unterhaching Re does not continue to support us. In short, we are not prepared to accept higher rates next year, and if you insist on raising the rates to their previous level, we'll take our business to another reinsurance company.'

Start like this: *Mr Lubbers pointed out that his business was still profitable despite …*

8 Proportional reinsurance – quota share

In proportional reinsurance the reinsurer takes a share of the cedant's original gross premium. The following text and diagram explain how proportional reinsurance works.

This is the **Agreement**:
The reinsurer has a 50% quota share treaty with a cedant. This means the reinsurer receives 50% of the cedant's gross premium for the year and pays 50% of all claims. The reinsurer must pay commission to the cedant to pay for the latter's expenses for the reinsurer's share. The reinsurance commission is 30% for the reinsurer's share of the premium.

Basic terms of the reinsurance agreement
Reinsurer's liability: 50% Reinsurance commission: 30%
Profit commission: 30% profit sharing after reinsurance expenses of € 50,000

Reinsurance results
Cedants annual premium: €1,000,000 Claims: €400,000
Result before profit commission: €150,000 Result after Profit commission: €150,000

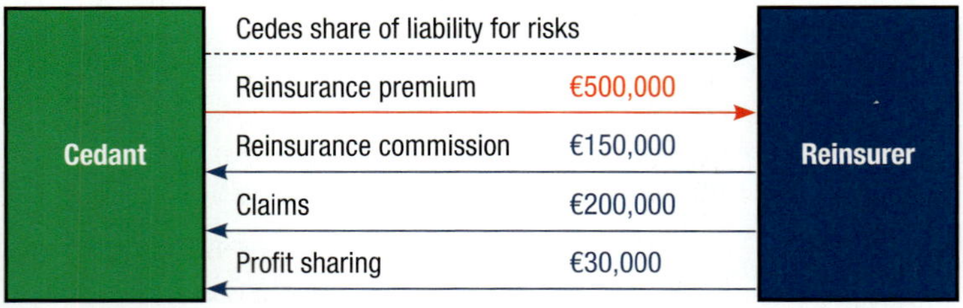

This is **what happened**:
The accounts for the year show that the cedant's premium was €1 million and that claims amounted to €400,000. Consequently, the reinsurance premium is 50% of €1 million – €500,000 – and its share of the claims was €200,000, i.e. 50% of €400,000. The reinsurance commission is 30% of the reinsurer's premium, i.e. €150,000. The reinsurer has made a profit of €150,000: that is €500,000 premium minus €200,000 claims minus €150,000 commission. There is a profit commission, however. Now the reinsurer does not return any profit unless its minimum profit requirements have been met. For this treaty this requirement is €50,000. This item is usually called 'reinsurer's expenses'. €50,000 having been taken away from the €150,000 profit leaves €100,000 to share, and the reinsurer has promised to pay 30% of this amount to the cedant, and so in the cash flow diagram €30,000 has been credited to the cedant. The annual result is therefore favourable for the reinsurer. It has earned €50,000 for the so-called reinsurer's expenses and it retains €70,000 of the profit. €50,000 and €70,000 make a total of €120,000.

A Answer the following questions on the text and diagram.

1. If an insurer has a 30% quota share treaty, what proportion of claims does it pay?
2. Why is a proportional treaty called 'proportional'?
3. If the reinsurer had a 40% share of the business and all other conditions stayed the same, how much profit would the reinsurer have returned to the cedant?
4. If claims for the year were €800,000 and all other conditions stayed the same, what would have been the reinsurer's result?

B Discuss the following questions about reinsurance commission with a partner.

1. Why might a reinsurer agree to a reinsurance commission that is greater than the cedant's expenses?
2. What is the risk for the reinsurer if it agrees to such a high reinsurance commission?

9 Proportional reinsurance – surplus

In this unit we have covered one form of proportional reinsurance – quota share – and one form of non-proportional reinsurance – risk excess of loss (Risk XL). It has also been mentioned that catastrophe excess of loss reinsurance (Cat XL) is a form of non-proportional reinsurance, because the reinsurance premium is calculated separately from the original premium received by the cedant from the policyholder. There is, however, another form of proportional reinsurance cover that has not been mentioned, and that is the surplus. Let's begin by comparing this with the quota share.

A quota share is an appropriate form of reinsurance if an insurer's results are threatened by high loss frequency and if the reinsured portfolio of risks is well balanced: that is, if the variation in the sums insured is not too great. However, if the portfolio contains a number of high sums insured, the retained amount may be too large in the event of a high claim. Furthermore, much of the premium transferred to the reinsurer may result from smaller risks that the cedant may feel it could keep itself. For these reasons, an insurance company may decide to retain a fixed amount in monetary terms (its retention) and cede only that share of each risk that exceeds it.

The maximum capacity provided by a surplus treaty reinsurer is expressed as a multiple of the retention. In property reinsurance this is called a line. For example, in a nine line treaty if the cedant's retention were €100,000, the obligatory acceptance of the reinsurer would be limited to €900,000. If the cedant lowered its retention to €50,000, the reinsurance capacity would be reduced proportionately to €450,000. If the retention were €100,000 and the cedant accepted three new risks (A, B & C) with sums insured of €50,000, €200,000 and €500,000 respectively, Risk A would not be ceded, and so there would be no liability for the reinsurer in the event of a claim. For Risk B the reinsurer would receive 50% of the gross premium and pay 50% of any claim. In the case of Risk C, the reinsurer would receive 80% of the premium and it would pay 80% of any claim. From these examples it can be seen that this is a very elegant form of risk management. Small risks that an insurer can keep itself are not reinsured, only those that exceed the retention being reinsured – the higher the sum insured, the greater the percentage that is ceded.

A rather unbalanced portfolio, such as is covered by surplus, could of course, be reinsured by a Risk XL. If an insurance company prefers to have a longer-term relationship with its reinsurer so that it has some continuity of cover, a surplus will be preferred, however. Surplus treaties are priced by the reinsurance commission for the reinsurer's share of each risk, analogue to the quota share. Surplus treaties very often have profit commissions.

A Answer these questions on the text.

1. What is a surplus retention in property insurance called?
2. An insurer's retention is €50,000 and in its portfolio there are two risks – Risk A and Risk B. The sum insured of Risk A is €75,000 and Risk B €200,000. There are two claims from Risk A amounting to €12,000 and €30,000 and two claims from Risk B amounting to €20,000 and €36,000. How will the claim payments be shared between cedant and reinsurer for each claim?
3. Why may a surplus be preferred to 1) a quota share and 2) a risk excess of loss treaty?

Applying for a job

Having to apply for a job doesn't have to be a negative experience. It might mean the start of your professional career after you have completed a vocational qualification. Or you may decide during the course of your career that it is time for a new challenge, as it is rare nowadays for people to remain in the same job for their whole working lives. Whatever the reason, knowing how to successfully apply for a job is a useful skill to have.

The insurance industry offers a wide range of jobs, including actuarial work, sales, surveying, claims handling and investigation, underwriting, risk management, investment management and pensions management. Insurance companies also recruit for general management functions such as accountancy, marketing, management services and human resources.

There are a number of different methods of finding and applying for a job. A lot of companies in the UK use employment agencies. They are hired by companies to connect them with the most suitable applicants for the vacant job.

There are general employment agencies for most industries and sectors of work, but also specialist agencies for jobs in certain industries like the insurance sector. Employment agencies work very efficiently for both sides-employers and applicants. They only send appropriate applicants for job interviews to the insurance company and will prepare the jobseekers before sending them to attend an interview. Using an employment agency is free of charge for the applicant. When a position has been successfully filled by the agency, the employer pays the agency an agreed fee, which is usually based on a percentage of the annual salary.

Many newspapers have job vacancy advertisements in their 'classified' section. A lot of local companies advertise in local newspapers. The big national papers often run specials on certain days of the week, like IT jobs on Thursdays.

More important than newspapers nowadays are employment websites. They are run as a database for current job vacancies. There are general websites for all kinds of jobs, but also specialist websites dedicated to certain sectors of the economy. They allow jobseekers to set up their own accounts where they are able to upload their CV and specify their search criteria, like company location or range of pay. These websites also enable jobseekers to apply for jobs directly through the website itself.

Another way of applying for a job is to approach a company directly, which is known as a 'speculative approach'. In this case a jobseeker writes a letter of application encouraging a potential employer to consider their application for now or the near future.

1 The job search

KMK **A** Lesen Sie den Text auf Seite 122 und beantworten Sie die Fragen.

1	Nennen Sie drei spezifische Tätigkeitsfelder in der Versicherungswirtschaft.	...
2	Welcher allgemeine Unternehmensbereich wird im Text nicht genannt? a) Rechnungswesen b) Rechtsabteilung c) Personalwesen d) Marketing	
3	Was ist die Hauptaufgabe einer Jobvermittlungsagentur? a) Durchführung der Vorstellungsgespräche b) Sichtung der Bewerbungen c) Herstellen des Kontaktes zwischen Unternehmen und geeigneten Bewerbern d) Erstellen der Stellenanzeige	
4	Wer bezahlt die Jobvermittlungsagentur?	...
5	Wonach richtet sich in der Regel die Vermittlungsgebühr?	...
6	Welchen Schwerpunkt hat laut Text der Stellenmarkt in britischen Tageszeitungen am Donnerstag?	...
7	Welches Medium für Stellenangebote ist heute wichtiger als Zeitungsanzeigen?	...
8	Welchen besonderen Service bieten Anbieter in diesem Medium?	...
9	Welche Suchkriterien werden im Text genannt?	...
10	Welches ist kein Kennzeichen einer Initiativbewerbung? a) Bewerbung, um eine Firma auf sich aufmerksam zu machen b) Bewerbung auf eine Stellenanzeige c) Bewerber/in erhofft sich, auch für zukünftige offene Stellen berücksichtigt zu werden	

B Discuss these questions with a partner.

1 Do you know any other ways of finding a new job?
2 Which method do you think is the most effective?
3 Which method would you prefer to use? Explain why.

INFO The application process

Before you start the application process, it is important to follow the instructions given in the job advertisement on how to apply. Some companies or organizations may ask you to post or email a CV with a covering letter or contact them to request an application pack.

2 Finding the perfect match

Julia Schmidt has now finished her training as an insurance clerk. Since she qualified, she has been working in the motor claims department of Proximus Versicherungs AG. However, she is interested in acquiring work experience abroad. While browsing an employment website, the following job vacancy attracts her attention:

Jobs at Insurance Jobs Board UK recruitment site

ecruiters.co.uk/jobboard/cand/canlogin.asp

Google

MOTOR CLAIMS NEGOTIATOR

Job title:	International Motor Claims Negotiator
Industry Sector:	Claims
Job Type:	Permanent
Region:	South East
Area:	Essex
Salary:	£20000 to £23000 per annum

Our client, a multi-site insurance company, is currently looking to recruit a Motor Claims Negotiator, to join their Essex based team.
The suitable candidate will possess previous motor claims experience either in accident damage or third-party claims, together with at least one foreign language and basic IT skills. You will be a driven, hardworking and motivated team player with a positive and helpful attitude. Working to tight deadlines, you will work well under pressure and have excellent customer service skills.
Within this fast paced environment, enthusiasm, toughness and a good sense of fun will stand you in good stead for a role within this lively and helpful team.
With your understanding of customer requirements and with a natural flair for identifying the best solution in line with company processes and procedures, you will contribute to the delivery of the team targets by achieving your own objectives effectively. You will handle and resolve technical or complex claims cases or complaints within your own authority limit.
This is a great opportunity for you to further your knowledge and to develop your career. If you are interested in applying, please contact Paul Scott on 0777 0399953 or email insurance@therecruiters.co.uk.

A Read the job description and write down the key factors needed for this job. In your opinion, which five factors are the most important? Explain why.

B Look at Julia's CV on page 125 and give at least two reasons why Julia is qualified for the job.What do you think is her most important qualification for the job?

Julia Schmidt

Regenstr. 56, 90455 Nuremberg, Germany
Phone (+49) 911 440371 • E-mail julia.schmidt@usernet.com

Objective

Highly-motivated, team-orientated insurance clerk, with experience in motor claims handling. Seeking experience on the British insurance market using language skills and pursuing a career in insurance

Work Experience

2009–2010	Proximus Versicherungs AG, Nuremberg, Motor Claims Adviser Handling third-party motor claims, negotiating with customers, third parties and lawyers.
2006–2009	Proximus Versicherungs AG, Nuremberg Training as Kauffrau für Versicherungen und Finanzen, certified by the Chamber of Commerce Nuremberg

Education

2006–2009	Berufsschule 4 Nuremberg – Part-time vocational school
1997–2006	Neues Gymnasium Nuremberg Abitur (Final exams similar to A-Levels) Main subjects: Maths and English

Skills

Excellent IT-Skills (MS Office)
Used to working under pressure, team orientated, friendly
Fluent Spanish; very good English (oral and written); conversational French
Driving licence for cars

References

References and letters of recommendation available on request.

INFO A winning CV

A CV is a summary of your abilities, work experience, education and qualifications. You could think of it as a sales brochure that highlights your unique selling points (USPs). There is no set format for a CV in the UK, but it should cover the following features:

Personal details

- name
- address
- telephone number(s) (home/mobile)
- email address

Personal statement or objective

This should be a single paragraph that captures the attention of the reader and summarizes your skills and experience relevant to the job you are applying for. Never use *I* or *we* in your personal statement. Instead, write in the third person throughout. This helps to keep your CV more focused and direct, for example: *Motivated insurance clerk with experience in telesales. Seeking experience on the British insurance market using various language skills and pursuing a career in insurance.*

Work experience

As a general rule, CVs should be in reverse chronological order, listing the most recent position first. For each position held you should provide:

- start and end of employment
- job title
- employer's name (and address)
- main duties, responsibilities and achievements

Education

Give a brief description of qualifications (school, academic and/or professional). State the grades achieved and give the names of schools or colleges, again in reverse chronological order.

Skills and achievements

Here you should write about common skills gained throughout your education and work experience, such as languages, IT skills or a full, clean driving licence. These skills are of interest for any employer. You should use words like *communicating, organizing, team-orientated, flexible, energetic, ...*

Hobbies and interests

This feature is optional, but could help to create a more rounded picture of your personality and provide something more personal to discuss at an interview. But think about your hobbies first: a dangerous sport or *socializing with friends* may not be what an employer wants to hear!

References

Due to data protection laws, candidates should not provide referees' names, addresses or any other contact details on CVs, but should state that details are available on request. Always ask your referees' permission before you give someone their details. Many employers will write by post to your referees and expect a reply, so it is in your interest to warn them that this might happen. Remember to provide referees who will comment on you favourably – and who are easy to contact.

3 Do's and Don'ts

Copy the table and put the following recommendations under the correct heading. Add any further ideas of your own.

Do ...	Don't ...

ask someone to read your CV and give you honest feedback | be positive | check your spelling and grammar | choose a sensible email address | focus on what you can offer | give details of your religion and political interests | give dishonest information to get the job | include a covering letter with details of the job you are applying for | include negative aspects | keep your CV honest and factual | keep your CV to two pages | mention the salary you earned in your last job | provide a photograph | provide detailed information of all the schools you have attended | provide details about your family | use a clear and simple layout | use a font size and style that is easy to read | use short sentences

4 Writing your own CV

A Work with a partner. What differences can you find between the CV Julia sends (page 125) and a normal German CV?

B Write your own CV using the information from the infobox and your list of do's and don'ts from exercise 3.

5 A covering letter

A Choose the most appropriate word or phrase in brackets to complete the sentences.

1 I would like to … (ask/request/apply) for the position of claims adjustor.
2 After three years of training, I … (left/completed/qualified) as a Kaufmann für Versicherungen und Finanzen and was … (recommended/certified/qualified) by the Chamber of Commerce.
3 At present I'm … (employed by / taken from / working for) Proximus Insurance Group.
4 Please find … (attached/enclosed/added) my CV for the … (position/vacancy/work) as call centre agent.
5 I would be grateful if you could send me an application … (form/sheet/paper).
6 I'm available for … (an interview / a discussion / a talk) at short … (time/notice/request).
7 Please … (ask/contact/tell) me if you require any … (extra/new/further) information.
8 I … (can't wait to hear / look forward to hearing / want to hear) from you.

B Complete Julia Schmidt's covering letter with the following phrases.

I completed my training | I refer to | I've been working | I studied | I'm looking forward to | Enclosed please find | My Spanish is fluent | My present job involves

Julia Schmidt

Regenstr. 56, 90455 Nuremberg, Germany

julia.schmidt@usernet.com, Phone: +49 911 440371

June 27, 20..

Attention: Mr Paul Scott
Personnel Manager
Victoria Insurance PLC
165 London Road
Colchester
CO1 7XJ
Great Britain

Dear Mr Scott

International Motor Claims Negotiator

…[1] the position of International Motor Claims Negotiator advertised on www.the recruiters.co.uk.

…[2] in the insurance industry last May with the examination by the Chamber of Commerce. Since then …[3] for Proximus Versicherungs AG in Nuremberg . …[4] handling third-party motor claims and negotiating with customers, third parties and lawyers.

…[5] my CV, a diploma from the Chamber of Commerce, a diploma from my vocational school, a Europass and an English language certificate showing my professional and language qualifications.

…[6] English for nine years at grammar school and Insurance English for a further three years as part of my training at vocational school. Last year I also attended a three-week business course in London which was certified with a Europass.

…[7] as my mother is Spanish and I was raised bilingual. Furthermore I studied French for five years at school.

This position has a definite appeal for me, both on a personal and career basis. I believe I can add value to your International Motor Claims team through my experience in the insurance industry and my language skills. Please contact me should you require any further information.

…[8] hearing from you.

Yours sincerely

Julia Schmidt

Encl.

6 Preparing for an interview

24

The next stage in Julia's application process is the interview. Paul Scott is impressed by her CV and covering letter, so he invites her for a face-to-face interview. As he will be in Germany on a business trip, they are going to meet at a restaurant in Munich. Julia finds a podcast on the Internet with some useful tips on face-to-face interviews.

KMK Hören Sie sich die folgende Radiosendung an und beantworten Sie im Anschluss die Fragen.

1	Nennen Sie den Namen des Radiosenders:	...
2	In welcher Stadt ist der Radiosender?	...
3	Für welches Unternehmen arbeitet Simon Bennett?	...
Sind die folgenden Aussagen richtig oder falsch?		
4	Grundsätzlich erfolgt zuerst ein Telefoninterview.	
5	Ein Grund für Telefoninterviews ist die Ersparnis bei den Reisekosten.	
6	Im Rahmen einer Bewerbung muss man auch mit einem Telefoninterview rechnen.	
7	Zur Auswahl der Bewerber/innen werden auch Gruppeninterviews eingesetzt.	
8	Gruppeninterviews werden meist von der Abteilung durchgeführt, die neue Mitarbeiter/innen sucht.	
9	Man sollte auch damit rechnen, am Telefon nach einem Gehaltswunsch gefragt zu werden.	
10	Welche (3) Teilaufgaben eines Assessment Centers werden in der Radiosendung genannt?	...
11	Vorstellungsgespräche können an unterschiedlichen Orten stattfinden. Welche werden genannt?	...
Sind die folgenden Aussagen richtig oder falsch?		
12	Bei einem Vorstellungsgespräch im Restaurant sollte man nie das teuerste Essen bestellen.	
13	Man sollte immer das gleiche bestellen, wie der/die Interviewpartner/in.	
14	Alkoholische Getränke sollte man nur bestellen, wenn der/die Interviewpartner/in auch Alkohol trinkt.	
15	Man sollte sich nichts bestellen, bei dem man sich leicht schmutzig macht.	

7 Role-play: a job interview

Julia Schmidt and Paul Scott are now at the restaurant in Munich.

Role-play the interview with a partner.
Partner A: Look at this page.
Partner B: Look at File 3 on page 130.

Partner A:
You are Julia Schmidt. Look at the job advert (page 124), your CV (page 125) and your covering letter (page 128). Prepare yourself to answer Paul Scott's interview questions.

Partner files

File 1 Unit 1, Ex 9

Partner B:
Ihr Name ist Magnus/Ida Andersson. Sie arbeiten bei einem schwedischen Versicherungsunternehmen. Zurzeit machen Sie ein Auslandspraktikum bei einem Tochterunternehmen ihrer Firma in München. Dort nehmen Sie an einer überbetrieblichen Fortbildungsveranstaltung teil. Während der Pause kommen Sie mit einer jungen Deutschen / einem jungen Deutschen aus einem anderen Unternehmen ins Gespräch. Sie stellen sich kurz vor und unterhalten sich mit ihr/ihm auf Englisch. Ihr Gespräch kann z. B. folgende Punkte umfassen:

- Ihre derzeitigen Aufgaben im Betrieb und Ihr Ausbildungsunternehmen;
- Ihre Freizeitaktivitäten;
- Vorteile eines Auslandspraktikums.

Verabreden Sie sich nach dem Arbeitstag zum Essen. Vereinbaren Sie Ort und Zeit.

File 2 Unit 3, Ex 2C

Partner A:
Dictate these email and website addresses to Partner B. Then check his/her answers.

1 jane.winterbourne@speed-mail.ie
2 www.stonehill-consulting.co.uk
3 your email address
4 your company's website address or a website address you often visit (if your partner works with the same company)

File 3 Unit 12, Ex 7

Partner B:
You are Paul Scott. Look at these interview notes and think of some other typical interview questions you could ask Julia Schmidt.

Interview questions for Julia Schmidt

1 *How would you describe yourself?*
2 *What are your short-term and long-term goals and objectives?*
3 *What do you see yourself doing five years from now?*
4 *How well do you work with people? Do you prefer working alone or in a team?*
5 *What do you consider to be your greatest strengths and weaknesses?*
6 *How would a good friend describe you?*
7 *What makes you qualified for this position?*

File 4 Unit 5, Ex 4

Partner B:
Sie sind Sachbearbeiter/in der Versicherungsagentur Hagen. Nehmen Sie den Anruf entgegen und vereinbaren Sie einen Termin, um den Anrufer / die Anruferin zu Hause zu besuchen.
Sie haben schon folgende Termine für die kommende Woche:

Date	AM	PM
Montag, 26. Juni		
Dienstag, 27. Juni	*Schmidt 10 Uhr*	
Mittwoch, 28. Juni	*Frau Hagen 11–12*	
Donnerstag, 29. Juni	*Huber 11 Uhr*	*14–16 Uhr Teammeeting*
Freitag, 30. Juni	*Fuchs 10.30 Uhr*	*Radtour zum Chiemsee! (bis Sonntag)*

File 5 Unit 6, Ex 7

Partner B:
You are Stanley Lu. Your wife read the email from Proximus Health (Partner A) before you did. She knows the whole background to your accident and the treatment. You have a hopeless memory, so use her notes below and write a reply to the email.

Zu 1 *Der Unfall geschah gegen 07.30 Uhr auf dem Weg zur S-Bahn. Stanley rutschte auf Eis aus und schlug mit dem Kopf gegen einen Baum. Arzttermin erst am frühen Nachmittag. 1. Telefonat: Erste Hilfe. 2. Telefonat: Am nächsten Tag nach dem Arztermin: Kopfweh – was tun (nichts oder Aspirin)?*

Zu 7 *Augentest, ob Gehirnerschütterung (concussion) festzustellen; Herz (pulse) und Blutdruck (blood pressure) geprüft*

Zu 3?5 *Neu. Die Impfung ist die erste von 3. – Nr. 2 nach einem Monat – Nr. 3 nach einem Jahr.*

File 6 Unit 10, Ex 6A

Partner B:
You are Roger Bell. Rearrange the meeting with Alison Kent's secretary. These are your appointments for the next week.

No appointment before 10.00 a.m. or that finishes after 16.30 (Friday 14.30).
No appointment can last more than 60 minutes.
On Tuesday and Thursday you are not available in the morning.
On Monday and Wednesday you are not available in the afternoon.
Lunch lasts from 12.00 to 14.00 every day, except Friday, when it finishes at 13.30.

File 7 Unit 6, Ex 10

Student B:
You are an agent of Proximus Health.
Use the additional information in this brochure to show Mr Kuromito how the benefits of Proximus Health are far superior to those of his statutory health provider. Give Mr Kuromito any other additional information about the health top-up benefits that you know to be true.

Benefits	Private Health Insurance	Public Health Scheme
Contact lenses & glasses	80% costs up to €200 within 2 yrs	Nothing, expect visually impaired
Medication, treatments, aids	up to €500 p.a.	€5/€10, 10% of costs for aids
Naturopathy	80% costs of naturopath	Nothing
Hospital accommodation	1 or 2 bed room with telephone. Consultant. Special treatment	Wichever hospital is the nearest
Payments in hospital	Nothing	€10 per day paid by patient
False teeth, implants	65–80% paid for	€50%–65% paid for
Sickness benefit	70% income limit for assessment of contributions	70% gross salary, 90% net salary Must pay social security, which means benefit is 75% net salary
Foreign travel	Worldwide for up to 6 weeks per journey. Emergency evacuation included.	Benefits only in EU countries with reciprocal agreements. No emergency evacuation.

File 8 Unit 3, Ex 12

Partner B:
Sie sind Sachbearbeiter/in in der Schadenabteilung der Proximus Versicherung und erhalten die telefonische Schadenmeldung eines Kunden / einer Kundin. Nehmen Sie den Anruf entgegen und stellen Sie dem Kunden / der Kundin situationsadäquate Fragen, z. B. Policenummer, Schadenhergang und Schadenhöhe, usw.

File 9 **Unit 7, Ex 5**

Partner B:
Sie sind Anke Müller.
Eine Deckung für Schlüssel ist prinzipiell möglich; auch wenn sie in der Standardpolice nicht gedeckt wird. Sie müssen wissen, welche Summe gedeckt werden soll.
Bei einer Deckungssumme von EUR 25.000 wäre eine Selbstbeteiligung von EUR 150 nötig. Dies ist risikogerecht und steht in den Zeichungsrichtlinien ihres Hauses, da solche Schäden häufiger vorkommen als man denkt.

File 10 **Unit 8, Ex 7**

Partner B:
You are Mr Andrew Fox. You and your wife Tess have both had a driving licence for more than 10 years. You have a 12 year-old son, Tim.
Address: Nordring 44, Hamburg
Vehicle: Smart Forfour, first registered 10/2006, manufacturer's key 9891, model key 015, reg. no. HH-TB 484. The car will be parked on the street.
You would like to have comprehensive cover with an excess of € 300. In England you had a no claims discount of 5 years.
Ask for confirmation of the insurance cover to register the car.
Give any other information if required.

File 11 **Unit 3, Ex 2C**

Partner B:
Dictate these email and website addresses to Partner A. Then check his/her answers.
1 henry_lexington@fast-net.com
2 www.maryland-investment.ie
3 your email address
4 your company's website address or a website address you often visit (if your partner works with the same company)

1 Mediation

Sie sind Mitarbeiter/in des Versicherungsmaklers Beckschlager.

Da sich Ihr Unternehmen auch an englischsprachige Kunden wenden möchte, sollen Sie die wichtigsten Informationen im folgenden Text für die Homepage Ihres Unternehmens in Stichpunkten auf Englisch schreiben.

http://beckschlager_v_f.de

Google

über uns

Wer sind wir?
Beckschlager Versicherungen & Finanzen ist ein Versicherungsmakler mit Sitz in Nürnberg. Der Geschäftsführer des Unternehmens ist Moritz Beckschlager. Er hat das Unternehmen 1992 gegründet. Somit besitzt Herr Beckschlager mehr als 20 Jahre Erfahrung im Versicherungsgeschäft. Ein Team bestehend aus vier qualifizierten Beratern sowie einem Auszubildenden unterstützt ihn.

Was bieten wir?
Da wir unabhängig sind von Versicherungsunternehmen, liefern wir objektive Beratung. Wir sind stets auf Ihrer Seite, sowohl beim Abschluss von neuen Verträgen als auch im Schadenfall. Die Zufriedenheit unserer Kunden ist unser wichtigstes Ziel. Wir bieten maßgeschneiderten Versicherungsschutz zu günstigen Preisen. Zu unserer Produktpalette gehören alle Arten von Versicherungen für Privatkunden und Geschäftskunden sowie Finanzprodukte.

Wie erreichen wir dies?
- Wir analysieren sorgfältig Ihren Versicherungsbedarf.
- Wir überprüfen die Preise und die Qualität des Versicherungsschutzes Ihrer bestehenden Verträge.
- Wir sagen Ihnen auch, welche Versicherungsverträge Sie überhaupt nicht brauchen.
- Beim Abschluss neuer Versicherungsverträge holen wir stets Angebote von den besten Versicherern ein, um für Sie einen optimalen und preiswerten Versicherungsschutz zu finden.
- Wenn sich Ihre Lebenssituation ändert, passen wir Ihren Versicherungsschutz sofort an.
- Im Schadenfall kümmern wir uns um eine schnelle und faire Schadenregulierung.

2 Rezeption: Hörverstehen*

Webcode: INSMU0101

A British radio show is doing a feature on career possibilities in the insurance field.

Since you are planning to do some work experience in an English-speaking country, you make notes on the following questions.

1 How many people work in the insurance industry in the UK?
2 What is David's job?
3 What is he responsible for?
4 Name two of his typical work activities.
5 Could you start your own business as an underwriter?
6 Where are most of the underwriting jobs offered in the UK?
7 What does David like about his job?
8 What does he dislike about his job?
9 Does David's job require him to travel?
10 How much is the entry salary of an underwriter?

*Geben Sie den Webcode im Webcode-Suchfeld auf www.cornelsen.de/matters ein, um den Hörtext anzuhören bzw. herunterzuladen.

Rezeption: Leseverstehen

Sie arbeiten in der Marketingabteilung eines Versicherungsunternehmens. Da viele Verbraucher beim Kauf von Versicherungsprodukten Preisvergleichsportale nutzen, sollen Sie die Informationen hierzu auf der folgenden Internetseite für Ihren Vorgesetzten auswerten.

How to use comparison sites

Step 1 – Work out what policy and cover you need
Use comparison sites to get quotes, not to judge the quality of a policy. Look at best buy surveys from other sources or use our 'What does a good policy look like?' pages to work out what cover you need. Once you know the kind of insurance policy and level of cover you're looking for, you'll be able to use comparison sites to help you get a good deal.

Step 2 – Pay attention to which answers are pre-filled
Insurance is complex and relies on many details that are specific to you, but comparison sites often make assumptions so they can make the process simpler for you. They sometimes use pre-filled answers to give you a standard set of results.

The policies they suggest might not be suitable if you have any non-standard requirements – for example if your house has a thatched roof or you're over or under a certain age – so check all the questions have been answered correctly. You must make sure the details are right or you might not be covered if you need to make a claim.

Step 3 – Use more than one comparison site
Comparison websites cover different providers and products – remember not all providers appear on comparison sites. […]

Step 4 – Don't get spammed
It's up to you to opt out of email and other marketing by making sure you tick or un-tick the relevant boxes. If you don't, you could get both marketing emails and phone calls, so read everything carefully.

Top tip
Use a different email address when getting comparison site quotes – that way your inbox won't fill up with junk mail. Just remember if you do take out a policy, your insurer will need to email you to confirm cover, policy schedule and wording and send out renewal notices.

Step 5 – Always check before you buy
When you are transferred from the comparison site to the insurer's site, it is essential that you check all the information is correct. If you don't do this and incorrect information has been given to the insurer, you may end up paying for invalid insurance.

Finally, always read the documentation before you buy a policy. If the documents aren't available on the comparison site, click through to the insurance company's own website to find and read the documents. If you can't find them, don't buy the policy. You need to make sure it will actually cover you if you need to claim.

(Source: abridged from https://www.moneyadviceservice.org.uk/en/articles/how-to-buy-insurance-using-comparison-sites)

Beantworten Sie die folgenden Verständnisfragen zum Text auf Deutsch.

1. Wofür kann der Kunde ein Preisvergleichsportal einsetzen? (1)
2. Was muss der Kunde entscheiden, bevor er das Preisvergleichportal nutzen kann? (2)
3. Warum geben die Preisvergleichsportale bei manchen Fragen die Antworten vor? (2)
4. Welche Nachteile können sich daraus für manche Kunden ergeben? (2)
5. Warum sollte der Kunde immer mehr als ein Preisvergleichsportal benutzen? (1)
6. Wie kann man vermeiden, dass man mit Werbe-E-Mails und Telefonaten bombardiert wird? (2)
7. Worauf muss der Kunde achten, wenn er vom Preisvergleichsportal auf die Seite des Versicherers geleitet wird? (1)
8. Was sollte der Kunde machen, bevor er die Versicherung kauft? (1)

1 Produktion

Der Kunde Howard Wilson hat per E-Mail mitgeteilt, dass er seit kurzem ein begeisterter Fahrradfahrer ist. Er hat sich ein Fahrrad für € 990,00 gekauft und möchte wissen, ob es in seiner Hausratversicherung gegen Diebstahl versichert ist.

Ihre Vorgesetzte beauftragt Sie, Herrn Wilson per E-Mail zu antworten. Berücksichtigen Sie dabei folgende Punkte.

- Betreffzeile
- Anrede und Dank für die E-Mail
- In der Hausratversicherung ist das Fahrrad gegen Einbruchdiebstahl versichert, nicht aber gegen einfachen Diebstahl
- Beispielsweise kein Versicherungsschutz, solange das Fahrrad vor einem Restaurant oder Laden abgestellt wird
- Für zusätzlichen Beitrag von 60,40 € könnte er eine Klausel vereinbaren, durch welche das Fahrrad gegen Diebstahl versichert ist
- Klausel gewährt Versicherungsschutz zum Neuwert bis zu einer bestimmten Obergrenze
- Da Kaufpreis des Fahrrads 990 € betrug, empfehlen wir eine Obergrenze von 2 % der Versicherungssumme
- Klausel verlangt, dass das Fahrrad immer mit eigenständigem Schloss gesichert wird, wenn es nicht in Gebrauch ist
- Kunde sollte Rahmennummer, Kaufbeleg und andere Nachweise der Eigentümerschaft des Fahrrads aufbewahren
- Falls Kunde unserem Vorschlag zustimmt, ändern wir den Vertrag und schicken ihm eine neue Police
- Passender Schlusssatz

2 Rezeption: Hörverstehen*

You work in a large insurance call centre, where part of the job is to deal with English-speaking customers. A customer calls.

Webcode: INSMU0301

Make notes about the following points/questions.

Reason for call (1)	...
Name and address of policyholder (1)	...
Type of insurance (1)	...
Cause of damage (1)	...
Why did the policyholder not notice the fire? (2)	...
What did the neighbour do? (2)	...
Alternative accommodation in a hotel: – Daily limit of expenses (1) – Length of time the insurer is willing to pay (1)	...
Duties of the loss adjuster (3)	...
Contact phone number (1)	...

*Geben Sie den Webcode im Webcode-Suchfeld auf www.cornelsen.de/matters ein, um den Hörtext anzuhören bzw. herunterzuladen.

Produktion

Ihre Kundin Fiona Clark, eine Journalistin, ist erst seit wenigen Wochen in Deutschland. Sie wird in einem Monat Ihren deutschen Freund heiraten und sich in Deutschland niederlassen. Da sie sich Gedanken um ihre Zukunft macht, hat sie um ein Angebot für eine private Rentenversicherung gebeten. Anhand der Angaben der Kundin wurde ein Angebot errechnet.

Schreiben Sie einen Begleitbrief zu diesem Angebot mit folgenden Angaben.

- Angebot basiert auf folgenden Angaben:

Versicherte Person:	Fiona Clark
Geburtsdatum:	10.10.1980
Versicherungsbeginn:	01.06.2013
Rentenbeginn:	01.06.2047
Ablauf Beitragszahlung:	01.06.2047
Ablauf Garantiezeit:	01.06.2057
Monatliche Prämie:	200,00 EUR

- Vorteile der Flexi-Rente für die versicherte Person:
  - lebenslange garantierte Rente in Höhe von 335,18 EUR oder stattdessen einmalige garantierte Kapitalzahlung in Höhe von 95.263,85 EUR bei Rentenbeginn
  - zusätzliche Überschussrente *(surplus annuity)* durch Beteiligung an Überschüssen des Versicherers; Höhe der Überschüsse kann aber nicht garantiert werden
  - Vorverlegung oder Hinausschieben des Rentenbeginns um bis zu 5 Jahre möglich, Änderung des vereinbarten Rentenbeginns (01.06.2047) hat jedoch Auswirkungen auf die Höhe der garantierten Leistungen

- Leistungen für ihre Hinterbliebenen:
  - Bei Tod der Kundin vor Rentenbeginn erhalten ihre Hinterbliebenen die eingezahlten Prämien als Einmalzahlung zurückerstattet
  - Bei Tod der Kundin nach Rentenbeginn erhalten ihre Hinterbliebenen die Rente bis zum Ende der vereinbarten Rentengarantiezeit (01.06.2057)

- beiliegende Unterlagen: ausführliches Angebot in deutscher Sprache, Bedingungen für die Rentenversicherung und Antragsformular
- Hilfe anbieten
- geeigneter Schlusssatz

Mediation

Als Versicherungsmakler/in betreuen Sie ein deutsches Unternehmen, das allgemeines Infomaterial zu englischen Unfallversicherungen benötigt. Das Unternehmen schickt regelmäßig Mitarbeiter für längere Zeit zu seiner britischen Niederlassung. Ihr Vorgesetzter bittet Sie daher, die wesentlichen Inhalte des folgenden Textes zu übertragen.

Übertragen Sie die wesentlichen Inhalte dieses Textes ins Deutsche.

Which policy is right for me?

Do not confuse income protection and personal accident protection. Personal accident policies tend to pay out a lump sum, compared to monthly payments under an income protection policy.

The aim is to find the best value-for-money cover, not the cheapest. A cheap policy may offer "budget" cover: with limitations and restrictions. A "budget" cover may be all you need, which is fine if you understand what you do and do not have protection against.

It is not critical illness insurance. Critical Illness (CI) insurance pays out a lump sum if you suffer one of a number of specific medical problems, such as a heart attack, cancer or stroke. The definition of accident varies hugely.

Neither Personal Accident nor Critical illness would pay out for stress, depression or back problems.

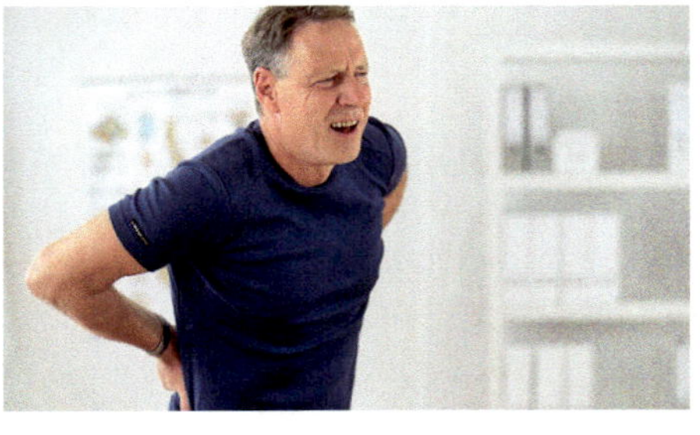

If you have or suspect you have a medical condition, a history of problems, or are in a job which is not acceptable to insurers, then there is a huge temptation to avoid telling the insurer this information. Even if they do not specifically ask a question relating to something which could be a problem, you must tell them. Insurers are very tough on people who fail to tell the whole story. If found out, they will certainly refuse to pay all or part of the claim, and may even prosecute you for attempted fraud.

"Non-disclosure" could lead to a claim being denied, just when you need the money the most. Mention any and all aspects of your medical history, and leave the insurer to decide which are trivial and which are important. If they have a query on a possible problem, they may seek to increase the premium or impose limitations on cover.

If during the term of your policy you change occupation, you must usually tell the insurer. If you were a shop assistant when taking the cover out, but are a roofer or fireman when you claim, insurers will not pay up.

A lot depends on what you want to cover and why.

In other classes of health insurance, policies from one provider can be very similar to those from a competitor. In personal accident policies there is a huge variety of products from a relatively small number of providers.

Personal Accident is an area where there are no official insurance body committees trying to dictate wordings and cover, so every provider goes their own way.

(Source: http://www.privatehealth.co.uk/healthinsurance/personal-accident-insurance/guide/choosing-policy/)

1 Interaktion

Ein Kunde / Eine Kundin aus England möchte telefonisch ein Angebot für eine Krankenversicherung einholen.

Erstellen Sie in Partnerarbeit einen Dialog aus folgenden Rollenkarten.

Student A

Sie heißen Julia/Julian McArthur. Sie sind kürzlich von England nach Deutschland gezogen und haben ihre Tätigkeit als selbstständige/r Musiklehrer/in aufgenommen. Sie rufen eine Agentur der Proximus Versicherung an, um ein Angebot für eine Krankenversicherung einzuholen. Sie bitten den Mitarbeiter / die Mitarbeiterin der Agentur, Englisch zu sprechen.
Machen Sie die folgenden Angaben, wenn Sie gefragt werden:

- 28 Jahre alt und unverheiratet
- keine akuten oder chronischen Erkrankungen
- Interesse besteht an Versicherung für stationäre und ambulante Behandlung
- Prämie sollte möglichst niedrig sein
- Ihre E-Mail-Adresse: j.mcarthur@google.de

Student B

Sie sind Mitarbeiter/in der Agentur Schiller der Proximus Versicherung. Als das Telefon klingelt, ist ein Kunde / eine Kundin am Apparat und möchte bei Ihnen ein Angebot für eine Krankenversicherung einholen.
Erklären Sie dem/der Anrufer/in, dass Sie zur Erstellung eines Angebots einige Informationen benötigen, die teilweise sehr persönlich sind.
Sie stellen Fragen zu folgenden Aspekten:

- Alter, Beruf, Familienstand
- Vorerkrankungen
- Gewünschter Leistungsumfang (ambulante bzw. stationäre Behandlung, zahnärztliche Behandlung, Chefarztbehandlung)
- In den nächsten Tagen schicken Sie ein Angebot per E-Mail. Adresse?
- Bedanken Sie sich abschließend für das Interesse an Ihrem Unternehmen und verabschieden Sie sich.

2 Produktion

Sie sind Mitarbeiter/in der Agentur Schiller der Proximus Versicherung. Die Kundin / Der Kunde Julia/Julian McArthur hat sich bei Ihnen telefonisch nach einer Krankenversicherung erkundigt. Sie haben zugesagt, ihr/ihm per E-Mail ein Angebot zu schicken.

Verfassen Sie dieses Schreiben mit den folgenden Inhalten.

- Betreffzeile
- Anrede und Dank für den Anruf
- Wie besprochen, bieten Sie eine Police mit Deckung für ambulante und stationäre Heilbehandlung an
- Beitrag ambulante Heilbehandlung: 155,30 € pro Monat für den Tarif A0
- Alternative: jährliche Selbstbeteiligung für die ambulante Heilbehandlung von z. B. 580,00 €, Beitrag dann nur 104,50 € pro Monat (Tarif A2)
- Vorschlag stationäre Heilbehandlung: Tarif S3 (Mehrbettzimmer), Beitrag nur 62,70 € pro Monat
- Wenn Tarif S1 (Einzelzimmer): Beitrag 84,50 € pro Monat
- Sie legen eine Informationsbroschüre zu den genannten Tarifen bei
- Formulieren Sie einen geeigneten Schluss

Interaktion

Die Agentur Hagen vermittelt Versicherungsprodukte der Proximus Versicherung AG. Vor wenigen Wochen hat die Proximus Versicherung AG eine neue Privathaftpflichtversicherung auf den Markt gebracht, die im Test einer unabhängigen Verbraucherzeitschrift mit „Gut" bewertet wurde. Die Agenturinhaberin Frau Hagen möchte nun mit einer Vertriebsaktion ihre Bestandskunden auf dieses Produkt aufmerksam machen und möglichst viele Verkaufsabschlüsse erzielen.

Mit der Organisation dieser Vertriebsaktion beauftragt Frau Hagen ihre/n Auszubildende/n sowie eine englische Studentin / einen englischen Studenten, die/der ein Praktikum in der Agentur macht.

Sie übernehmen mit Ihrem/Ihrer Gesprächspartner/in die Rollen der beiden. Das Gespräch ist in englischer Sprache zu führen. Besprechen Sie, wie Sie bei der Vertriebsaktion vorgehen würden. Dabei können Sie folgende Punkte in Ihr Gespräch einbeziehen:

- Wo und von wem könnten Sie Informationen über die neue Haftpflichtversicherung der Proximus Versicherung erhalten? (z. B. Broschüren der Vertriebsabteilung? Artikel der Testzeitschrift? usw.)
- Welche Merkmale sollten die Kunden haben, die Sie für die Aktion auswählen wollen? (Altersgruppe? Familienstand? usw.)
- Was sollte in dem Werbebrief stehen, den die Kunden erhalten? (z. B. Hinweis auf gutes Testergebnis? Typische Schadenbeispiele? Prämie? Versicherungssummen? usw.)
- Bevor Sie die Kunden anrufen, stellen Sie sich hierfür einen Leitfaden zusammen. Welche Punkte würden Sie aufnehmen? (Wie Sie sich vorstellen? Wie Sie ihre Kunden auf den Brief ansprechen? Wie Sie auf unentschlossene Kunden reagieren? Wie Sie Beratungstermine vereinbaren? usw.)
- Welche Informationen bräuchten Sie von den Kunden im Rahmen des Beratungsgesprächs, damit Sie ihnen ein bedarfsgerechtes Angebot machen können? (z. B. Familienstand? Hobbies? Beschäftigt im öffentlichen Dienst? Hundebesitzer? usw.)

Rezeption: Leseverstehen

Young women to see insurance premiums 'double'

Women face paying higher car insurance premiums from today due to new European rules. But men, particularly young drivers, should see a fall when they come to renew policies.

Experts have warned that some young female motorists could see their premiums almost double.

The new gender-neutral rules stem from a European Court of Justice ruling last year which means insurers are no longer able to consider a customer's gender when calculating how much they pay for their car or life insurance, or what their retirement income should be. Women have benefited from smaller car insurance premiums due to their lower accident rates, and predictions as to how they will be affected have varied widely.

Young women are likely to bear the brunt of the increases, due to the higher accident rates of young men, which experts warn could force many younger female drivers off the road. Meanwhile, some men could see a small reduction in their premiums.

[...] Comparison website, MoneySupermarket, said that although it is yet to see any great spike in prices, this could change quickly as insurers jostle for position in the fast-moving market. The website's insurance expert, Kevin Pratt, said: "There may be a period of a few days or weeks when the market adjusts. There are over 100 companies trying to get business and they will inevitably monitor what the others are doing." Mr Pratt said he hopes insurers will place greater emphasis on other factors to make sure drivers can still get a reasonable price, such as their job, type of car, driving record, any security measures on the car and age. [...]

Seven ways to help cut your car insurance costs

The Association of British Insurers (ABI) has set out some tips on reducing your premiums.

1. Shop around. It is often useful to get quotes from different insurers, using a broker or comparison websites. Don't just buy on price, but on the policy best suited to your needs. Make sure you check the details of the cover.
2. Make sure your vehicle is secure. Premium discounts are often available when an approved alarm or immobiliser is fitted and parking the car in a garage overnight can also reduce costs.
3. Pay a higher voluntary excess, which is the first part of any claim that you pay yourself. This can mean a lower premium.
4. Limit the car's use. Using your vehicle in connection with any business ramps up the cost. Limit use to social, domestic and pleasure purposes if this is possible.
5. If you are a young driver, consider taking the Pass Plus course, which helps people to drive more safely. Some insurers may offer lower premiums for completing the course.
6. Pay the premium in one go if you can afford to, as you may be charged more by paying in instalments.
7. Choose a lower powered car. Lower engine sizes often mean lower premiums.

(Source: abridged from http://www.telegraph.co.uk/finance/personalfinance/insurance/motorinsurance/9760222/Young-women-to-see-insurance-premiums-double.html)

Beantworten Sie die folgenden Verständnisfragen zum Text auf Deutsch.

1 Was ist der Grund für den Anstieg der Prämien in der Kraftfahrversicherung?
2 Wen werden die Prämienerhöhungen vor allem treffen? Warum?
3 Wie lange wird es laut Kevin Pratt von der Preisvergleichsseite *MoneySupermarket* dauern, bis sich der Markt auf die neue Situation einstellt? Wie wird begründet, dass es sich um diese Zeitspanne handelt?
4 Welche weiteren Faktoren, die die Preise für die Kraftfahrversicherung beeinflussen können, nennt Kevin Pratt?
5 Die *Association of British Insurers* gibt Konsumenten Hinweise, wie sie die Kosten für die Kfz-Prämie senken können. Zählen Sie diese Tipps in Stichworten auf.

Interaktion

Der/Die Versicherungs- und Finanzmakler/in Frau/Herr Schwertfeger erhält einen Anruf von einem/einer neuen Kunden/Kundin, Frau/Herr Shearer.

Führen Sie ein Telefongespräch mit folgendem Ablauf.

Student A – Frau/Herr Schwertfeger	Student B – James/Jane Shearer
Melden Sie sich mit Namen und fragen Sie, was Sie für den Kunden / die Kundin tun können?	
	Sie melden sich mit Ihrem Namen. Sagen Sie, dass Ihnen Frau/Herr Schwertfeger von Ihrem Freund Andrew Harper empfohlen wurde.
Sie freuen sich, wenn die Kunden mit Ihrem Service zufrieden sind. Bitten Sie Frau/Herr Shearer, Grüße an Herrn Harper auszurichten.	
	Sagen Sie, dass Sie vor zwei Wochen von einer Tante Geld geerbt haben. Sie möchten wissen, wie Sie das Geld am besten anlegen können.
Sagen Sie, dass Sie als unabhängige/r Finanzberater/in viele verschiedene Produkte anbieten können. Fragen Sie, welchen Betrag er/sie anlegen möchte.	
	Sagen Sie, dass Sie vorhaben, 40.000 Euro anzulegen.
Fragen Sie, wie lange er/sie das Geld anlegen möchte.	
	Sagen Sie, dass Sie Ihr Geld ungefähr 10 Jahre anlegen möchten.
Fragen Sie, welche Geldanlageformen er/sie bisher genutzt hat.	
	Erklären Sie, dass Sie bisher Ihr Geld auf Sparkonten, Festgeldkonten oder in deutschen Staatsschuldverschreibungen angelegt haben. Diese Produkte bieten aber nur niedrige Zinssätze.
Sagen Sie, dass diese Produkte andererseits aber sehr sicher sind. Wenn man sich für ein Produkt mit höherem Ertrag entscheidet, muss man auch ein steigendes Risiko akzeptieren.	
	Weisen Sie darauf hin, dass Sie durchaus auch offen für risikoreichere Anlageformen wie Aktien oder Aktienfonds wären. Bisher haben Sie gezögert, weil Sie zu wenig über solche Produkte wissen.
Schlagen Sie Herrn/Frau Shearer ein Beratungsgespräch vor, indem Sie ihm/ihr mehr über diese Produkte sagen können. Sie benötigen auch noch weitere Informationen über die persönliche Situation des Kunden / der Kundin, damit Sie ihn/sie gut beraten können.	
	Fragen Sie, ob der/die Makler/in am 23. Juni gegen 15.00 Uhr Zeit hat.
Sagen Sie, dass der Termin für Sie in Ordnung geht. Fragen Sie, ob der Kunde / die Kundin zu Ihnen ins Büro kommen möchte oder ob Sie ihn/sie zu Hause besuchen sollen.	
	Sagen Sie, dass Sie zu ihm/ihr ins Büro kommen, Herr Harper hat Ihnen die Adresse gegeben, und verabschieden Sie sich.
Bedanken Sie sich für das Gespräch und verabschieden Sie sich.	

Mediation

Sie arbeiten für ein Maklerunternehmen, das auch Klein- und Mittelbetriebe betreut.

Ihre Vorgesetzte bittet Sie, die wesentlichen Inhalte der folgenden Tipps für die Kunden ins Deutsche zu übertragen.

5 Ways to Save Money on Business Insurance

How much did your business insurance premium increase last year? Thirty percent? Forty percent? According to a survey by the CFIB (Canadian Federation of Independent Business), you're one of the luckier small businesses. Some have had their small business insurance premiums increase by as much as 600 percent. [...]

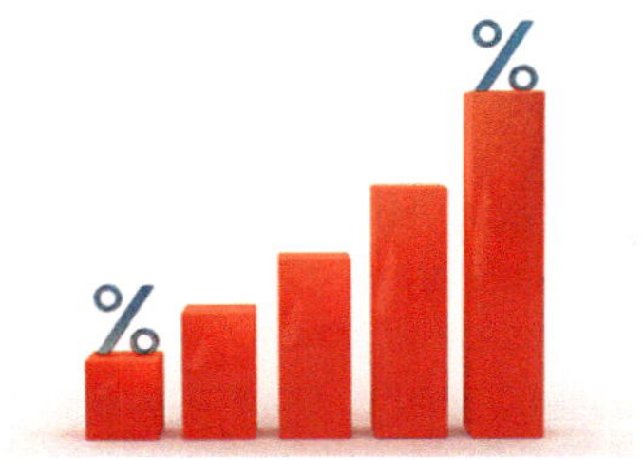

Check this list of ways to save money on business insurance. [...]

1) **Reduce your business insurance coverage.**
Comb through your business insurance policy and see what areas of business insurance you can prune. For instance, are there deductibles that you can increase to lower your insurance rates? If you are carrying fleet or vehicle insurance, are you carrying [...] collision insurance on older vehicles?

2) **Take advantage of group rates by purchasing your business insurance through a business or professional organization.**
Many different business organizations, such as Chambers of Commerce and the CFIB, offer insurance plans and/or discounts on business insurance to their members. The bigger the group, the more diffuse the risk and the lower the insurance rates are. You will have to pay to become a member of the group or association, of course, but you could still end up saving money compared to the cost of purchasing the same kind of business insurance the group offers on your own.

3) **Lower your liability risk as much as possible.**
Talk to your insurance agent or broker to find out what you could do to lower your business insurance cost. Would installing a security system reduce your business insurance premiums, for instance?
Are you offering particular products or services that are increasing the risk of insuring your business from the insurer's point of view? By eliminating these "risky" products, you could dramatically lower your premiums.

4) **Avoid the U.S. market.**
It sounds harsh and it is, but the increases in business insurance premiums for Canadian small exporters have been especially high. Insurers consider doing business with the U.S. extremely risky because it is highly litigious.

5) **Relocate your business to an area with lower insurance rates.**
The costs of various types of business insurance vary, depending on where your business is located. Vehicle insurance, for instance, is much more inexpensive in Alberta and B.C. than in the Maritimes. Do the research and see if relocating is worth your while.

These are only some of the things you can do to save money on the cost of small business insurance. [...] The most important thing you can do to reduce the cost of your business insurance, however, is to shop around. Instead of just sticking with the same company, go through an insurance broker and/or get quotes from different companies.

(Source: Susan Ward, About.com Guide, http://sbinfocanada.about.com/od/insurance/a/bizinsurance1.htm)

Rezeption: Leseverstehen

Sie arbeiten bei einem Rückversicherungsunternehmen und erhalten den Auftrag, den folgenden Marktbericht auszuwerten.

Trends in the reinsurance industry

Due to an economic downturn in 2011, there was a slight decrease in demand for insurance cover in industrialized countries. This was not true for emerging countries, although changing legal framework conditions did have a negative effect on life insurance premiums. Overall, there was a slight global growth only in casualty, property accident and health insurance.

Capital base in the insurance industry slowed down due to high expenditures following natural disasters. This, however, did not stop market conditions from improving slightly for reinsurers.

Casualty, property and accident reinsurance

At the beginning of 2011, there was a decrease in price on renewal of reinsurance contracts. However, in the course of the year, reinsurers increased reinsurance premiums when they renewed contracts and this trend seemed to continue in 2012. Rising claims expenses forced reinsurers to raise prices, particularly for insurance against natural disasters. Some devastating natural disasters in 2011, such as earthquakes in Japan and New Zealand, floods in Australia and Thailand, and tornados in the USA, drove the number of claims to a record level.

Life and health reinsurance

In 2011, premium income increased in both life insurance and in life reinsurance. The reasons for this development are as follows: just as in previous years, a growing number of people took out annuities, income protection and long-term care policies from private insurers (in Germany). On top of that, the insurance markets in Asia experienced an enormous growth.

In fact, the health care market is one of the fastest-growing on a global scale and will continue to grow for several reasons: we're now living longer, more and more medical breakthroughs are being made, and more is being done to develop health care markets in emerging countries. Health reinsurance will continue to benefit from this trend.

(Source: based on information from, GDV, p. 74)

Beantworten Sie die folgenden Verständnisfragen zum Text auf Deutsch.

1 Was war die Ursache für die abnehmende Nachfrage nach Versicherungsschutz in den Industriestaaten?

2 Worauf ist in den Schwellenländern der Rückgang des Wachstums bei Lebensversicherungsprämien zurückzuführen?

3 In welchen Versicherungssparten gab es weltweit einen Prämienanstieg?

4 Wie haben sich die Marktbedingungen der Rückversicherer insgesamt entwickelt?

5 Was verursachte den Preisanstieg bei der Rückversicherung im Laufe des Jahres 2011?

6 Welche Naturkatastrophen verursachten in den folgenden Ländern erhebliche Schäden?
   a Neuseeland
   b Thailand
   c USA

7 Welchen Einfluss haben die asiatischen Märkte auf das Lebensrückversicherungsgeschäft?

8 Wodurch wird sich das Wachstum auf dem weltweiten Gesundheitsmarkt in Zukunft verstärken?

Interaktion

There is a job vacancy at The Hastings Insurance Company Ltd in England. The Head of Human Resources, Sophie/Steve Green, calls an applicant for a telephone interview.

Use the cards below to act out the roles.

Student A

- You are Sophie/Steve Green. Introduce yourself.
- Suitable time for telephone interview?
- Ask the applicant to talk about their CV
- Ask the applicant to describe themselves
- Strengths and weaknesses?
- Like working in a team? Why?
- How would the applicant's colleagues describe him/her?
- Hobbies?
- What does applicant expect of the job?
- Why did the applicant train as an insurance business management assistant?
- Ask the applicant why you should choose him/her for the job
- Any further questions?

Student B

- You are the applicant. Answer the phone and introduce yourself
- Say that this is a suitable time for telephone interview
- Talk about your CV
- Describe yourself
- Talk about your strengths and weaknesses
- Say whether you like working in a team or not and give reasons
- Describe yourself from the point of view of your colleagues
- Talk about your hobbies
- Describe what you expect of the job
- Explain why you chose to become an insurance business management assistant
- Give reasons why you should be chosen for the job
- Ask any questions you may have

Rezeption I (Hörverstehen)

Erreichbare Punkte: (hier) 20

Situation: You work for XX Insurance and will soon be taking care of car insurance claims. Since you have many English-speaking customers, you decide to find some information on the topic in English. You come across the following podcast.

Aufgabe: Complete the following table with information from the podcast. You will hear it twice.

How to file an insurance claim	– Contact … during … (2) – Call … (1) – File claim … (1)
Information needed to report an insurance claim	– When and where … (1) – How … (1) – Vehicle/vehicles … (1) – Description of … (1) – The names and contact information of … (1) – The names and contact information of … (1) – Whether the police … (1)
Reason why handling processes of claims vary	– … (1)
Typical steps a claim goes through after report	– Discuss … (1) – Determine … (1) – … damages (1) – … damages (1) – … (1)
What happens after an insurance claim has been reported?	– A claims representative will be … (1) – Claims representative will contact … (1) – Usually within … (1)

Rezeption II (Leseverstehen)

Erreichbare Punkte: (hier) 20

Situation: Während einer Fachtagung werden Informationsblätter und Werbematerial zu Versicherungsleistungen für Auslandspraktika verteilt.

TR Insurance offers working abroad travel insurance

If you are planning to take a work placement abroad, you need the right type of insurance to cover your travel arrangements, the type of work you are doing, and any holiday or activities you plan during your time away.

When should I buy my insurance?

Once you have your work placement confirmed, you will be thinking about organising your travel plans and accommodation […]. Make sure you buy your insurance as soon as you commit to these costs. This may be a number of weeks before your trip starts, but it means that, once you have purchased your insurance policy, you will be covered to claim back any irrecoverable costs if you have to unexpectedly cancel your work placement abroad.

[We offer a] specialist travel insurance policy which will cover:

- **you at your work placement, including volunteer work** – should you become injured.
- **your course fees** – we will reimburse you of any irrecoverable unused pre-paid course fees, if you have to cancel or curtail your work placement due to the death, injury or illness of either you or a close relative.
- **your belongings** – protect communication and entertainment essentials such as your laptop, tablet, mobile phone, and gadgets as well as any other personal possessions you take with you from theft or damage.
- **your accommodation costs** – like your course fees if you have to unexpectedly cancel or curtail your work placement abroad, we will reimburse you of any irrecoverable unused prepaid accommodation costs; we will also cover any costs you are liable to pay for theft or fire damage to a landlord's property.
- **your travel costs** – for things such as delayed or missed departures, and reimbursement of your travel costs if you have to unexpectedly cancel your trip.
- **medical costs** – this will cover any medical costs if you are unwell or injured whilst abroad, as well as cover the costs to return you home if you are seriously unwell, and back again once you are recovered – all supported by a 24-hour English-speaking helpline.

(Source: http://www.endsleigh.co.uk/Travel/Pages/work-abroad-insurance.aspx)

Aufgabe: Beantworten Sie die Fragen bzw. machen Sie die gewünschten Angaben stichwortartig in folgender Tabelle auf Deutsch.

Wann sollten Sie die Versicherung kaufen?	...
Was wird von TR Insurance abgedeckt?	...
Gebühren	...
Besitztum	...
Unterkunftskosten	...
Fahrtkosten	...
Medizinische Kosten	...

Mediation

Erreichbare Punkte: (hier) 30

Situation: Um die Internetseite Ihrer Versicherungsgesellschaft zu ergänzen, werden u. a. folgende Informationen wiedergegeben.

Aufgabe: Fassen Sie die Informationen über den Versicherungsschutz in privaten Haushalten auf Deutsch zusammen.

As private households and businesses are exposed to many risks every day, the insurance industry offers a wide range of insurance products and solutions, from contracts for old age provision and the assurance of personal risks, to insurance against damage to buildings and contents, and insurance against liability incidents, such as traffic accidents caused by policyholders.
People can assure their property as well as themselves and their families. Alongside families, networks of friends, neighbourhoods and government social security schemes, private insurance protection represents a core pillar of social assurance in the free market economy.
Insurance requirements of households are very different and depend on household composition, age of household members, income and precise living situations, as well as on individual preferences and mentalities.

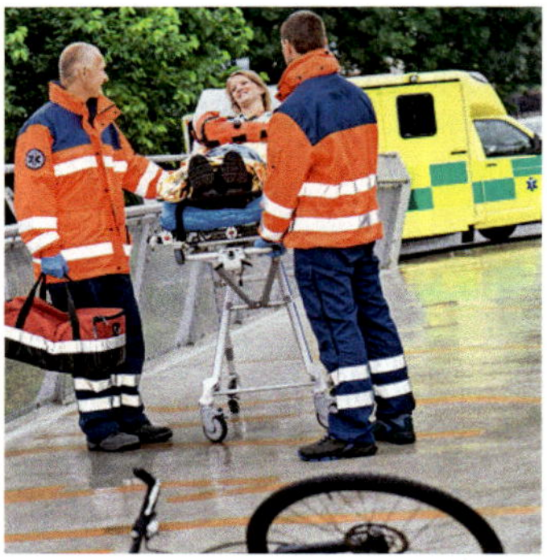

For most households, it makes sense to assure against risks that can threaten their financial livelihood. Many people are not sufficiently insured when it comes to risks to basic livelihood, such as families with children who are not insured against the death of the main provider in the family.

Part of the population still refrains from taking out private liability insurance, even though an accident caused by a pedestrian or cyclist injuring a third party can lead to financial ruin.

Produktion

Erreichbare Punkte: (hier) 30

Situation: Ein Kunde, Herr Brown, hat Ihnen per E-Mail mitgeteilt, dass er für den Kauf seines Hauses ein Darlehen in Höhe von 150.000 Euro aufnehmen muss. Er möchte für den Fall seines vorzeitigen Todes eine günstige Absicherung für seine Familie. Seine Frau ist nicht berufstätig, und er hat zwei Töchter im Alter von 5 und 7 Jahren.

Aufgabe: Schreiben Sie einen Brief an Ihren Kunden John Brown mit folgendem Inhalt.

- Begrüßung
- Betreffzeile
- Nehmen Sie Bezug auf seine E-Mail. Bedanken Sie sich für sein Interesse an den Produkten Ihrer Gesellschaft.
- Bieten Sie eine Risiko-Lebensversicherung in Höhe des Darlehensbetrages mit 20 Jahren Laufzeit an.
- Weisen Sie ihn darauf hin, dass
  - die monatliche Prämie 25 Euro beträgt
  - diese Police keinen Rückkaufswert und keine Erlebensfall-Leistung enthält
  - die Möglichkeit besteht, die Police innerhalb der ersten 10 Jahre ohne erneute Gesundheitsprüfung in eine gemischte Lebensversicherung umzuwandeln
  - die Möglichkeit besteht, neben dem Todesfall auch unheilbare Krankheiten einzuschließen gegen einen kleinen Zusatzbeitrag
- Fragen Sie an, ob er schon eine Berufsunfähigkeitsversicherung besitzt. Angesichts der Tatsache, dass seine Frau nicht berufstätig ist, wäre es wichtig, neben dem Todesfall auch dieses Risiko miteinzuschließen. Teilen Sie ihm mit, dass Ihre Gesellschaft ihm auf Wunsch hier sicher auch ein günstiges Angebot machen kann.
- geeigneter Schlusssatz

Mündliche Prüfung Teil II

Situation

Sie möchten sich nach Ihrer Ausbildung auf folgende Anzeige bewerben (siehe S. 149). Da Sie wissen, dass ein Bewerbungsgespräch auf Englisch stattfinden wird, üben Sie mit Ihrem/Ihrer Partner/in dieses Gespräch.

Wir suchen eine/n

Versicherungskauffrau/-mann für den Versicherungsinnendienst
in der Fachabteilung Haftpflichtversicherung

Ihr Aufgabengebiet
- Risikoanalyse, Prüfung, Dokumentierung von Versicherungsverträgen im Segment Haftpflichtversicherung
- Neuordnung von Verträgen nach Vorgaben der Abteilungsleitung
- Schadenmanagement (Bearbeitung und Begleitung von Schäden)
- Verhandlungen mit Versicherern

Unsere Anforderungen
- abgeschlossene Ausbildung im Bereich Versicherungen und Finanzen
- selbstständiges und eigenverantwortliches Arbeiten
- Flexibilität, Kommunikations- und Teamfähigkeit
- ein ausgeprägtes Organisationsgeschick und gute MS-Office-Kenntnisse
- gute Englischkenntnisse

Unser Angebot
- eine gut bezahlte Innendienstposition in einem mitarbeiterfreundlichen Unternehmen
- diverse Weiterbildungs- und Qualifizierungsmöglichkeiten
- gute Sozialleistungen, Weihnachts- und Urlaubsgeld

Wir haben Ihr Interesse geweckt? Wir freuen uns auf Ihre aussagekräftige Bewerbung.
Für weitere Informationen steht Ihnen unser Personalberater Herr Stefan Hinz gerne zur Verfügung. Bitte senden Sie Ihre Bewerbungsunterlagen unter Angabe Ihrer Einkommensvorstellung mit Anschreiben, Lebenslauf und den relevanten Zeugnissen an: bewerbung@HV_versicherung.de

Student A

You are the personnel manager at HV Versicherung. You are responsible for holding the job interviews. Give the applicant enough time to respond to your questions and use your imagination to make up possible answers.

- Introduce yourself
- Small talk
- Motivation to work for your company?
- Which department(s) worked in during apprenticeship?
- Outline main principles of company policy (team work / customer orientation)
- Strengths?
- Company welcomes motivated employees / supports qualification opportunities
- Questions?

Student B

You are an applicant for the vacant job. You are invited for a job interview. Be prepared to ask and answer questions and use your imagination to make up possible answers.

- Introduce yourself
- Small talk
- State motivation to work for HV Versicherung
- Give details about apprenticeship and departments worked in
- Customer orientation a main principle for you (give example from daily routine)
- Describe your strengths
- Ask about "Weiterbildungs- und Qualifizierungsmöglichkeiten" mentioned in advertisement
- Expectations concerning employees?

Glossary of insurance terms

The number after each entry refers to the unit in which the term first occurs.

ageing reserve 6 Money set aside from the insurance premium of private health insurers to subsidize the risk premium at older ages. *Alterungsrückstellungen*

agent 1 A person who sells insurance policies for one or more insurance companies. *Agent/in*

aggregator 1 An Internet instrument used mainly for price comparison of insurance premiums. *Vergleichsrechner*

all risks 10 A property policy that covers all perils except the ones that are excluded. *Allgefahrenpolice*

annuity 4 A contract that in Germany provides a monthly payment for life (life annuity) in return for a single premium payment or a series of premiums. *Rente, Annuität*

arson 10 The crime of deliberately setting fire to something, particularly a building. *Brandstiftung*

balanced portfolio 11 A group of risks whose sums insured are fairly similar. *ausgewogener Bestand*

benefit 3 A payment made under an insurance policy. *Leistung*

broker 1 A representative of a person or organization seeking insurance cover *Makler/in*

buildings insurance 3 Insurance that covers the fabric of a building: the walls, roof, etc. *(Wohn-)Gebäudeversicherung*

burden of proof 10 The duty to provide evidence or proof in order to make a claim. *Beweislast*

business insurance 1 An insurance programme for a company. *Versicherungsprogramm für Unternehmen*

business interruption insurance 10 A form of insurance that compensates an insured for loss of income if a place of production is damaged by an insured peril *Betriebsunterbrechungversicherung*

cedant (UK), cedent (USA) 11 First/Direct/Primary insurer that lays off risks or shares of risks to a reinsurer. *Zedent*

cede 11 To lay off a share of a risk to a reinsurer. *zedieren*

commission 11 The money paid to an agent by an insurance company for acquiring a new policy or on the renewal of a policy; the money paid to a cedant by a reinsurer for its share of proportional reinsurance. *Provision*

comprehensive policy 8 A motor insurance policy that covers own damage to the insured vehicle. *Vollkaskopolice*

contents insurance 2 Insurance for the contents of a house or flat. *Hausratversicherung*

conversion option 4 An arrangement which allows the policyholder to change the cover at an agreed point of time, often used in life insurance for switching from a term insurance benefit to a savings benefit of some kind. *Umtauschoption*

cover, coverage 11 The amount of insurance an insurer provides its policyholder; the amount of reinsurance a reinsurer provides its cedant. *Deckung*

deductible (in USA & UK) 10 Cf. excess. A deductible is also the share of each claim that a cedant keeps in non-proportional reinsurance. *Abzugsfranchise, Selbstbeteiligung*

endowment insurance 4 A life insurance policy that pays the benefit on maturity or on death if that occurs first. *gemischte Versicherung, kapitalbildende Versicherung*

environmental impairment insurance 7 A liability policy that pays if the insured negligently causes environmental pollution. *Umwelthaftpflichtversicherung*

escalator clause 10 An indexed clause that may be linked to inflation. *Gleitklausel*

excess (not USA) 3 The part of a claim that a policyholder has to pay. *Abzugsfranchise, Selbstbeteiligung*

first party 4 In the liability class this means the policyholder. *erste Partei, d. h. ein Versicherungsnehmer im Rahmen der Haftpflichtversicherung*

fortuity 7 Fortune, chance, luck *Zufall*

frequency of loss 6 How often a loss event occurs, usually measured per thousand or as a percentage. *Schadenhäufigkeit*

gross negligence 7 Acting in a careless way although the possibility of bodily injury or property damage is known. *grobe Fahrlässigkeit*

hard market 10 An insurance market where the premium rates are high and the insurer has a profit expectation; a sellers' market. *Verkäufermarkt*

health insurance *1* Insurance that covers medicine, hospital stays and other medical expenses. *(private) Krankenversicherung*
indemnification *1* Compensation for loss: the money paid or the replacement supplied. *Entschädigung*
indemnify *3* To compensate; to put someone in the same financial position as s/he was before a loss occurred. *entschädigen*
indemnity *1* 1) Cf. indemnification. 2) The principle of providing compensation for loss. *Entschädigung*
level term insurance *4* A life insurance policy covering the death risk with a sum insured that does not change for the duration of the policy. *Risikoversicherung mit gleichbleibender Summe*
liability *1* Responsibility towards other people, *Haftpflicht*
loading *11* The factor for expenses that is added to the net premium: net premium + loading = gross premium. *Aufschlag*
loss frequency *11* How often a loss event occurs, usually measured per thousand or as a percentage. *Schadenhäufigkeit*
loss severity *11* The degree of seriousness of a claim measured as a monetary value. *Schwere des Risikos*
marine insurance *11* Insurance of all goods in transit except aviation (i.e. not only cargo at sea) + hull insurance. *Transportversicherung*
moral hazard *6* A change of behaviour by the policyholder after s/he has taken out an insurance policy. That is, the person does not take such good care of his or her property. *subjektives Risiko*
motor insurance *1* Insurance of vehicles which travel on public roads that can travel above a legally defined minimum speed. *Kraftfahrtversicherung, Kfz-Versicherung*
negligence *7* An act of carelessness that a person of normal intelligence having reasonable foresight would have avoided. *Fahrlässigkeit*
over-insured *3* The sum insured is higher than the value of the property being insured. *Überversicherung*
penetration rate *7* The percentage of people in a market who could buy a given good or service (e.g. insurance) who actually do so. *Marktdurchdringung*
pension *9* An annuity that is provided on retirement by an organization such as the state (statutory pension) or a company. *Rente*
peril *2* A danger such as fire, lightning, explosion. *Gefahr*
personal accident insurance *10* An accident policy for individuals. *private Unfallversicherung*
personal pension plan *4* An annuity that begins on retirement paid for by a company or the policyholder. *private Rentenversicherung*
policy *1* A contract of insurance describing term, coverage, premium, etc. *Police*
policyholder *1* The owner of an insurance policy. *Versicherungsnehmer/in*
portability *6* Being able to transfer the ageing reserve of a comprehensive private health insurance policy to another company if the policyholder changes his/her health provider. *Portabilität*
portfolio *11* A group of risks covered by a reinsurer in one contract. *Bestand, Portefeuille*
premium *1* The sum of money a policyholder pays in order to be insured. *Prämie*
product liability insurance *7* A form of liability policy that protects a company if its products cause property damage or bodily injury to third parties. *Produkthaftpflichtversicherung*
product recall (cost) insurance *10* Insurance that compensates a company that has to ask its customers to return goods that have been sold to them, because of a defect that could cause bodily injury or property damage. *Rückrufkostenversicherung*
product tamper insurance *10* A form of liability policy that protects a company if a malicious person or persons change its products so that they cause bodily injury or property damage to members of the public. *Manipulationsversicherung*
professional indemnity insurance *7* A form of liability policy that protects certain professions against professional negligence. *Berufshaftpflichtversicherung*
protection policy *4* A form of life insurance that provides cover against death or disability without a savings component. *Lebensversicherung ohne Sparanteil*
public liability insurance *7* A form of liability policy that protects a company if its employees cause property damage or bodily injury to third parties. *Betriebshaftpflichtversicherung*

qualified intention *7* In German law a form of intention: knowing that an action could cause bodily injury or property damage, but doing it nevertheless. *bedingter Vorsatz*

quota share *11* A form of proportional reinsurance whereby the insurance company cedes the same share of each risk in the portfolio of reinsured risks to the reinsurer. *Quote*

rate *11* The parameter in an insurance premium calculation – usually per thousand – that indicates how frequently a loss is expected to occur. *Prämiensatz*

recklessness *1* Cf. gross negligence *grobe Fahrlässigkeit*

reimbursement *7* Paying a policyholder for a claim which the policyholder has already paid for. This is usual in private health insurance. *Kostenrückerstattung*

reinsurance *11* The insurance of insurance companies. *Rückversicherung*

replacement value *8* The cost of putting someone in the same financial position after a loss as s/he was before the loss occurred. *Wiederbeschaffungswert*

retention *10* The share of any claim that a policyholder keeps for his own account. *Selbstbehalt*

rider *3* An additional benefit to a life policy, such as accidental death or income protection. *Zusatzversicherung (in der Lebensversicherung)*

risk excess of loss *11* A non-proportional form of reinsurance whereby a reinsurer pays the amount of all claims that exceed a certain amount (the deductible) up to an agreed upper limit. *Einzelschadenexzedent*

risk of random loss *11* The risk that a much higher than average loss occurs. *Zufallsrisiko*

second party *4* In the liability class this means the insurance company. *zweite Partei, d.h. eine Versicherungsgesellschaft im Rahmen der Haftpflichtversicherung*

severity of loss *1* Seriousness of loss, which in insurance is measured in money. *Schwere des Verlustes*

soft market *10* An insurance market where the premium rates are low and the insurer does not expect to make a profit. *Käufermarkt*

submission *10* A proposal made to a broker by an insurance company. *Angebotsabgabe*

surplus *11* A form of proportional reinsurance whereby the insurance company cedes only that proportion of risks to the cedant that exceed its retention. *Summenexzedent*

term (life) insurance *1* A life insurance policy that covers the death risk for a limited period only. *Risikoversicherung*

third party *4* In the liability class this means the person who the first party has allegedly injured or whose property s/he has allegedly damaged. *dritte Partei, d.h. der (vermeintlich) Geschädigte im Rahmen der Haftpflichtversicherung*

third party fire and theft *8* A motor policy that covers fire damage to the insured vehicle or theft, in addition to the liability cover. *Kfz-Haftpflicht- und Teilkaskoversicherung*

tied agent *1* An insurance agent who only sells the policies of one company. *Einfirmenvertreter/in*

top-up benefit *6* An additional policy that supplements the main policy, usually a health policy. *Zusatzversicherung*

unbalanced portfolio (of risks) *11* A group of risks with great variation in the sums insured. *unausgewogener Bestand*

under-insured *3* The sum insured is lower than the value of the property being insured. *unterversichert*

underrate *11* To calculate a risk incorrectly by making it too cheap, so that the premium is too low. *unterbewerten*

underwrite *6* To assess whether a risk should be accepted or declined. *(ein Risiko) zeichnen*

whole of life insurance *4* A form of life insurance policy that continues and provides a sum insured on death. *lebenslängliche Todesfallversicherung*

Unit word list

Die neuen Wörter sind in der Reihenfolge ihres Vorkommens im Text verzeichnet. Hier sind jedoch die Wörter, die zum Grundwortschatz gehören, nicht aufgeführt.

P = das Wort befindet sich im *Partner file*.
T = das Wort befindet sich im *Transcript*.

Die Zahl am linken Rand gibt die Seitenzahl an.

UNIT 1

6	**insurance** [ɪn'ʃʊərəns]	Versicherung
	company ['kʌmpəni]	Gesellschaft, Unternehmen, Firma
	take over [ˌteɪk 'əʊvə]	übernehmen
	insurer [ɪn'ʃʊərə]	Versicherer
	invite [ɪn'vaɪt]	einladen
	attend [ə'tend]	*(Schule, usw.)* besuchen, *(Veranstaltung)* teilnehmen
	parent company [ˌpeərənt 'kʌmpəni]	Muttergesellschaft
	profile ['prəʊfaɪl]	Porträt, Profil
	found [faʊnd]	gründen
	public limited company (plc) [ˌpʌblɪk ˌlɪmɪtɪd 'kʌmpəni]	Aktiengesellschaft (AG)
	founder ['faʊndə]	Gründer/in
	Saxonian [sæ'ksəʊniən]	sächsisch
	businessman ['bɪznəsmən]	Geschäftsmann
	provide [prə'vaɪd]	bieten, anbieten
	class [klɑːs]	Art, Kategorie, Klasse
	fire insurance ['faɪər ɪnʃʊərəns]	Feuerversicherung
	marine insurance [məˌriːn ɪn'ʃʊərəns]	Transportversicherung
	liability insurance [ˌlaɪə'bɪləti ɪnʃʊərəns]	Haftpflichtversicherung
	acquire [ə'kwaɪə]	erwerben, akquirieren, kaufen
	difficulty ['dɪfɪkəlti]	Schwierigkeit, Problem
	move [muːv]	verlegen
	Head Office [ˌhed 'ɒfɪs]	Zentrale
	business ['bɪznəs]	Geschäft, Geschäfts-
	mutual insurance company [ˌmjuːtʃuəl ɪn'ʃʊərəns kʌmpəni]	Versicherungsverein auf Gegenseitigkeit (VVaG)
	several ['sevrəl]	einige, mehrere
	chamber of handicraft [ˌtʃeɪmbər əv 'hændikrɑːft]	Handwerkskammer
	merge [mɜːdʒ]	fusionieren
	leading ['liːdɪŋ]	führend
	provider [prə'vaɪdə]	Anbieter
	life insurance ['laɪf ɪnʃʊərəns]	Lebensversicherung
	establish [ɪ'stæblɪʃ]	gründen
	turn out to be [ˌtɜːn 'aʊt tə bi]	sich (als etw) erweisen, sich (als etw) herausstellen
	branch out [ˌbrɑːntʃ 'aʊt]	das Geschäftsfeld erweitern
	financial services *pl* [faɪˌnænʃl 'sɜːvɪsɪz]	Finanzdienstleistungen
	building society ['bɪldɪŋ səsaɪəti]	Bausparkasse
	branch office ['brɑːntʃ ɒfɪs]	Niederlassung
	abroad [ə'brɔːd]	im/ins Ausland
	be based in [bi 'beɪst ɪn]	seinen Sitz haben in
	share [ʃeə]	Aktie, Anteil
	public ['pʌblɪk]	Öffentlichkeit
	policyholder ['pɒləsihəʊldə]	Versicherungsnehmer/in
7	**headquarters** [ˌhed'kwɔːtəz]	Zentrale
	combine [kəm'baɪn]	zusammenschließen, vereinigen
	health insurance ['helθ ɪnʃʊərəns]	Krankenversicherung
	distribution [ˌdɪstrɪ'bjuːʃn]	Vertrieb, Versand
	billion ['bɪliən]	Milliarde
	operations *pl* [ˌɒpə'reɪʃnz]	Geschäftsbereiche, -felder
	comprehensive [ˌkɒmprɪ'hensɪv]	umfassend
	range [reɪndʒ]	Angebot, Palette
	within [wɪ'ðɪn]	innerhalb
	indemnity [ɪn'demnəti]	Entschädigung
	indemnity insurance [ɪn'demnəti ɪnˌʃʊərəns]	Schadenversicherung
	accident ['æksɪdənt]	Unfall
	policy ['pɒləsi]	Police
	in addition [ɪn ə'dɪʃn]	darüber hinaus, außerdem
	serve [sɜːv]	versorgen
	motor insurance ['məʊtər ɪnʃʊərəns]	Kfz-Versicherung
	employee [ɪm'plɔɪiː]	Angestellte/r, Mitarbeiter/in
	channel of distribution [ˌtʃænl əv ˌdɪstrɪ'bjuːʃn]	Vertriebskanal
	agent ['eɪdʒənt]	Agent/in, Vertreter/in
	tied agent [ˌtaɪd 'eɪdʒənt]	Einfirmenvertreter/in
	independent [ˌɪndɪ'pendənt]	unabhängig
	broker ['brəʊkə]	Makler/in
	direct selling [dəˌrekt 'selɪŋ]	Direktvertrieb
	amount to [ə'maʊnt tə]	*(Geldsumme)* sich belaufen auf
	premium ['priːmiəm]	Prämie
	income ['ɪnkʌm]	Einkommen
	figure ['fɪgə]	Zahl, Ziffer
	deal with ['diːl wɪð]	zu tun haben mit, umgehen mit

Abkürzungen			
	AE = American English	*jdm* = jemandem	*pl* = plural noun
	BE = British English	*jdn* = jemanden	*sb* = somebody
	etw = etwas	*jdn* = jemandes	*sth* = something

8	**own** [əʊn]	besitzen
	control [kən'trəʊl]	kontrollieren, führen, leiten
	serve [sɜːv]	dienen
	administrative [əd'mɪnɪstrətɪv]	Verwaltungs-
	be owned by sb [bi 'əʊnd baɪ]	jdm gehören
	structure ['strʌktʃə]	Struktur
	stake [steɪk]	Anteil, Beteiligung
	majority [mə'dʒɒrəti]	Mehrheit
	subsidiary [səb'sɪdiəri]	Tochtergesellschaft
	operate ['ɒpəreɪt]	betreiben, unterhalten
	regional office [ˌriːdʒnəl 'ɒfɪs]	Landesdirektion
	report to sb [rɪ'pɔːt tə]	jdm unterstehen
	be located in [bi ləʊ'keɪtɪd ɪn]	seinen Sitz haben in
	local office [ˌləʊkl 'ɒfɪs]	Bezirksdirektion
	apart from [ə'pɑːt frəm]	außer, abgesehen von
	operate ['ɒpəreɪt]	operieren, geschäftlich tätig sein
9	**introduce** [ˌɪntrə'djuːs]	vorstellen, (miteinander) bekannt machen
	colleague ['kɒliːg]	Kollege/-in
	surname ['sɜːneɪm]	Nachname
	head [hed]	Leiter/in, Chef/in
	pleasure ['pleʒə]	Vergnügen, Freude
	take part in [teɪk 'pɑːt ɪn]	teilnehmen an
	reception [rɪ'sepʃn]	Empfang, Rezeption
	appointment [ə'pɔɪntmənt]	Termin, Verabredung
	stay [steɪ]	bleiben; wohnen, übernachten
	trade fair ['treɪd feə]	(Handels-)Messe
	Managing Director [ˌmænɪdʒɪŋ də'rektə]	Geschäftsführer/in
	department [dɪ'pɑːtmənt]	Abteilung
	agency ['eɪdʒənsi]	Agentur
	continue [kən'tɪnjuː]	weitergehen, (sich) fortsetzen
	later on ['leɪtər ɒn]	später, nachher
	human resources [ˌhjuːmən rɪ'sɔːsɪz]	Personal(abteilung)
	take a seat [ˌteɪk ə 'siːt]	Platz nehmen
	trouble ['trʌbl]	Schwierigkeiten, Probleme
	at all [ət 'ɔːl]	überhaupt
	directions *pl* [də'rekʃnz]	Wegbeschreibung
	business trip ['bɪznəs trɪp]	Geschäftsreise
	sight [saɪt]	Sehenswürdigkeit
	get to know [ˌget tə 'nəʊ]	kennen lernen
	insight ['ɪnsaɪt]	Einblick
	Bavarian [bə'veəriən]	bayerisch
	sound [saʊnd]	klingen
	promising ['prɒmɪsɪŋ]	vielversprechend
	stay [steɪ]	Aufenthalt
	division [dɪ'vɪʒn]	Abteilung
	call [kɔːl]	nennen, rufen; anrufen
	in particular [ɪn pə'tɪkjələ]	insbesondere
	exception [ɪk'sepʃn]	Ausnahme
	Chief Executive Officer (CEO) [ˌtʃiːf ɪg'zekjətɪv ɒfɪsə]	Vorstandsvorsitzende/r
	trainee [treɪ'niː]	Auszubildende/r, Trainee
	senior ['siːniə]	vorgesetzt, ranghöher
	staff [stɑːf]	Personal, Mitarbeiter
	member of staff [ˌmembər əf 'stɑːf]	Mitarbeiter/in
	prefer [prɪ'fɜː]	vorziehen
	address [ə'dres]	*hier:* Anrede
10	**visitor** ['vɪzɪtə]	Gast, Besucher/in
	arrival [ə'raɪvl]	Ankunft
	left (over) [ˌleft 'əʊvə]	übrig
	on time [ɒn 'taɪm]	pünktlich
	worry ['wʌri]	sich Sorgen machen
	pleasant ['pleznt]	angenehm
	traffic ['træfɪk]	Verkehr
	mind [maɪnd]	etwas dagegen haben
	delayed [dɪ'leɪd]	verspätet
	apologize [ə'pɒlədʒaɪz]	sich entschuldigen
	delay [dɪ'leɪ]	Verspätung, Verzögerung
	Don't worry. [ˌdəʊnt 'wʌri]	Keine Sorge.
	journey ['dʒɜːni]	Reise, Fahrt
	bumpy ['bʌmpi]	holprig, unruhig
	rather ['rɑːðə]	ziemlich
11	**hospitality** [ˌhɒspɪ'tæləti]	Gastfreundschaft
	appropriate [ə'prəʊpriət]	passend, angemessen
	response [rɪ'spɒns]	Reaktion, Antwort
	questionnaire [ˌkwestʃə'neə]	Fragebogen
	on one's own [ɒn ˌwʌnz 'əʊn]	allein
12	**present** [prɪ'zent]	vorstellen, präsentieren
	imagine [ɪ'mædʒɪn]	sich vorstellen, annehmen, glauben
	challenging ['tʃælɪndʒɪŋ]	fordernd, anspruchsvoll
	manage ['mænɪdʒ]	es schaffen
	face sth [feɪs]	mit einer Sache zu kämpfen haben
	competition [ˌkɒmpə'tɪʃn]	Wettbewerb
	tough [tʌf]	*(Wettbewerb)* hart
	invisible [ɪn'vɪzəbl]	unsichtbar
	customer ['kʌstəmə]	Kunde/Kundin
	compare [kəm'peə]	(miteinander) vergleichen
	quote [kwəʊt]	Angebot, Kostenvoranschlag
	uncertain [ʌn'sɜːtn]	unsicher
	cover ['kʌvə]	Versicherungsschutz
	needs *pl* [niːdz]	Bedarf, Bedürnisse
	advice [əd'vaɪs]	Beratung, Rat
	convince [kən'vɪns]	überzeugen
	trust [trʌst]	vertrauen
	skills *pl* [skɪlz]	Fähigkeiten, Fertigkeiten, Kenntnisse
	essential [ɪ'senʃl]	unabdingbar, wesentlich
	success [sək'ses]	Erfolg
	wide range [waɪd 'reɪndʒ]	große Auswahl
	competitive [kəm'petətɪv]	konkurrenzfähig
	enable [ɪ'neɪbl]	in die Lage versetzen, ermöglichen, befähigen
	tailor-made [ˌteɪlə'meɪd]	maßgeschneidert
	solution [sə'luːʃn]	Lösung
	individual [ˌɪndɪ'vɪdʒuəl]	Einzelperson
	personal ['pɜːsənl]	privat, persönlich
	various ['veəriəs]	verschieden
	client ['klaɪənt]	Kunde/Kundin

investment fund [ɪn'vestmənt fʌnd]	Investmentfonds
mortgage ['mɔ:gɪdʒ]	Hypothek
experience [ɪk'spɪəriəns]	Erfahrung, Berufserfahrung
qualified ['kwɒlɪfaɪd]	qualifiziert
adviser [əd'vaɪzə]	Berater/in
certain ['sɜ:tn]	bestimmte/r/s
area ['eəriə]	Gebiet, Bereich
responsible [rɪ'spɒnsəbl]	zuständig, verantwortlich
be involved in sth [bi ɪn'vɒlvd ɪn]	sich mit etw befassen, mit etw zu tun haben
support [sə'pɔ:t]	Unterstützung
in charge of [ɪn 'tʃɑ:dʒ əv]	zuständig für
traineeship [treɪ'ni:ʃɪp]	Ausbildung
professional training [prə,feʃənl 'treɪnɪŋ]	Berufsausbildung
carry out [,kæri 'aʊt]	ausführen, durchführen
sponsoring company [,spɒnsərɪŋ 'kʌmpəni]	Ausbildungsbetrieb
aspect ['æspekt]	Aspekt
vocational school [vəʊ,keɪʃənl 'sku:l]	Berufsschule
provide [prə'vaɪd]	liefern, sorgen für
theoretical [,θɪə'retɪkl]	theoretisch
necessary ['nesəsəri]	nötig
qualification [,kwɒlɪfɪ'keɪʃn]	Abschluss
graduate ['grædʒueɪt]	einen Abschluss machen
13 **set up** [,set 'ʌp]	gründen
survive [sə'vaɪv]	überleben
gain [geɪn]	erwerben
task [tɑ:sk]	Aufgabe
claim [kleɪm]	Schadensfall, Versicherungsanspruch
settlement (of claims) ['setlmənt]	(Schaden-)Regulierung
agreement [ə'gri:mənt]	Vereinbarung, Abkommen
entitle [ɪn'taɪtl]	berechtigen
settle (a claim) ['setl]	(Schaden) regulieren
case [keɪs]	Fall
investigate [ɪn'vestɪgeɪt]	untersuchen
compensation [,kɒmpən'seɪʃn]	Entschädigung
(on) the condition (that) [kən'dɪʃn]	(unter der) Bedingung (, dass)
loss [lɒs]	Verlust
cover ['kʌvə]	decken, versichern
terms *pl* [tɜ:mz]	Bedingungen, Konditionen
involve [ɪn'vɒlv]	umfassen, mit sich bringen
collection [kə'lekʃn]	Inkasso
payment ['peɪmənt]	Zahlung
method of payment [,meθəd əv 'peɪmənt]	Zahlungsweise
collect [kə'lekt]	kassieren, einziehen
direct debit [də,rekt 'debɪt]	Einzug(sverfahren), Lastschrift
transfer [træns'fɜ:]	überweisen
account [ə'kaʊnt]	Konto
mention ['menʃn]	erwähnen, nennen
14 **cancel** ['kænsl]	*(Vertrag, usw.)* kündigen
cancellation [,kænsə'leɪʃn]	Kündigung

competitor [kəm'petɪtə]	Konkurrent/in, Konkurrenz
proposer [prə'pəʊzə]	Antragsteller/in
review [rɪ'vju:]	prüfen, überprüfen
include [ɪn'klu:d]	einschließen, umfassen
proposal form [prə'pəʊzl fɔ:m]	Antrag(s)formular
take care [teɪk 'keə]	dafür sorgen
rights and duties *pl* [,raɪts ən 'dju:tiz]	Rechte und Pflichten
contract ['kɒntrækt]	Vertrag
additional [ə'dɪʃnəl]	zusätzlich, Zusatz-
whether ['weðə]	ob
affect sth [ə'fekt]	sich auf etw auswirken
improve [ɪm'pru:v]	verbessern
duty ['dju:ti]	Aufgabe, Pflicht
contact sb ['kɒntækt]	sich mit jdm in Verbindung setzen
reason ['ri:zn]	Grund
reject [rɪ'dʒekt]	ablehnen
change your mind [,tʃeɪndʒ jɔ: 'maɪnd]	seine Meinung ändern
assist [ə'sɪst]	behilflich sein, unterstützen
demanding [dɪ'mɑ:ndɪŋ]	anstrengend, anspruchsvoll
undemanding [,ʌndɪ'mɑ:ndɪŋ]	anspruchslos
satisfying ['sætɪsfaɪɪŋ]	befriedigend, erfüllend
unsatisfying [,ʌn'sætɪsfaɪɪŋ]	unbefriedigend
varied ['veərid]	abwechslungsreich
monotonous [mə'nɒtənəs]	monoton
industry ['ɪndəstri]	*hier:* Branche
underwriter ['ʌndəraɪtə]	Versicherer; *hier:* Risikoprüfer/in, Antragsprüfer/in
loss adjuster [,lɒs ə'dʒʌstə]	Schadensachverständige/r, Gutachter/in
actuary ['æktʃuəri]	Aktuar/in
15 **Underwriting Department** [,ʌndə'raɪtɪŋ dɪpɑ:tmənt]	Antragsabteilung
Claims Department ['kleɪmz dɪpɑ:tmənt]	Schadenabteilung
Legal Department [,li:gl dɪ'pɑ:tmənt]	Rechtsabteilung
Mathematical Department [mæθə,mætɪkl dɪ'pɑ:tmənt]	Mathematische Abteilung
Actuarial Department [æktʃu,eəriəl dɪ'pɑ:tmənt]	Mathematische Abteilung
Accounting Department [ə'kaʊntɪŋ dɪpɑ:tmənt]	Rechnungswesen
Sales and Marketing Department [,seɪlz ənd 'mɑ:kɪtɪŋ dɪpɑ:tmənt]	Marketing und Vertrieb
Personnel Department [,pɜ:sə'nel dɪpɑ:tmənt]	Personalabteilung
Investment Department [ɪn'vestmənt dɪpɑ:tmənt]	Abteilung Vermögensanlagen
profit ['prɒfɪt]	Gewinn, Profit
demographic [,demə'græfɪk]	demographisch
advise [əd'vaɪz]	beraten, raten

	revenue ['revənju:]	Einkünfte, Einnahmen
	bond [bɒnd]	Wertpapier, Anleihe
	fraud [frɔ:d]	Betrug
	insurance fraud [ɪn'ʃʊərəns frɔ:d]	Versicherungsbetrug
	percentage [pə'sentɪdʒ]	(prozentualer) Anteil, Prozentsatz
	decline [dɪ'klaɪn]	ablehnen
	statistics *pl* [stə'tɪstɪks]	Statistik
	tariff ['tærɪf]	Tarif
	campaign [kæm'peɪn]	Werbekampagne
	promote [prə'məʊt]	bewerben
16	**negotiate** [nɪ'gəʊʃieɪt]	verhandeln
	decrease [dɪ'kri:s]	sinken, zurückgehen
	due to ['dju: tə]	aufgrund von
	fierce [fɪəs]	*(Wettbewerb)* hart
	accept [ək'sept]	akzeptieren
	application [,æplɪ'keɪʃn]	Antrag
	refuse [rɪ'fju:z]	sich weigern
	state of health [,steɪt əv 'helθ]	Gesundheitszustand
	quotation [kwəʊ'teɪʃn]	Angebot, Kostenvoranschlag
	sales [seɪlz]	Vertrieb
	waste of time [,weɪst əv 'taɪm]	Zeitverschwendung
17	**hire sb** ['haɪə]	jdn einstellen
	part-time [,pɑ:t'taɪm]	Teilzeit
	whereas [,weər'æz]	während, dagegen
	represent [,reprɪ'zent]	vertreten, repräsentieren
	obtain [əb'teɪn]	erzielen, erlangen, erhalten
	generic term [dʒə,nerɪk 'tɜ:m]	Gattungsbegriff, Oberbegriff
	intermediary [,ɪntə'mi:diəri]	Mittelsmann
	insured [ɪn'ʃʊəd]	Versicherte/r
	development [dɪ'veləpmənt]	Entwicklung
	alternative [ɔ:l'tɜ:nətɪv]	andere/r/s, alternative/r/s
	spring up [,sprɪŋ 'ʌp]	aus dem Boden schießen
	acquisition [,ækwɪ'zɪʃn]	Akquisition
	purchase ['pɜ:tʃəs]	kaufen
	aid [eɪd]	Hilfe
	outlet ['aʊtlet]	Verkaufsstelle
	association [ə,səʊsi'eɪʃn]	Verband
	car dealer ['kɑ: di:lə]	Autohändler/in
	access sb ['ækses]	an jdn herantreten, jdn erreichen
	potential [pə'tenʃl]	potenziell
	proportion [prə'pɔ:ʃn]	Anteil
	in contrast (to) [ɪn 'kɒntrɑ:st tə]	im Gegensatz zu/dazu
	retailer ['ri:teɪlə]	(Einzel-)Händler
	account for [ə'kaʊnt fə]	ausmachen
	increase [ɪn'kri:s]	steigen, zunehmen
	remaining [rɪ'meɪnɪŋ]	verbleibend, übrig
	available [ə'veɪləbl]	erhältlich, verfügbar
	aggregator ['ægrɪgeɪtə]	Vergleichsrechner
	term life insurance [,tɜ:m 'laɪf ɪnʃʊərəns]	Risikolebensversicherung
	coverage ['kʌvərɪdʒ]	Deckung, Versicherungsschutz, Versicherung

UNIT 2

18	**result** [rɪ'zʌlt]	Ergebnis
	survey ['sɜ:veɪ]	Umfrage, Befragung
	receive [rɪ'si:v]	erhalten, bekommen
	attitude ['ætɪtju:d]	Einstellung, Haltung
	overall [,əʊvər'ɔ:l]	insgesamt
	satisfied ['sætɪsfaɪd]	zufrieden
	confidence ['kɒnfɪdəns]	Vertrauen
	not applicable [nɒt ə'plɪkəbl]	nicht zutreffend
	value ['vælju:]	Wert
	perception [pə'sepʃn]	Wahrnehmung
	uncomplicated [,ʌn'kɒmplɪkeɪtɪd]	unkompliziert
	claims procedure ['kleɪmz prəsi:dʒə]	Schadensbearbeitung, -abwicklung
	honesty ['ɒnəsti]	Ehrlichkeit
	trustworthiness ['trʌstwɜ:ðinəs]	Vertrauenswürdigkeit
	documentation [,dɒkjumen'teɪʃn]	Unterlagen, Dokumentation
	competent ['kɒmpɪtənt]	kompetent
	adjust [ə'dʒʌst]	anpassen
	local proximity [,ləʊkl prɒk'sɪməti]	räumliche Nähe
19	**rank (second)** [ræŋk]	den (zweiten) Platz belegen
	valuable ['væljuəbl]	wertvoll
	define [dɪ'faɪn]	definieren
	consider [kən'sɪdə]	erachten, halten für
	influence ['ɪnfluəns]	beeinflussen
	behave [bɪ'heɪv]	sich verhalten
	slightly ['slaɪtli]	ein bisschen, etwas
	suitable ['su:təbl]	geeignet, passend
	reliable [rɪ'laɪəbl]	zuverlässig
	responsible [rɪ'spɒnsəbl]	verantwortungsbewusst
	previous ['pri:viəs]	vorherig
	contents insurance ['kɒntents ɪnʃʊərəns]	Hausratversicherung
	ruin ['ru:ɪn]	zerstören
	arrest [ə'rest]	verhaften
	embezzlement [ɪm'bezlmənt]	Veruntreuung, Unterschlagung
	require [rɪ'kwaɪə]	verlangen, vorschreiben
	report [rɪ'pɔ:t]	anzeigen
	break-in ['breɪkɪn]	Einbruch
20	**seek** [si:k]	suchen
	willing ['wɪlɪŋ]	bereit
	shop around for [,ʃɒp ə'raʊnd fə]	sich umsehen nach
	personalized ['pɜ:sənəlaɪzd]	persönlich zugeschnitten
	trust [trʌst]	Vertrauen
	convenience [kən'vi:niəns]	Komfort
	uninterested [ʌn'ɪntrəstɪd]	desinteressiert
	price-sensitive [,praɪs 'sensətɪv]	preisbewusst
	relationship [rɪ'leɪʃnʃɪp]	Beziehung, Verhältnis
	oriented ['ɔ:riəntɪd]	orientiert
	voice [vɔɪs]	Stimme
	table ['teɪbl]	Tabelle
	bargain ['bɑ:gɪn]	Schnäppchen
	leave sb alone [,li:v ə'ləʊn]	jdn in Ruhe lassen

	according to [ə'kɔ:dɪŋ tə]	gemäß, nach
	priority [praɪ'ɒrəti]	Priorität
	exchange [ɪks'tʃeɪndʒ]	austauschen
21	**offer** ['ɒfə]	Angebot
	pie chart ['paɪ tʃɑ:t]	Tortendiagramm
	breakdown ['breɪkdaʊn]	Aufschlüsselung
22	**slight** [slaɪt]	leicht, gering
	sales *pl* [seɪlz]	Umsatz
	stable ['steɪbl]	stabil
	remain [rɪ'meɪn]	bleiben
	constant ['kɒnstənt]	konstant, gleich
	even out [ˌi:vn 'aʊt]	sich einpendeln
	drop [drɒp]	zurückgehen
	change [tʃeɪndʒ]	Veränderung
	negligible ['neglɪdʒəbl]	vernachlässigbar
	significant [sɪg'nɪfɪkənt]	bedeutend, signifikant, erheblich
	considerable [kən'sɪdərəbl]	beträchtlich
	sharp [ʃɑ:p]	drastisch, rapide
	dramatic [drə'mætɪk]	dramatisch
	graph [grɑ:f]	Diagramm
	from ... onwards [ˌfrəm 'ɒnwədz]	von ... an
	growth [grəʊθ]	Wachstum
	growth rate ['grəʊθ reɪt]	Wachstumsrate
	slow down [ˌsləʊ 'daʊn]	(sich) verlangsamen
23	**spread** [spred]	Verteilung
24	**structure** ['strʌktʃə]	strukturieren
	visuals *pl* ['vɪʒuəlz]	visuelle Hilfsmittel
	conclusion [kən'klu:ʒn]	Schluss
	interrupt [ˌɪntə'rʌpt]	unterbrechen
	purpose ['pɜ:pəs]	Zweck, Absicht
	objective [əb'dʒektɪv]	Ziel, Zweck
	aim [eɪm]	Ziel
	segment ['segmənt]	Segment
	indicate ['ɪndɪkeɪt]	zeigen, hindeuten auf
	divide [dɪ'vaɪd]	teilen, unterteilen
	talk [tɔ:k]	Vortrag
	stage [steɪdʒ]	Abschnitt
	turn to sth ['tɜ:n tə]	sich einer Sache zuwenden
	consist of [kən'sɪst əv]	bestehen aus
	draw sb's attention to sth [ˌdrɔ: sʌmbədiz ə'tenʃn tə]	jds Aufmerksamkeit auf etw lenken
25	**combine** [kəm'baɪn]	kombinieren
	transparency [træns'pærənsi]	Transparenz
	expect [ɪk'spekt]	erwarten
	brief [bri:f]	kurz, knapp, bündig
	exclusion [ɪk'sklu:ʒn]	Ausschluss(klausel)
	target ['tɑ:gɪt]	zielen auf
	differ ['dɪfə]	sich unterscheiden
	take into account [ˌteɪk ɪntu ə'kaʊnt]	berücksichtigen
	vary ['veəri]	variieren, schwanken
	avoid [ə'vɔɪd]	vermeiden
T	**jargon** ['dʒɑ:gən]	Jargon, Fachchinesisch
	on the one hand [ɒn ðə 'wʌn hænd]	einerseits
	increased [ɪn'kri:st]	gesteigert, vermehrt
	on the other hand [ɒn ði 'ʌðə hænd]	andererseits
	relevant ['reləvənt]	relevant, wichtig
	requirement [rɪ'kwaɪəmənt]	Wunsch, Anforderung
T	**apply to** [ə'plaɪ tə]	zutreffen auf
	effective [ɪ'fektɪv]	effektiv
	variation [ˌveəri'eɪʃn]	Unterschied, Schwankung
26	**pronunciation** [prəˌnʌnsi'eɪʃn]	Aussprache
	volume ['vɒlju:m]	Lautstärke
	pitch [pɪtʃ]	Tonhöhe, Tonlage
	pace [peɪs]	Geschwindigkeit, Tempo
	audience ['ɔ:diəns]	Publikum
	prompt card ['prɒmpt kɑ:d]	Moderationskarte
	address [ə'dres]	ansprechen
	point out [ˌpɔɪnt 'aʊt]	deuten auf, hinweisen auf
	OHP transparency [ˌəʊ eɪtʃ 'pi: trænspærənsi]	Overheadfolie
	conscious ['kɒnʃəs]	bewusst
	turn one's back to sb [ˌtɜ:n wʌnz 'bæk tə]	jdm den Rücken zuwenden
	facial expression [ˌfeɪʃl ɪk'spreʃn]	Gesichtsausdruck
	gesture ['dʒestʃə]	Geste
	reinforce [ˌri:ɪn'fɔ:s]	verstärken
	message ['mesɪdʒ]	Botschaft
	crossed arms [ˌkrɒst 'ɑ:mz]	verschränkte Arme
	clenched fist [ˌklentʃt 'fɪst]	geballte Faust
	visual aids *pl* ['vɪʒuəl eɪdz]	visuelle Hilfsmittel
	flow chart ['fləʊtʃɑ:t]	Flussdiagramm
	make sure [ˌmeɪk 'ʃʊə]	sicherstellen, sich vergewissern
	font size ['fɒnt saɪz]	Schriftgröße
	sufficiently [sə'fɪʃntli]	ausreichend, genügend
	contrasting [kən'trɑ:stɪŋ]	kontrastierend, Kontrast-
	limit ['lɪmɪt]	beschränken, begrenzen
	focus ['fəʊkəs]	Mittelpunkt
	be meant to [bi 'ment tə]	dazu dienen
	express [ɪk'spres]	ausdrücken, äußern
	opinion [ə'pɪniən]	Meinung, Ansicht
	view [vju:]	Ansicht
	point of view [ˌpɔɪnt əv 'vju:]	Standpunkt, Perspektive, Sicht
27	**crime** [kraɪm]	Verbrechen
	coalition [ˌkəʊə'lɪʃn]	Bündnis
	estimate ['estɪmət]	schätzen
	property ['prɒpəti]	Eigentum
	fraudulent ['frɔ:djələnt]	betrügerisch
	occur [ə'kɜ:]	*(Tatbestand)* vorliegen, *(Fall)* eintreten
	deceive [dɪ'si:v]	täuschen
	lower ['ləʊə]	senken
	severity [sɪ'verəti]	Schwere
	common ['kɒmən]	verbreitet, häufig
	annually ['ænjuəli]	jährlich
	inflate [ɪn'fleɪt]	aufblähen
	pad [pæd]	*(Rechnung, usw.)* fälschen
	homeowner ['həʊməʊnə]	Hausbesitzer/in
	exaggerate [ɪg'zædʒəreɪt]	übertreiben
	burglary ['bɜ:gləri]	Einbruch
	fake [feɪk]	vortäuschen
	pension ['penʃn]	Rente

disability pension [dɪsəˌbɪləti 'penʃn]	Invaliditätsrente
invent [ɪn'vent]	erfinden
injury ['ɪndʒəri]	Verletzung
stage [steɪdʒ]	inszenieren
cause [kɔːz]	verursachen
intentional [ɪn'tenʃənl]	absichtlich
collision [kə'lɪʒn]	Zusammenstoß, Kollision
innocent ['ɪnəsnt]	unschuldig
non-existent [ˌnɒn ɪg'zɪstənt]	nicht existierend
passenger ['pæsɪndʒə]	Mitfahrer/in, Beifahrer/in
suffer ['sʌfə]	erleiden, leiden
whiplash ['wɪplæʃ]	Schleudertrauma
loss of earnings [ˌlɒs əv 'ɜːnɪŋz]	Verdienstausfall
commit [kə'mɪt]	*(Straftat)* begehen
crook [krʊk]	Gauner/in, Kriminelle/r
organized crime ['ɔːgənaɪzd kraɪm]	organisiertes Verbrechen
honest ['ɒnɪst]	ehrlich
little white lies *pl* [lɪtl ˌwaɪt 'laɪz]	Notlügen
make up for [ˌmeɪk 'ʌp fə]	ausgleichen, wieder gutmachen
victim ['vɪktɪm]	Opfer
victimless ['vɪktɪmləs]	ohne Opfer
consumer goods *pl* [kən'sjuːmə gʊdz]	Konsumgüter
services *pl* ['sɜːvɪsɪz]	Dienstleistungen
pass sth on [ˌpɑːs 'ɒn]	weiterreichen, weitergeben
average ['ævərɪdʒ]	Durchschnitt, durchschnittlich
hidden ['hɪdn]	verborgen
tax [tæks]	Steuer
widespread ['waɪdspred]	verbreitet
back off [ˌbæk 'ɒf]	nachgeben
encourage [ɪn'kʌrɪdʒ]	fördern
suspicious [sə'spɪʃəs]	verdächtig
court [kɔːt]	Gericht
risk [rɪsk]	Risiko
swindler ['swɪndlə]	Betrüger/in
view [vjuː]	sehen, betrachten
get caught [ˌget 'kɔːt]	erwischt werden
legal ['liːgl]	rechtlich, gesetzlich
prosecutor ['prɒsɪkjuːtə]	Strafverfolger/in
violence ['vaɪələns]	Gewalt
high-profile [ˌhaɪ 'prəʊfaɪl]	in der Öffentlichkeit stehend
conduct [kən'dʌkt]	*(Studie, usw.)* durchführen

UNIT 3

28 **building** ['bɪldɪŋ]	Gebäude
retail ['riːteɪl]	Einzelhandel
chain [tʃeɪn]	Kette
rent [rent]	mieten
request sth [rɪ'kwest]	um etw bitten, etw anfordern
enquiry [ɪn'kwaɪəri]	Anfrage
panel ['pænl]	Liste
in order to [ɪn 'ɔːdə tə]	um ... zu
enclosed [ɪn'kləʊzd]	*(Brief)* beigefügt
to the best of your knowledge [tə ðə ˌbest əv jɔː 'nɒlɪdʒ]	nach bestem Wissen
return [rɪ'tɜːn]	zurückschicken
asap = as soon as possible [ˌeɪ es eɪ 'piː]	so bald wie möglich, baldmöglichst
attachment [ə'tætʃmənt]	*(Brief)* Anlage, *(E-Mail)* Attachment
calculate ['kælkjuleɪt]	berechnen
work out [ˌwɜːk 'aʊt]	ausrechnen, herausfinden
replacement cost [rɪ'pleɪsmənt kɒst]	Wiederbeschaffungskosten
belongings *pl* [bɪ'lɒŋɪŋz]	Eigentum, Besitz, Sachen
current ['kʌrənt]	aktuell
entry ['entri]	Eintrag
sum [sʌm]	Summe
sum insured [ˌsʌm ɪn'ʃʊəd]	Versicherungssumme
under-insured [ˌʌndər ɪn'ʃʊəd]	unterversichert
over-insured [ˌəʊvər ɪn'ʃʊəd]	überversichert
look forward to [ˌlʊk 'fɔːwəd tə]	sich freuen auf
hesitate ['hezɪteɪt]	zögern
wish [wɪʃ]	Wunsch
abbreviation [əˌbriːvi'eɪʃn]	Abkürzung
procedure [prə'siːdʒə]	Verfahren, Vorgehen
29 **hyphen** ['haɪfn]	Bindestrich
dash [dæʃ]	Binde-/Gedankenstrich
slash [slæʃ]	Schrägstrich
underscore [ˌʌndə'skɔː]	Unterstrich
salutation [ˌsælju'teɪʃn]	*(Brief)* Anrede
close [kləʊs]	*(Brief)* Schlussformel
recipient [rɪ'sɪpiənt]	Empfänger/in
sender ['sendə]	Absender/in
contraction [kən'trækʃn]	Kurzform
contain [kən'teɪn]	enthalten
inform [ɪn'fɔːm]	informieren
appreciate [ə'priːʃieɪt]	zu schätzen wissen, schätzen
30 **regarding** [rɪ'gɑːdɪŋ]	betreffend, bezüglich
discuss [dɪ'skʌs]	diskutieren, erörtern, besprechen
prompt [prɒmpt]	Stichwort
death [deθ]	Tod
peril ['perəl]	Gefahr, Risiko
limit ['lɪmɪt]	Obergrenze, Limit
veterinary ['vetnri]	tierärztlich
expense(s) [ɪk'spensɪz]	Kosten, Auslagen
burst pipe [bɜːst 'paɪp]	Rohrbruch
damage ['dæmɪdʒ]	Schaden, Beschädigung, Schädigung
water damage [ˌwɔːtə 'dæmɪdʒ]	Wasserschaden
arrange [ə'reɪndʒ]	vereinbaren, abmachen
assessment [ə'sesmənt]	Schätzung, Bewertung
subject ['sʌbdʒɪkt]	Thema; *(E-Mail)* Betreff
concise [kən'saɪs]	knapp, prägnant
content [kən'tent]	Inhalt
body ['bɒdi]	*(Brief, usw.)* Haupttext
to the point [tə ðə 'pɔɪnt]	treffend, sachbezogen
idea [aɪ'dɪə]	Gedanke
break [breɪk]	Zeilenumbruch

	capital letter ['kæpɪtl letə]	Großbuchstabe
	register ['redʒɪstə]	Ton
	signature ['sɪgnətʃə]	Unterschrift
31	**home contents** *pl* [ˌhəʊm 'kɒntents]	Hausrat
	fixed [fɪkst]	fest
	feature ['fi:tʃə]	Merkmal, Eigenschaft
	put [pʊt]	formulieren
	protect [prə'tekt]	schützen
	domestic appliances *pl* [dəˌmestɪk ə'plaɪənsɪz]	Haushaltsgeräte
	valuables *pl* ['væljuəblz]	Wertsachen
	jewellery ['dʒu:əlri]	Schmuck
	lightning ['laɪtnɪŋ]	Blitzschlag
	earthquake ['ɜ:θkweɪk]	Erdbeben
	flood [flʌd]	Überschwemmung
	attempted [ə'temptɪd]	versucht
	malicious [mə'lɪʃəs]	mutwillig
	subsidence [səb'saɪdns]	Absacken *(eines Gebäudes)*
	involving [ɪn'vɒlvɪŋ]	mit, unter Beteiligung von
	aircraft ['eəkrɑ:ft]	Flugzeug
	vehicle ['vi:əkl]	Fahrzeug
	aerial ['eəriəl]	Antenne
	escape [ɪ'skeɪp]	entweichen
	remove [rɪ'mu:v]	entfernen
	accidental [ˌæksɪ'dentl]	zufällig
	accidental damage [æksɪˌdentl 'dæmɪdʒ]	unbeabsichtigte Beschädigung
	tabletop ['teɪbltɒp]	Tischplatte
	legal liability [ˌli:gl laɪə'bɪləti]	gesetzliche Haftpflicht
	occupier ['ɒkjupaɪə]	Bewohner/in
	injure ['ɪndʒə]	(sich) verletzen
	accommodation [əˌkɒmə'deɪʃn]	Unterkunft
	alternative accommodation [ɔ:lˌtɜ:nətɪv əkɒmə'deɪʃn]	Ausweichunterkunft, -quartier
	flooding ['flʌdɪŋ]	Überschwemmung
	replacement [rɪ'pleɪsmənt]	Ersatz
	lawn mower ['lɔ:n məʊə]	Rasenmäher
	break down [ˌbreɪk 'daʊn]	kaputtgehen
	outbuilding ['aʊtˌbɪldɪŋ]	Nebengebäude, Anbau
	shed [ʃed]	Schuppen
	temporary ['temprəri]	befristet, vorübergehend
	increase ['ɪŋkri:s]	Steigerung
	excess ['ekses]	Selbstbeteiligung, Selbstbehalt
	apply [ə'plaɪ]	gelten
	specify ['spesɪfaɪ]	(genau) angeben, spezifizieren
	compulsory [kəm'pʌlsəri]	obligatorisch
	opt for ['ɒpt fə]	sich entscheiden fur
	voluntary ['vɒləntri]	freiwillig
	reduce [rɪ'dju:s]	reduzieren
	except for [ɪk'sept fə]	außer, ausgenommen
	durable ['djʊərəbl]	langlebig
	linen ['lɪnɪn]	Bettwäsche
	repair [rɪ'peə]	reparieren
	replace [rɪ'pleɪs]	ersetzen
	equivalent [ɪ'kwɪvələnt]	gleichwertig

	compensate ['kɒmpenseɪt]	entschädigen
	wear and tear [ˌweər ən 'teə]	Abnutzung, Verschleiß
	portion ['pɔ:ʃn]	Teil
32	**principle** ['prɪnsəpl]	Prinzip
	occur [ə'kɜ:]	geschehen
	unexpected [ˌʌnɪk'spektɪd]	unerwartet
	use [ju:s]	Gebrauch
	law [lɔ:]	Gesetz
	rule [ru:l]	Vorschrift, Bestimmung, Regel
	danger ['deɪndʒə]	Gefahr
	claim on sth ['kleɪm ɒn]	eine Versicherung in Anspruch nehmen
	reduction [rɪ'dʌkʃn]	Abzug
	crack [kræk]	Riss
	strike [straɪk]	treffen, erschlagen
	increase [ɪn'kri:s]	erhöhen
	leak [li:k]	*(Wasser)* austreten
	gardening tool ['gɑ:dnɪŋ tu:l]	Gartengerät
33	**detached house** [dɪ'tætʃt haʊs]	freistehendes Haus
	joined to ['dʒɔɪnd tə]	verbunden mit
	semi-detached house [ˌsemi dɪ'tætʃt haʊs]	Doppelhaushälfte
	terraced house [ˌterəst 'haʊs]	Reihenhaus
	row [rəʊ]	Reihe
	level ['levl]	Etage, Geschoss
	entrance ['entrəns]	Eingang
	studio flat ['stju:diəʊ flæt]	Einzimmerwohnung
	former ['fɔ:mə]	ehemalige/r/s
	factory ['fæktəri]	Fabrik
	warehouse ['weəhaʊs]	Lagerhaus
	make suitable [ˌmeɪk 'su:təbl]	*(Haus, usw.)* umbauen
	landlord ['lændlɔ:d]	Vermieter
	owner-occupied flat [ˌəʊnər 'ɒkjupaɪd flæt]	Eigentumswohnung *(BE)*
	condominium/condo [ˌkɒndə'mɪniəm/ 'kɒndəʊ]	Eigentumswohnung *(AE)*
34	**permanent** ['pɜ:mənənt]	dauerhaft
	fixture ['fɪkstʃə]	eingebautes Inventar, dauerhafte Ausstattung
	chartered surveyor [ˌtʃɑ:təd sə'veɪə]	Bausachverständige/r
	postcode ['pəʊstkəʊd]	Postleitzahl
T	**Hold the line.** [ˌhəʊld ðə 'laɪn]	Bleiben Sie am Apparat.
T	**put sb through** [ˌpʊt 'θru:]	*(Telefon)* jdn durchstellen
T	**convenient** [kən'vi:niənt]	angenehm
T	**residential area** [reziˌdenʃl 'eəriə]	Wohngegend
T	**catch** [kætʃ]	verstehen
T	**particular** [pə'tɪkjələ]	bestimmte/r/s, spezielle/r/s, besondere/r/s
T	**grant** [grɑ:nt]	gewähren, einräumen
T	**discount** ['dɪskaʊnt]	Rabatt
T	**pay** [peɪ]	sich auszahlen

	take out insurance [teɪk ˌaʊt ɪn'ʃʊərəns]	einer Versicherung abschließen
	recommend [ˌrekə'mend]	empfehlen
	competitive [kəm'petətɪv]	konkurrierend
	structure ['strʌktʃə]	Bau(werk), Konstruktion
	built-in kitchen unit [bɪlt ˌɪn 'kɪtʃɪn ju:nɪt]	Einbauküche
	fittings *pl* ['fɪtɪŋz]	(sanitäre) Installationen
	fence [fens]	Zaun
	gate [geɪt]	Tor, Tür
	depend on [dɪ'pend ɒn]	davon abhängen, darauf ankommen
	escape of water [ɪˌskeɪp əv 'wɔ:tə]	Wasseraustritt
	rebuilding [ˌri:'bɪldɪŋ]	Wiederaufbau
	calculator ['kælkjuleɪtə]	Rechner
	free of charge [ˌfri: əv 'tʃɑ:dʒ]	kostenlos, gebührenfrei, gratis
	drawback ['drɔ:bæk]	Nachteil, Haken
	rough [rʌf]	ungefähr, grob
	hire ['haɪə]	engagieren
	accurate ['ækjərət]	genau, exakt
	handy ['hændi]	praktisch
	polite [pə'laɪt]	höflich
	digit ['dɪdʒɪt]	Ziffer
	area code ['eəriə kəʊd]	Vorwahl
	extension [ɪk'stenʃn]	Durchwahl
	landline ['lændlaɪn]	Festnetz
35	**identify yourself** [aɪ'dentɪfaɪ jɔ:self]	sich zu erkennen geben
	available [ə'veɪləbl]	*(Telefon)* zu sprechen sein
	reach [ri:tʃ]	erreichen
	connection [kə'nekʃn]	Verbindung
	engaged [ɪn'geɪdʒd]	*(Leitung)* belegt
	busy ['bɪzi]	*(Leitung)* belegt
	dial ['daɪəl]	*(Telefon)* wählen
	speak up [ˌspi:k 'ʌp]	lauter sprechen
	repeat [rɪ'pi:t]	wiederholen
	cut off [ˌkʌt 'ɒf]	unterbrechen
37	**drill** [drɪl]	bohren
	drive [draɪv]	Zufahrt, Auffahrt
	patio ['pætiəʊ]	Terrasse
	fitted ['fɪtɪd]	eingebaut
	benefit ['benɪfɪt]	(Versicherungs-)Leistung
	drain [dreɪn]	Abwasserleitung
	cable ['keɪbl]	Kabel
	breakage ['breɪkɪdʒ]	Bruch
	washbasin ['wɒʃbeɪsn]	Waschbecken
38	**vandal** ['vændl]	Vandale
	restoration work [ˌrestə'reɪʃn wɜ:k]	Reparaturarbeiten
	power cut ['paʊə kʌt]	Stromausfall
	fire brigade ['faɪə brɪgeɪd]	Feuerwehr
	extinguish [ɪk'stɪŋgwɪʃ]	*(Feuer)* löschen
	spill [spɪl]	verschütten
39	**cut (costs, risk)** [kʌt]	(Kosten, Risiko) senken
	dependent on [dɪ'pendənt ɒn]	abhängig von
	circumstances *pl* ['sɜ:kəmstənsɪz]	Umstände
	pay out [ˌpeɪ 'aʊt]	auszahlen
	security [sɪ'kjʊərəti]	Sicherheit
	measure ['meʒə]	Maßnahme
	fit [fɪt]	einbauen
	burglar alarm ['bɜ:glər əlɑ:m]	Alarmanlage
	install [ɪn'stɔ:l]	installieren
	time switch ['taɪm swɪtʃ]	Zeitschalter
	neighbourhood ['neɪbəhʊd]	Nachbarschaft
	watch [wɒtʃ]	Wache
	scheme [ski:m]	Plan, Projekt
	maintain [meɪn'teɪn]	warten, unterhalten
	smoke alarm ['sməʊk əlɑ:m]	Rauchmelder
	research [rɪ'sɜ:tʃ]	Nachforschungen, Recherche
	comparison [kəm'pærɪsn]	Vergleich
	effort ['efət]	Mühe, Aufwand
	reputation [ˌrepju'teɪʃn]	Ruf
	be prepared to [bi prɪ'peəd tə]	bereit sein
	nationwide ['neɪʃnwaɪd]	landesweit
	Automobile Association (AA) [ˌɔ:təməbi:l əˌsəʊsi'eɪʃn]	*brit. Automobilklub*

UNIT 4

40	**self-employed** [ˌself ɪm'plɔɪd]	selbstständig
	carpenter ['kɑ:pəntə]	Tischler/in
	depend on [dɪ'pend ɒn]	abhängig sein von, abhängen von
	responsibility [rɪˌspɒnsə'bɪləti]	Verantwortung, Verantwortlichkeit
	dependant [dɪ'pendənt]	(finanziell abhängige/r) Angehörige/r
	disaster [dɪ'zɑ:stə]	Katastrophe
	pregnant ['pregnənt]	schwanger
	pensioner ['penʃənə]	Rentner/in
	funeral ['fju:nərəl]	Trauerfeier
	burial ['beriəl]	Beerdigung
	beneficiary [ˌbenɪ'fɪʃəri]	Nutznießer, Begünstigte/r
	cash value [ˌkæʃ 'vælju:]	Barwert
	inheritance [ɪn'herɪtəns]	Erbe
	insist on [ɪn'sɪst ɒn]	bestehen auf
	term [tɜ:m]	Laufzeit
	duration [dju'reɪʃn]	Dauer, Laufzeit
	debt(s) [dets]	Schulden
	shop assistant ['ʃɒp əsɪstənt]	Verkäufer/in
	retirement [rɪ'taɪəmənt]	Ruhestand
	tax benefits *pl* ['tæks benɪfɪts]	Steuervergünstigungen, -vorteile
	tax-free [ˌtæks'fri:]	steuerfrei
	to be honest [tə bi 'ɒnɪst]	ehrlich gesagt
	tax deferred [ˌtæks dɪ'fɜ:d]	latente Steuer, aufgeschobene Steuer
41	**bank loan** ['bæŋk ləʊn]	Kredit
	assets *pl* ['æsets]	Vermögen, Vermögenswerte
	reliant on [rɪ'laɪənt ɒn]	angewiesen auf, abhängig von
	be liable to sth [bi 'laɪəbl tə]	mit etw (einer Steuer) belegt werden können
	refer to sth [rɪ'fɜ: tə]	von etw sprechen, auf etw verweisen
	lend [lend]	leihen

	state pension [ˌsteɪt ˈpenʃn]	staatliche Pensionskasse, gesetzliche Rente
42	**in the meantime** [ɪn ðə ˈmiːntaɪm]	in der Zwischenzeit
	endowment insurance [ɪnˈdaʊmənt ɪnʃʊərəns]	kapitalbildende Lebensversicherung, *auch* gemischte Versicherung
	unit-linked [ˈjuːnɪt lɪŋkt]	fondsgebunden
	investment risk [ɪnˈvestmənt rɪsk]	Investitionsrisiko
	conversion option [kənˈvɜːʃn ɒpʃn]	Umtauschoption
	savings *pl* [ˈseɪvɪŋz]	Ersparnisse
	rider [ˈraɪdə]	Zusatzversicherung
	annuity [əˈnjuːəti]	(Kapital-)Rente, Annuität
	terminal illness [ˌtɜːmɪnl ˈɪlnəs]	tödliche/unheilbare Krankheit
	secure [sɪˈkjuə]	sichern
	lump sum [ˌlʌmp ˈsʌm]	Pauschalbetrag
	tend to [ˈtend tə]	dazu neigen
	avoider [əˈvɔɪdə]	Vermeider
	speculative [ˈspekjuleɪtɪv]	spekulativ
43	**select** [sɪˈlekt]	wählen, auswählen
	payable [ˈpeɪəbl]	zahlbar
	expire [ɪkˈspaɪə]	*(Vertrag, usw.)* auslaufen
	regard [rɪˈgɑːd]	betrachten
	cash-in value [kæʃ ˌɪn ˈvæljuː]	Rückkaufswert
	level term [ˌlevl ˈtɜːm]	mit gleichbleibender Versicherungssumme
	collateral [kəˈlætərəl]	Sicherheit, Kollateral
	evidence [ˈevɪdəns]	Nachweis
	convert [kənˈvɜːt]	umwandeln
	renewal [rɪˈnjuːəl]	Verlängerung
	extend [ɪkˈstend]	ausdehnen, erweitern
	agreed [əˈgriːd]	vereinbart
	intended for [ɪnˈtendɪd fə]	gedacht für, dazu gedacht
	regardless of [rɪˈgɑːdləs əv]	ungeachtet, egal
	certainty [ˈsɜːtnti]	Gewissheit, Sicherheit
	uncertain [ʌnˈsɜːtn]	ungewiss
	long-term [ˌlɒŋˈtɜːm]	langfristig, Langzeit-
	guarantee [ˌgærənˈtiː]	garantieren
	bonus [ˈbəʊnəs]	Prämie, Bonus
	quarterly [ˈkwɔːtəli]	vierteljährlich
	premature [ˈprematʃə]	vorzeitig
	invest [ɪnˈvest]	investieren
	unit trust [ˌjuːnɪt ˈtrʌst]	Anlagefond, Investmentfond
	initial [ɪˈnɪʃl]	erste/r/s, anfänglich
	capital [ˈkæpɪtl]	Kapital
	level [ˈlevl]	Höhe
	employer [ɪmˈplɔɪə]	Arbeitgeber
	restriction [rɪˈstrɪkʃn]	Einschränkung
	be designed to [bi dɪˈzaɪnd tə]	dafür gedacht sein, dass
	disabled [dɪsˈeɪbld]	behindert
	occupational [ˌɒkjuˈpeɪʃənl]	beruflich, berufsbedingt
44	**choice** [tʃɔɪs]	Wahl
	repayment [rɪˈpeɪmənt]	Rückzahlung, Ratenzahlung
	male [meɪl]	männlich
	divorced [dɪˈvɔːst]	geschieden
	clerk [klɑːk]	Angestellte/r, Sachbearbeiter/in
	bank clerk [ˈbæŋk klɑːk]	Bankangestellte/r
	put away [ˌpʊt əˈweɪ]	*(Geld)* sparen, ansparen
	early retirement [ˌɜːli rɪˈtaɪəmənt]	Vorruhestand
	widow [ˈwɪdəʊ]	Witwe
	sickness [ˈsɪknəs]	Krankheit
	technician [tekˈnɪʃn]	Techniker/in
	renovate [ˈrenəveɪt]	renovieren
	Congratulations. [kənˌgrætʃʊˈleɪʃnz]	Herzlichen Glückwunsch!
	property [ˈprɒpəti]	Immobilie(n)
	interest [ˈɪntrəst]	Zinsen
	in cash [ɪn ˈkæʃ]	bar
	nurse [nɜːs]	Krankenschwester/-pfleger
T	**relative** [ˈrelətɪv]	Verwandte/r
	salary [ˈsæləri]	Lohn, Gehalt
45	**budget** [ˈbʌdʒɪt]	Budget, Etat
	tight [taɪt]	eng, knapp
	reasonable [ˈriːznəbl]	vernünftig
	advantage [ədˈvɑːntɪdʒ]	Vorteil
	catch [kætʃ]	Haken
	exchange rate [ɪksˈtʃeɪndʒ reɪt]	Wechselkurs
	currency [ˈkʌrənsi]	Währung
	medical report [ˌmedɪkl rɪˈpɔːt]	ärztliches Attest
	counselling [ˈkaʊnsəlɪŋ]	Beratung
	consider [kənˈsɪdə]	erwägen, in Betracht ziehen
46	**introduce** [ˌɪntrəˈdjuːs]	einführen
	take advantage of [ˌteɪk ədˈvɑːntɪdʒ əv]	sich etw zunutze machen
	agree on sth [əˈgriː ɒn]	sich auf etw einigen, etw vereinbaren
	quote sb for sth [ˈkwəʊt fə]	jdm ein Angebot für etw machen
	sum assured [ˌsʌm əˈʃʊəd]	Versicherungssumme *(brit. Lebensversicherung)*
	occupation [ˌɒkjuˈpeɪʃn]	Beruf, Beschäftigung
	competitive [kəmˈpetətɪv]	*(Preis, usw.)* günstig
47	**folder** [ˈfəʊldə]	Mappe
	terms and conditions *pl* [ˌtɜːmz ənd kənˈdɪʃnz]	Allgemeine Geschäftsbedingungen
	assistance [əˈsɪstəns]	Hilfe, Unterstützung
	enclosure [ɪnˈkləʊʒə]	*(Brief)* Anlage
48	**have in common** [ˌhəv ɪn ˈkɒmən]	gemeinsam haben
	addressee [ˌædreˈsiː]	Adressat, Empfänger/in
	for the attention of [fə ði əˈtenʃn əv]	*(Brief)* zu Händen
	reference [ˈrefərəns]	*(Brief)* Zeichen
	unless [ənˈles]	es sei denn, außer (wenn)
	state [steɪt]	angeben, sagen, erklären
49	**enquire about** [ɪnˈkwaɪər əbaʊt]	sich erkundigen nach
	concerning [kənˈsɜːnɪŋ]	bezüglich, betreffend
	remark [rɪˈmɑːk]	Bemerkung
	approximately [əˈprɒksɪmətli]	ungefähr
	immediately [ɪˈmiːdiətli]	sofort, unmittelbar
	order [ˈɔːdə]	Reihenfolge

	delete [dɪ'li:t]	löschen, tilgen
	impression [ɪm'preʃn]	Eindruck
50	**preferred** [prɪ'fɜ:d]	bevorzugt
	period of payment [ˌpɪəriəd əv 'peɪmənt]	Zahlungszeitraum
	tick [tɪk]	ankreuzen, mit einem Häkchen versehen
	spouse [spaʊz]	Gatte/Gattin
	Fire away. [ˌfaɪər ə'weɪ]	Schießen Sie los!
	disease [dɪ'zi:z]	Krankheit
T	**medical complaints** *pl* [ˌmedɪkl kəm'pleɪnts]	gesundheitliche Beschwerden
	healthy ['helθi]	gesund
	for ages [fər 'eɪdʒɪz]	eine Ewigkeit
	surgery ['sɜ:dʒəri]	Operation, chirurgischer Eingriff
	awkward ['ɔ:kwəd]	peinlich, unangenehm
	medication [ˌmedɪ'keɪʃn]	Medikamente
	addiction [ə'dɪkʃn]	Sucht
	addicted [ə'dɪktɪd]	abhängig
51	**furthermore** [ˌfɜ:ðə'mɔ:]	außerdem, darüber hinaus
	tax break ['tæks breɪk]	Steuererleichterung
	considerable [kən'sɪdərəbl]	beträchtlich, erheblich
	pension funds *pl* ['penʃn fʌndz]	Rentenfonds
	immediate [ɪ'mi:diət]	sofort zahlbar
	payout ['peɪaʊt]	Auszahlung
	comprise [kəm'praɪz]	ausmachen
	adapted [ə'dæptɪd]	bearbeitet
	market share [ˌmɑ:kɪt 'ʃeə]	Marktanteil

UNIT 5

52	**leisure** ['leʒə]	Freizeit
	statutory ['stætʃətri]	gesetzlich (vorgeschrieben)
	treatment ['tri:tmənt]	Behandlung
	restore [rɪ'stɔ:]	wiederherstellen
	ability [ə'bɪləti]	Fähigkeit
	earning capacity ['ɜ:nɪŋ kəpæsəti]	Erwerbsfähigkeit
53	**nursery school** ['nɜ:səri sku:l]	Kindergarten, Kindertagesstätte
	after-school care centre [ɑ:ftə ˌsku:l 'keə sentə]	Hort
	prevention [prɪ'venʃn]	Prävention
	resources *pl* [rɪ'sɔ:sɪz]	Mittel, Ressourcen
	prevent [prɪ'vent]	verhüten, verhindern
	take steps [ˌteɪk 'steps]	Schritte unternehmen, Maßnahmen ergreifen
	cut off [ˌkʌt 'ɒf]	abschneiden
	thumb [θʌm]	Daumen
	operate ['ɒpəreɪt]	bedienen, arbeiten mit
	saw [sɔ:]	Säge
	ankle ['æŋkl]	Knöchel
54	**single parent** [ˌsɪŋgl 'peərənt]	Alleinerziehende/r
	in-company ['ɪn kʌmpəni]	betriebsintern
	suit [su:t]	passen
	suggestion [sə'dʒestʃən]	Vorschlag
	tied up [ˌtaɪd 'ʌp]	beschäftigt
55	**chest** [tʃest]	Brust
	chin [tʃɪn]	Kinn
	elbow ['elbəʊ]	Ellbogen
	heel [hi:l]	Ferse
	hip [hɪp]	Hüfte
	knee [ni:]	Knie
	neck [nek]	Hals
	shin [ʃɪn]	Schienbein
	thigh [θaɪ]	Oberschenkel
	toes [təʊz]	Zehen
	waist [weɪst]	Taille
	wrist [rɪst]	Handgelenk
	burn [bɜ:n]	(sich) verbrennen
	fracture ['fræktʃə]	(sich etw) brechen
	hit [hɪt]	stoßen, schlagen
	paralyse ['pærəlaɪz]	lähmen
	scald [skɔ:ld]	(sich) verbrühen
	sprain [spreɪn]	verstauchen
	wheelchair ['wi:ltʃeə]	Rollstuhl
	confined to a wheelchair [kənˌfaɪnd tu ə 'wi:ltʃeə]	an den Rollstuhl gefesselt
	X-ray ['eksreɪ]	Röntgenstrahlen, -bild
	pan [pæn]	Pfanne
	awkwardly ['ɔ:kwədli]	ungeschickt
	jump [dʒʌmp]	Sprung
	bleed [bli:d]	bluten
	concussion [kən'kʌʃn]	Gehirnerschütterung
56	**disability benefit** [ˌdɪsə'bɪləti benɪfɪt]	Invaliditätsleistung
	disablement benefit [dɪs'eɪblmənt benɪfɪt]	Invaliditätsleistung
	accidental death [æksɪˌdentl 'deθ]	Unfalltod
	bridging benefit ['brɪdʒɪŋ benɪfɪt]	Übergangsleistung
	degree [dɪ'gri:]	Grad
	plastic surgery [ˌplæstɪk 'sɜ:dʒəri]	kosmetische Operationen, plastische Chirurgie
	rescue ['reskju:]	Rettung
	rescue operations *pl* ['reskju: ɒpəreɪʃnz]	Rettungsmaßnahmen
	casualty ['kæʒuəlti]	Verletze/r, Unfallopfer
	dead body [ded 'bɒdi]	Leichnam
	hospital daily benefit [ˌhɒspɪtl ˌdeɪli 'benɪfɪt]	Krankenhaustagegeld
	daily accident benefit [ˌdeɪli 'æksɪdənt benɪfɪt]	Unfalltagegeld
	unable [ʌn'eɪbl]	unfähig
	unable to work [ʌnˌeɪbl tə 'wɜ:k]	arbeitsunfähig
	accident annuity ['æksɪdənt ənju:əti]	Unfallrente
	double ['dʌbl]	sich verdoppeln
	hearing ['hɪərɪŋ]	Gehör
	rent [rent]	Miete
	groceries *pl* ['grəʊsəri:z]	Lebensmittel
	scene of an accident [ˌsi:n əv ən 'æksɪdənt]	Unfallort
	scar [skɑ:]	Narbe
	employ [ɪm'plɔɪ]	beschäftigen, anstellen
	housekeeper ['haʊski:pə]	Haushälterin
57	**adapt** [ə'dæpt]	anpassen, umbauen
	terminate ['tɜ:mɪneɪt]	enden, auslaufen
	vocational training [vəʊˌkeɪʃənl 'treɪnɪŋ]	Berufsausbildung

58	**be entitled to** [bi ɪn'taɪtld tə]	Anspruch haben auf
	confirm [kən'fɜ:m]	bestätigen
	limb [lɪm]	Gliedmaß
	separation [ˌsepə'reɪʃn]	Trennung, Abtrennung
	sight [saɪt]	Sehvermögen
	forefinger ['fɔ:fɪŋgə]	Zeigefinger
	entire [ɪn'taɪə]	gesamte/r/s, ganze/r/s
	anniversary [ˌænɪ'vɜ:səri]	Jahrestag
	miss [mɪs]	vermissen
	sufficient [sə'fɪʃnt]	ausreichend
59	**impairment** [ɪm'peəmənt]	Beeinträchtigung
	blood circulation ['blʌd sɜ:kjəleɪʃn]	Blutkreislauf
	proven ['pru:vn]	erwiesen
	condition [kən'dɪʃn]	Leiden
	assess [ə'ses]	schätzen, einschätzen, bewerten, feststellen
	bodily injury [ˌbɒdɪli 'ɪndʒəri]	Verletzung
	ophthalmic surgeon [ɒfˌθælmɪk 'sɜ:dʒən]	Augenarzt/-ärztin, Augenchirurg/in
	calculation [ˌkælkju'leɪʃn]	Rechnung, Berechnung
	vision ['vɪʒn]	Sehkraft
	sympathy ['sɪmpəθi]	Mitgefühl
	painful ['peɪnfl]	schmerzhaft
	recovery [rɪ'kʌvəri]	Genesung
	condolences *pl* [kən'dəʊlənsɪz]	Beileid
60	**vary with** ['veəri wɪð]	sich richten nach
	engaged in sth [ɪn'geɪdʒd ɪn]	mit etw beschäftigt
	sedentary ['sedntəri]	sitzend
	desk bound ['desk baʊnd]	am Schreibtisch
	manual work [ˌmænjuəl 'wɜ:k]	körperliche Arbeit, Handarbeit
	hazardous ['hæzədəs]	gefährlich, riskant
	office clerk ['ɒfɪs klɑ:k]	Büroangestellte/r
	tool [tu:l]	Werkzeug
	machinery [mə'ʃi:nəri]	Maschinen
	plumber ['plʌmə]	Klempner/in
	uninsurable [ˌʌnɪn'ʃʊərəbl]	nicht versicherbar, nicht versicherungsfähig
	diver ['daɪvə]	Taucher/in
	claims report ['kleɪmz rɪpɔ:t]	Schadenbericht
	make up [ˌmeɪk 'ʌp]	sich ausdenken
61	**waste of money** [ˌweɪst əv 'mʌni]	Geldverschwendung
	package ['pækɪdʒ]	im Paket anbieten
	give away [ˌgɪv ə'weɪ]	verschenken
	stand-alone policy [stænd əˌləʊn 'pɒləsi]	unabhängige Police, selbstständige Police
	freebie ['fri:bi]	Werbegeschenk
	in terms of ... [ɪn 'tɜ:mz əv]	was ... angeht, was ... betrifft
	queue [kju:]	(Warte-)Schlange
	be involved in sth [bi ɪn'vɒlvd ɪn]	an etw beteiligt sein
	mountaineering [ˌmaʊntə'nɪərɪŋ]	Bergsteigen
	rock climbing ['rɒk klaɪmɪŋ]	Felsklettern
	parachuting ['pærəʃu:tɪŋ]	Fallschirmspringen
	despite [dɪ'spaɪt]	trotz
	steady ['stedi]	stabil
	point out [ˌpɔɪnt 'aʊt]	darauf hinweisen
	(the) elderly [ði 'eldəli]	ältere Menschen
	vulnerable ['vʌlnərəbl]	verwundbar, anfällig
	proper ['prɒpə]	richtig
	retire [rɪ'taɪə]	in den Ruhestand treten
	review [rɪ'vju:]	Bericht
	Financial Services Authority (FSA) [faɪˌnænʃl 'sɜ:vɪsɪz ɔ:θɒrəti]	*brit. Aufsichtsbehörde für Finanzdienstleistungen*
	warning ['wɔ:nɪŋ]	Warnung, Warnhinweis
	limitation [ˌlɪmɪ'teɪʃn]	Beschränkung, Grenze
	regulator ['regjuleɪtə]	Regulierungsbehörde
	emphasize ['emfəsaɪz]	betonen, hervorheben
	anxiety [æŋ'zaɪəti]	Sorge
	ratio ['reɪʃiəʊ]	Verhältnis
	suggest [sə'dʒest]	andeuten
	be down to sth [bi 'daʊn tə]	an etw liegen
	excessive prices *pl* [ɪkˌsesɪv 'praɪsɪz]	überhöhte Preise
	lack [læk]	Mangel, Nichtvorhandensein
	concerned [kən'sɜ:nd]	besorgt
	pros and cons *pl* [ˌprəʊz ənd 'kɒnz]	Für und Wider

UNIT 6

62	**universal** [ˌju:nɪ'vɜ:sl]	allgemein
	citizen ['sɪtɪzn]	Bürger/in
	health care ['helθ keə]	Gesundheitswesen
	life expectancy ['laɪf ɪkspektənsi]	Lebenserwartung
	state [steɪt]	Staat, staatlich
	enormous [ɪ'nɔ:məs]	enorm
	pressure ['preʃə]	Druck
	recently ['ri:sntli]	in letzter Zeit
	comprehensive [ˌkɒmprɪ'hensɪv]	Vollkasko-
	top-up benefit [tɒp ˌʌp 'benɪfɪt]	Zusatzleistung
	strict [strɪkt]	streng, strikt
	underwritten [ˌʌndə'rɪtn]	gezeichnet
	ageing reserve ['eɪdʒɪŋ rɪzɜ:v]	Alterungsrückstellungen
	top-up cover [tɒp ˌʌp 'kʌvə]	Zusatzdeckung
	short-term [ˌʃɔ:t'tɜ:m]	kurzfristig, Kurzzeit-, befristet
	be prone to sth [bi 'prəʊn tə]	zu etw neigen, für etw anfällig sein
	exceed [ɪk'si:d]	überschreiten
	civil servant [ˌsɪvl 'sɜ:vənt]	Beamte/r
	be subject to sth [bi 'sʌbdʒekt tə]	einer Sache unterliegen
	a great deal [ə greɪt 'di:l]	eine Menge, viel
	interference [ˌɪntə'fɪərəns]	Einmischung
	favour sth ['feɪvə]	sich für etw aussprechen
63	**entitled** [ɪn'taɪtld]	mit dem Titel
	hardly ['hɑ:dli]	kaum
	opt out of sth [ˌɒpt 'aʊt əv]	aus etw aussteigen

	equivalent [ɪ'kwɪvələnt]	Gegenstück, Pendant
	National Health Service (NHS) [ˌnæʃnəl 'helθ sɜːvɪs]	*staatlicher Gesundheitsdienst Großbritanniens*
	dental ['dentl]	zahnärztlich, Zahn-
	medicine ['medsn]	Medizin
	guarantee [ˌgærən'tiː]	Garantie
	in-patient treatment [ɪnˌpeɪʃnt 'triːtmənt]	stationäre Behandlung
	consultant [kən'sʌltənt]	Chefarzt/-ärztin
	emergency evacuation [ɪ'mɜːdʒənsi ɪvækjueɪʃn]	Notevakuierung
	fail [feɪl]	versäumen, nicht schaffen
	consequently ['kɒnsɪkwəntli]	folglich, deshalb
	matter ['mætə]	Sache, Angelegenheit
	misleading [ˌmɪs'liːdɪŋ]	irreführend, missverständlich
	out of date [ˌaʊt əv 'deɪt]	veraltet, überholt
	pass (a law) [ˌpɑːs ə 'lɔː]	(ein Gesetz) verabschieden
	afford sth [ə'fɔːd]	sich etw leisten
	transfer [træns'fɜː]	wechseln
	basic ['beɪsɪk]	Grund-
	be afraid of [bi ə'freɪd əv]	Angst haben vor, sich fürchten vor
	raise [reɪz]	*(Tarif, usw.)* anheben
	error ['erə]	Fehler, Irrtum
	be affected by sth [bi ə'fektɪd baɪ]	von etw betroffen sein
64	**set up** [ˌset 'ʌp]	einrichten
	treat [triːt]	behandeln
	in-patient [ɪn'peɪʃnt]	stationäre/r Patient/in
	in the event of sth [ɪn ði ɪ'vent əv]	bei etw, im Falle von etw
	excerpt ['eksɜːpt]	Auszug, Ausschnitt
	consider [kən'sɪdə]	betrachten
	participant [pɑː'tɪsɪpənt]	Teilnehmer/in
65	**acute** [ə'kjuːt]	akut
	last [lɑːst]	dauern
	influenza [ˌɪnflu'enzə]	Grippe
	appendicitis [əˌpendə'saɪtɪs]	Blinddarmentzündung
	bone [bəʊn]	Knochen
	chronic ['krɒnɪk]	chronisch
	diabetes [ˌdaɪə'biːtiːz]	Diabetes
	asthma ['æsmə]	Asthma
	osteoporosis [ˌɒstiəʊpə'rəʊsɪs]	Osteoporose
	consequence ['kɒnsɪkwəns]	Folge, Konsequenz
	tax relief ['tæks rɪliːf]	Steuervergünstigung, -erleichterung, -nachlass
	restrict [rɪ'strɪkt]	beschränken, einschränken
	criticism ['krɪtɪsɪzəm]	Kritik, Kritikpunkte
	dissatisfied [dɪs'sætɪsfaɪd]	unzufrieden
	ridiculous [rɪ'dɪkjələs]	lächerlich
	face [feɪs]	sich stellen (müssen)
	kidney ['kɪdni]	Niere
	portability [ˌpɔːtə'bɪləti]	Portabilität
	rely on [rɪ'laɪ ɒn]	angewiesen sein auf
	force [fɔːs]	zwingen
	likely ['laɪkli]	wahrscheinlich
	shrink [ʃrɪŋk]	schrumpfen
	contribution [ˌkɒntrɪ'bjuːʃn]	Beitrag
	relieve sb of sth [rɪ'liːv əv]	jdm etw abnehmen
	population [ˌpɒpju'leɪʃn]	Bevölkerung
	question of principle [ˌkwestʃən əv 'prɪnsəpl]	Grundsatzfrage
	pure [pjʊə]	rein
	issue ['ɪʃuː]	Frage, Problem
	permit [pə'mɪt]	zulassen
	well-off [ˌwel 'ɒf]	wohlhabend
	subsidize ['sʌbsɪdaɪz]	subventionieren
66	**reimbursement** [ˌriːɪm'bɜːsmənt]	Erstattung
	bill [bɪl]	Rechnung
	prescription [prɪ'skrɪpʃn]	(ärztliches) Rezept
	reimburse [ˌriːɪm'bɜːs]	erstatten
	resident ['rezɪdənt]	Bewohner/in, Einwohner/in
67	**item** ['aɪtəm]	*(Liste)* Punkt
68	**hand in** [ˌhænd 'ɪn]	einreichen
	turn down [ˌtɜːn 'daʊn]	ablehnen
	policy administration department ['pɒləsi ədmɪnɪstreɪʃn dɪpɑːtmənt]	Policenverwaltung(sabteilung)
	issue ['ɪʃuː]	*(Dokument, usw.)* ausstellen
	electric kettle [ɪˌlektrɪk 'ketl]	Wasserkocher
	line manager [laɪn 'mænɪdʒə]	Vorgesetzte/r, Abteilungsleiter/in
69	**chemist** ['kemɪst]	Apotheker/in
	general practitioner [ˌdʒenrəl præk'tɪʃənə]	Allgemeinarzt/-ärztin, Hausarzt/-ärztin
	dentist ['dentɪst]	Zahnarzt/-ärztin
	optician [ɒp'tɪʃn]	Optiker/in
	surgeon ['sɜːdʒən]	Chirurg/in
	contact lenses *pl* ['kɒntækt lenzɪz]	Kontaktlinsen
	glasses *pl* ['glɑːsɪz]	Brille
	aids *pl* [eɪdz]	Hilfsmittel
	naturopathy [ˌneɪtʃə'rɒpəθi]	Naturheilkunde
	naturopath ['neɪtʃərəʊpæθ]	Naturheilkundler/in
	false teeth [fɔːls 'tiːθ]	Zahnprothese
	implant ['ɪmplɑːnt]	Implantat
	sickness benefit ['sɪknəs benɪfɪt]	Krankengeld
	intend [ɪn'tend]	beabsichtigen, vorhaben
	compare [kəm'peə]	sich vergleichen lassen
	superior to [suː'pɪəriə tə]	besser als
	visually impaired [ˌvɪʒuəli ɪm'peəd]	sehbehindert
	gross [grəʊs]	brutto, Brutto-
	net [net]	netto, Netto-
	social security [ˌsəʊʃl sɪ'kjʊərəti]	Sozialversicherung
	reciprocal [rɪ'sɪprəkl]	gegenseitig
70	**cancellation** [ˌkænsə'leɪʃn]	Stornierung, Kündigung
	curtailment [kɜː'teɪlmənt]	(Urlaubs-)Abbruch
	be made redundant [bi ˌmeɪd rɪ'dʌndənt]	den Arbeitsplatz verlieren

cut sth short [kʌt 'ʃɔ:t]	etw plötzlich abbrechen
incur [ɪn'kɜ:]	*(Kosten)* haben, anfallen
fare [feə]	Fahrpreis
subject to ['sʌbdʒɪkt tə]	abhängig von, je nach
legally liable [ˌli:gəli 'laɪəbl]	gesetzlich haftbar
legal assistance [ˌli:gl ə'sɪstəns]	Rechtsbeistand
71 physical well-being [ˌfɪzɪkl 'welbi:ɪŋ]	leibliches Wohl(ergehen)
carelessness ['keələsnəs]	Unachtsamkeit, Nachlässigkeit, Fahrlässigkeit
valid ['vælɪd]	gültig
frequency ['fri:kwənsi]	Häufigkeit
moral hazard [ˌmɒrəl 'hæzəd]	subjektives Risiko
shorten ['ʃɔ:tn]	kürzen

UNIT 7

72 party ['pɑ:ti]	Partei
involved [ɪn'vɒlvd]	beteiligt
contractual relationship [kənˌtræktʃuəl rɪ'leɪʃnʃɪp]	vertragliche Beziehung
pavement ['peɪvmənt]	Gehsteig
swerve [swɜ:v]	einen Schlenker machen, ausscheren
avoid sb [ə'vɔɪd]	*(Auto)* jdm ausweichen
load [ləʊd]	Ladung
gas cylinder [ˌgæs 'sɪlɪndə]	Gasflasche
loss of life [ˌlɒs əv 'laɪf]	Todesopfer
property damage ['prɒpəti dæmɪdʒ]	Sachschaden
unlikely [ʌn'laɪkli]	unwahrscheinlich
negligence ['neglɪdʒəns]	Fahrlässigkeit
human ['hju:mən]	menschlich
careless ['keələs]	unbedacht, fahrlässig
penetration rate [ˌpenə'treɪʃn reɪt]	*hier:* Marktdurchdringung
ignorance ['ɪgnərəns]	Unwissenheit
lack of imagination [ˌlæk əv ɪˌmædʒɪ'neɪʃn]	Phantasielosigkeit
process ['prəʊses]	Verfahren, Ablauf
claimant ['kleɪmənt]	Anspruchsberechtig-te/r, Antragsteller/in
commission [kə'mɪʃn]	Provision
73 hassle ['hæsl]	Schwierigkeiten, Ärger
for instance [fər 'ɪnstəns]	zum Beispiel
excluded [ɪk'sklu:dɪd]	ausgeschlossen, ausgenommen
benefit ['benɪfɪt]	profitieren
objection [əb'dʒekʃn]	Einwand, (Gegen-) Argument
administration [ədˌmɪnɪ'streɪʃn]	Verwaltung
injured party [ˌɪndʒəd 'pɑ:ti]	Geschädigte/r
incident ['ɪnsɪdənt]	Vorfall
account of the incident [əˌkaʊnt əv ði 'ɪnsɪdənt]	Schilderung des Vorfalls
demand [dɪ'mɑ:nd]	fordern, verlangen
74 damages *pl* ['dæmɪdʒɪz]	Schadenersatz
award [ə'wɔ:d]	zusprechen, zuerkennen
harm [hɑ:m]	Schaden
behaviour [bɪ'heɪvjə]	Verhalten
order ['ɔ:də]	anordnen, befehlen
repetition [ˌrepə'tɪʃn]	Wiederholung
75 crowded ['kraʊdɪd]	voll (besetzt)
briefcase ['bri:fkeɪs]	Aktenkoffer
forehead ['fɔ:hed]	Stirn
solicitor [sə'lɪsɪtə]	(Rechts-)Anwalt/Anwältin
be concussed [bi kən'kʌst]	eine Gehirnerschütterung haben
76 dresser ['dresə]	Garderobier/e
lock up [ˌlɒk 'ʌp]	abschließen
query ['kwɪəri]	Anfrage
78 indemnify [ɪn'demnɪfaɪ]	entschädigen
indemnification [ɪnˌdemnɪfɪ'keɪʃn]	Entschädigung
fault [fɔ:lt]	Schuld, Verschulden
intention [ɪn'tenʃn]	Absicht
direct intention [dəˌrekt ɪn'tenʃn]	Vorsatz
qualified intention [ˌkwɒlɪfaɪd ɪn'tenʃn]	bedingter Vorsatz
reckon with ['rekən wɪð]	rechnen mit
recklessness ['rekləsnəs]	grobe Fahrlässigkeit
gross negligence [ˌgrəʊs 'neglɪdʒəns]	grobe Fahrlässigkeit
deliberate [dɪ'lɪbərət]	absichtlich, bewusst, vorsätzlich
79 arise [ə'raɪz]	*(Tatbestand)* vorliegen, *(Fall)* eintreten
foreseeable [fɔ:'si:əbl]	vorhersehbar
thoughtlessness ['θɔ:tləsnəs]	Nachlässigkeit, Unaufmerksamkeit
partial fault [ˌpɑ:ʃl 'fɔ:lt]	Teilschuld
contributory negligence [kənˌtrɪbjʊtəri 'neglɪdʒəns]	Mitverschulden
fortuity [fɔ:'tju:ɪti]	Zufall
fortuitous [fɔ:'tju:ɪtəs]	zufällig
lead [li:d]	Kabel
frayed [freɪd]	abgewetzt, zerschlissen
fatal ['feɪtl]	tödlich, fatal
bribe [braɪb]	bestechen
overhear [əʊvə'hɪə]	(zufällig) hören
alcohol level ['ælkəhɒl levl]	Alkoholspiegel
per mille [pɜ: 'mɪl]	Promille
mentally ill [ˌmentəli 'ɪl]	geisteskrank
collide [kə'laɪd]	kollidieren, zusammenstoßen
fur coat ['fɜ: kəʊt]	Pelzmantel
wig [wɪg]	Perücke
cyclist ['saɪklɪst]	Radfahrer/in
80 come across sb [ˌkʌm ə'krɒs]	jdn (zufällig) treffen, jdn (zufällig) finden
be made liable [bi ˌmeɪd 'laɪəbl]	haftbar gemacht werden, in Haftung genommen werden
admit [əd'mɪt]	zugeben, eingestehen
blame sb [bleɪm]	jdm die Schuld geben, jdm (für etw) verantwortlich machen
claim [kleɪm]	*hier:* behaupten
warning ['wɔ:nɪŋ]	Mahnung
overdue [ˌəʊvə'dju:]	überfällig
81 casualty ['kæʒuəlti]	Haftpflicht *(AE)*

	trip sb up [ˌtrɪp ˈʌp]	jdm ein Bein stellen
	collapse [kəˈlæps]	einstürzen
	broken pipe [ˌbrəʊkən ˈpaɪp]	Rohrbruch
	slip [slɪp]	ausrutschen
	staircase [ˈsteəkeɪs]	Treppe
T	property owner [ˈprɒpəti əʊnə]	Grundbesitzer/in
T	motor third party liability [ˌməʊtə ˌθɜːd pɑːti laɪəˈbɪləti]	Kfz-Haftpflicht
T	public liability [ˌpʌblɪk laɪəˈbɪləti]	Betriebshaftpflicht
T	notice [ˈnəʊtɪs]	Hinweisschild
T	overlap [ˌəʊvəˈlæp]	sich überschneiden
T	workman [ˈwɜːkmən]	Arbeiter
T	product liability [ˈprɒdʌkt laɪəbɪləti]	Produkthaftpflicht
T	faulty [ˈfɔːlti]	fehlerhaft, defekt
T	manufacturer [ˌmænjuˈfæktʃərə]	Hersteller
T	distributor [dɪˈstrɪbjətə]	(Zwischen-)Händler, Vertreiber
T	similarity [ˌsɪməˈlærəti]	Ähnlichkeit
T	environmental impairment insurance [ɪnvaɪrənˌmentl ɪmˈpeəmənt ɪnʃʊərəns]	Umwelthaftpflicht-versicherung
T	professional indemnity insurance [prəˌfeʃənl ɪnˈdemnəti ɪnʃʊərəns]	Berufshaftpflicht-versicherung
T	lawyer [ˈlɔːjə]	(Rechts-)Anwalt/Anwältin
T	engineer [ˌendʒɪˈnɪə]	Ingenieur/in
T	profession [prəˈfeʃn]	Beruf, Berufsgruppe

UNIT 8

82	caravan [ˈkærəvæn]	Campingwagen
	trailer [ˈtreɪlə]	Anhänger
	attach [əˈtætʃ]	befestigen, anhängen
	make sense [meɪk ˈsens]	sinnvoll sein
	partial cover [ˌpɑːʃl ˈkʌvə]	Teilkaskoversicherung
	hail [heɪl]	Hagel
	breakage of glass [ˌbreɪkɪdʒ əv ˈglɑːs]	Glasbruch
	be at fault [bi ət ˈfɔːlt]	Schuld haben
	comprehensive cover [ˌkɒmprɪˈhensɪv kʌvə]	Vollkaskoversicherung
	occasional [əˈkeɪʒənl]	gelegentlich, Gelegenheits-
	no claim(s) discount [ˌnəʊ ˈkleɪms dɪskaʊnt]	Schadenfreiheitsrabatt
	unsuitable [ʌnˈsuːtəbl]	ungeeignet
	courtesy car [ˈkɜːtəsi kɑː]	Ersatzwagen, Mietwagen *(auf Kosten des Versicherers)*
	breakdown [ˈbreɪkdaʊn]	Panne
	approved repairer [əˌpruːvd rɪˈpeərə]	Vertragswerkstatt
	protected [prəˈtektɪd]	*hier:* garantiert
83	garage [ˈgærɑːʒ]	(Kfz-)Werkstatt
	license [ˈlaɪsns]	zulassen
	tow [təʊ]	ziehen, (ab)schleppen
	marten [ˈmɑːtɪn]	Marder
84	camper van [ˈkæmpə væn]	Wohnmobil *(BE)*
	convertible [kənˈvɜːtəbl]	Cabrio(let)
	estate (car) [ɪˈsteɪt kɑː]	Kombi *(BE)*
	four-wheel drive [ˌfɔːwiːl ˈdraɪv]	Vierradantrieb
	hatchback [ˈhætʃbæk]	Schrägheck, Fließheck
	limousine [ˈlɪməziːn]	Limousine
	motorhome [ˈməʊtəhəʊm]	Wohnmobil
	pick-up [ˈpɪkʌp]	Pritschenwagen
	people carrier [ˈpiːpl kæriə]	Minivan *(BE)*
	saloon [səˈluːn]	Limousine *(BE)*
	van [væn]	Lieferwagen
	liftback [ˈlɪftbæk]	Schrägheck, Fließheck
	MPV (multi-purpose vehicle) [em ˌpiː ˈviː / mʌlti ˌpɜːpəs ˈviːəkl]	Minivan *(AE)*
	off-road vehicle [ˌɒfrəʊd ˈviːəkl]	Geländewagen
	roadster [ˈrəʊdstə]	Sportwagen
	RV (recreational vehicle) [ɑː ˈvi / rekriˌeɪʃənl ˈviːəkl]	Wohnmobil
	sedan [sɪˈdæn]	Limousine *(AE)*
	station wagon [ˈsteɪʃn wægən]	Kombi *(AE)*
	SUV (sports utility vehicle) [ˌes juː ˈviː / spɔːts juːˈtɪləti viːəkl]	Geländewagen, -limousine
85	division [dɪˈvɪʒn]	*(Sport)* Liga
	company car [ˈkʌmpəni kɑː]	Firmenwagen
	scooter [ˈskuːtə]	Motorroller
	worth [wɜːθ]	wert, im Wert von
	driving test [ˈdraɪvɪŋtest]	Fahrprüfung
	pass (a test) [ˌpɑːs ə ˈtest]	(einen Test) bestehen
	(insurance) category [ɪnˈʃʊərəns kætəgəri]	(Versicherungs-)Klasse
	own-fault [əʊn ˈfɔːlt]	selbst verschuldet
	first-time [ˈfɜːsttaɪm]	Anfänger
	motorist [ˈməʊtərɪst]	Autofahrer/in
T	registration [ˌredʒɪˈstreɪʃn]	Anmeldung
T	urban area [ˌɜːbən ˈeəriə]	Stadtgebiet, Ballungs-raum
T	high-performance [ˌhaɪ pəˈfɔːməns]	leistungsstark
T	determine [dɪˈtɜːmɪn]	bestimmen
T	newly-qualified [ˌnjuːli ˈkwɒlɪfaɪd]	frisch qualifiziert
T	be considered sth [bi kənˈsɪdəd]	als etw gelten
T	implication [ˌɪmplɪˈkeɪʃn]	Konsequenz, Auswirkung
T	claims history [ˈkleɪmz hɪstri]	Schadenverlauf
T	first-timer [ˌfɜːstˈtaɪmə]	Anfänger/in
T	multi-car bonus [mʌlti ˌkɑː ˈbəʊnəs]	Rabatt für mehrere Fahr-zeuge, Mehrvertrags-rabatt
T	assumption [əˈsʌmpʃn]	Annahme, Vermutung
T	deductible [dɪˈdʌktəbl]	Selbstbeteiligung, Selbstbehalt
T	waive [weɪv]	verzichten auf, *(Gebühren)* erlassen
86	fortune [ˈfɔːtʃuːn]	Vermögen
	motoring [ˈməʊtərɪŋ]	Autofahren

	petrol ['petrəl]	Benzin
	recover [rɪ'kʌvə]	zurückbekommen, wiedererlangen
	condition [kən'dɪʃn]	Zustand
	replacement value [rɪ'pleɪsmənt vælju:]	Wiederbeschaffungswert
87 P	**driving licence** ['draɪvɪŋlaɪsns]	Führerschein
	cover note ['kʌvə nəʊt]	Deckungsbestätigung
	entitlement [ɪn'taɪtlmənt]	Anspruch, Anrecht
88	**answering machine** [,ɑ:nsərɪŋ mə'ʃi:n]	Anrufbeantworter
	bonnet ['bɒnɪt]	Motohaube *(BE)*
	hood [hʊd]	Motohaube *(AE)*
	boot [bu:t]	Kofferraum *(BE)*
	trunk [trʌŋk]	Kofferraum *(AE)*
	bumper ['bʌmpə]	Stoßstange
	wing [wɪŋ]	Kotflügel *(BE)*
	fender ['fendə]	Kotflügel *(AE)*
	headlight ['hedlaɪt]	Scheinwerfer
	hub-cap ['hʌb kæp]	Radkappe
	indicator ['ɪndɪkeɪtə]	Blinker
	rear-view mirror [,rɪəvju: 'mɪrə]	Rückspiegel
	steering wheel ['stɪərɪŋ wi:l]	Lenkrad
	tyre ['taɪə]	Reifen *(BE)*
	tire ['taɪə]	Reifen *(AE)*
	wipers *pl* ['waɪpəz]	Scheibenwischer
	wheel [wi:l]	Rad
	windscreen ['wɪndskri:n]	Windschutzscheibe *(BE)*
	windshield ['wɪndʃi:ld]	Windschutzscheibe *(AE)*
	claim report ['kleɪm rɪpɔ:t]	Schadenanzeige
T	**deer** [dɪə]	Hirsch, Reh
T	**front end** [frʌnt 'end]	*(Auto)* Front
T	**location** [ləʊ'keɪʃn]	Ort, Schauplatz
T	**direction** [də'rekʃn]	Richtung
T	**disappear** [,dɪsə'pɪə]	verschwinden
T	**report** [rɪ'pɔ:t]	melden
T	**police station** [pə'li:s steɪʃn]	Polizeiwache
T	**delicate** ['delɪkət]	heikel
	surveyor [sə'veɪə]	Gutachter/in
	ignore [ɪg'nɔ:]	ignorieren
	right of way [,raɪt əv 'weɪ]	Vorfahrt
	skid [skɪd]	schlittern
	slippery ['slɪpəri]	rutschig, glatt
	back [bæk]	*(Auto)* zurücksetzen
	overtake [,əʊvə'teɪk]	überholen
	dent [dent]	Beule
	scratch [skrætʃ]	Kratzer
	crack [kræk]	*(Glas)* Sprung
89	**drive** [draɪv]	antreiben
	grumble ['grʌmbl]	murren, meckern
	section ['sekʃn]	Abschnitt
	guide [gaɪd]	Ratgeber
	elsewhere [,els'weə]	anderswo
	outside circumstances *pl* [,aʊtsaɪd 'sɜ:kəmstənsɪz]	äußere Umstände
	soar [sɔ:]	*(Kosten)* in die Höhe schießen
	litigation [,lɪtɪ'geɪʃn]	Gerichtsverfahren, Rechtsstreitigkeiten
	personal injury [,pɜ:sənl 'ɪndʒəri]	Verletzung
	attempt [ə'tempt]	versuchen
	intervene [,ɪntə'vi:n]	eingreifen
	find in favour of sb [,faɪnd ɪn 'feɪvər əv]	zu jds Gunsten urteilen
	award [ə'wɔ:d]	Entschädigung(s-summe)
	emergency department [ɪ'mɜ:dʒənsi dɪpɑ:tmənt]	Notaufnahme
	ambulance ['æmbjələns]	Krankenwagen
	blameless ['bleɪmləs]	schuldlos, unschuldig
	opposite party [,ɒpəzɪt 'pɑ:ti]	Gegenpartei
	pick up the tab [pɪk ,ʌp ðə 'tæb]	für die Kosten aufkommen
	recent ['ri:snt]	neueste/r/s
	research [rɪ'sɜ:tʃ]	Untersuchungen
	suggest [sə'dʒest]	darauf hindeuten
	cold comfort [,kəʊld 'kʌmfət]	schwacher Trost
	Catch-22 (situation) [,kætʃ twenti 'tu:]	Dilemma, Teufelskreis
	tempting ['temptɪŋ]	verlockend

UNIT 9

90	**basic account** [,beɪsɪk ə'kaʊnt]	Standardkonto
	current account ['kʌrənt əkaʊnt]	Girokonto
	range [reɪndʒ]	Reihe, Auswahl
	term account ['tɜ:m əkaʊnt]	Festgeldkonto
	convenient [kən'vi:niənt]	praktisch, günstig
	tax credit ['tæks kredɪt]	Steuer(rück)erstattung
	cheque [tʃek]	Scheck
	cash card ['kæʃ kɑ:d]	Geldkarte
	withdraw [wɪð'drɔ:]	*(Geld)* abheben
	debit card ['debɪt kɑ:d]	Kundenkarte, Bankkarte
	cash back ['kæʃ bæk]	Bargeldauszahlung
	overdrawn [,əʊvə'drɔ:n]	*(Konto)* überzogen
	get overdrawn [,get əʊvə'drɔ:n]	das Konto überziehen
	overspend [,əʊvə'spend]	*(Etat, usw.)* überziehen
	act [ækt]	fungieren
	standing order [,stændɪŋ 'ɔ:də]	Dauerauftrag
	facility [fə'sɪləti]	Möglichkeit, Einrichtung
	one-off payment [wʌn ,ɒf 'peɪmənt]	Einmalzahlung
	in advance [ɪn əd'vɑ:ns]	im Voraus
	charge [tʃɑ:dʒ]	Gebühr
	apply [ə'plaɪ]	*(Gebühren)* anfallen
	rate [reɪt]	(Zins-)Satz
	savings account ['seɪvɪŋz əkaʊnt]	Sparkonto
91	**wage** [weɪdʒ]	Lohn, Gehalt
	put money aside [pʊt ,mʌni ə'saɪd]	Geld (an)sparen
	purchase ['pɜ:tʃəs]	Kauf, Erwerb
	deposit [dɪ'pɒzɪt]	Kaution, Anzahlung
	branch [brɑ:ntʃ]	Filiale, Zweigstelle
	ATM [,eɪ ti: 'em]	Geldautomat
	cash dispenser ['kæʃ dɪspensə]	Geldautomat

	information desk [ɪnfə'meɪʃn desk]	Informationsschalter
	leaflet ['li:flət]	Prospekt, Broschüre
	rack [ræk]	Regal, Ständer
	till [tɪl]	Schalter
	counter ['kaʊntə]	Schalter
	(bank) statement ['bæŋk steɪtmənt]	Kontoauszug
92	**means of payment** [ˌmi:nz əv 'peɪmənt]	Zahlungsmittel
	fine [faɪn]	Geldbuße, Geldstrafe
	membership fee ['membəʃɪp fi:]	Mitgliedsbeitrag
	sort code ['sɔ:t kəʊd]	Bankleitzahl
	balance ['bæləns]	Kontostand, Saldo
93	**denote** [dɪ'nəʊt]	bezeichnen, anzeigen
	transaction [træn'zækʃn]	(Geschäfts-)Vorgang, Überweisung
	deposit [dɪ'pɒzɪt]	Einzahlung
	credit ['kredɪt]	einzahlen, gutschreiben
	withdrawal [wɪð'drɔ:əl]	Abhebung
	debit ['debɪt]	abbuchen, belasten
	beneficiary [ˌbenɪ'fɪʃəri]	(Zahlungs-)Empfänger/in
94	**money market** ['mʌni mɑ:kɪt]	Finanzmarkt
	yield [ji:ld]	Ertrag, Zinsertrag
	instant access [ˌɪnstənt 'ækses]	Sofortzugang
	cope [kəʊp]	bewältigen, zurechtkommen
	notice account ['nəʊtɪs əkaʊnt]	Festgeld-, Termingeldkonto
	notice ['nəʊtɪs]	Mitteilung, Ankündigung
	prior ['praɪə]	vorherig
	penalty fee ['penlti fi:]	Strafgebühr
	certificate of deposit (CD) [səˌtɪfɪkət əv dɪ'pɒzɪt]	festverzinsliches Wertpapier, *hier:* Einlagenzertifikat
95	**return** [rɪ'tɜ:n]	Ertrag
	government paper ['gʌvənmənt peɪpə]	staatliches Wertpapier
	securities *pl* [sɪk'jʊərətiz]	Wertpapiere
	National Savings account [ˌnæʃnəl 'seɪvɪŋz əkaʊnt]	staatliches Einlagenkonto *(vergleichbar mit Bundeswertpapieren)*
	maturity [mə'tʃʊərəti]	Fälligkeit
	financial crisis [faɪˌnænʃl 'kraɪsɪs]	Finanzkrise
	safety-conscious ['seɪfti kɒnʃəs]	auf Sicherheit bedacht
96	**borrow** ['bɒrəʊ]	leihen
T	**overdraft facility** [ˌəʊvədrɑ:ft fə'sɪləti]	Dispositionskredit
T	**secured loan** [sɪˌkjuəd 'ləʊn]	abgesichertes Darlehen
T	**lender** ['lendə]	Kreditgeber
T	**force sth** [fɔ:s]	etw erzwingen
T	**keep sth up** [ˌki:p 'ʌp]	etw aufrechterhalten
T	**annual percentage rate (APR)** [ˌænjuəl pə'sentɪdʒ reɪt]	effektiver Jahreszins
T	**affordable** [ə'fɔ:dəbl]	erschwinglich
T	**instalment** [ɪn'stɔ:lmənt]	Rate
T	**spread** [spred]	verteilen
T	**discover** [dɪ'skʌvə]	entdecken
T	**headache** ['hedeɪk]	Kopfschmerz(en)
T	**owe** [əʊ]	schulden
T	**spread** [spred]	Überziehungsprovision, -zins
T	**goal** [gəʊl]	Ziel
T	**take out a loan** [teɪk ˌaʊt ə 'ləʊn]	einen Kredit aufnehmen
98	**final exam** [ˌfaɪnl ɪg'zæm]	Abschlussprüfung
	government bond ['gʌvənmənt bɒnd]	Staatsschuldverschreibung
	ensure [ɪn'ʃʊə]	gewährleisten, sicherstellen
T	**forecast** ['fɔ:kɑ:st]	vorhersagen, voraussagen
T	**persist** [pə'sɪst]	anhalten, fortbestehen
T	**phenomenon** [fə'nɒmɪnən]	Phänomen
99	**text message** ['tekst mesɪdʒ]	SMS
	fashionable ['fæʃnəbl]	in Mode
	access ['ækses]	zugreifen auf
	(industry) body ['ɪndəstri bɒdi]	(Branchen-)Verband
	chairman ['tʃeəmən]	Vorsitzender
	outcome ['aʊtkʌm]	Ergebnis
	striking ['straɪkɪŋ]	erstaunlich, hervorstechend
	irreversible [ˌɪrɪ'vɜ:səbl]	unumkehrbar
	decline [dɪ'klaɪn]	Abstieg
	go unchallenged [ˌgəʊ ʌn'tʃælɪndʒd]	nicht bestritten werden, nicht angegriffen werden
	merchant ['mɜ:tʃənt]	Kaufmann
	goldsmith ['gəʊldsmɪθ]	Goldschmied/in
	predict [prɪ'dɪkt]	vorhersagen, voraussagen
	fake [feɪk]	fälschen
	phase sth out [ˌfeɪz 'aʊt]	etw auslaufen lassen
	concern [kən'sɜ:n]	Sorge, Besorgnis
	viable ['vaɪəbl]	machbar, durchführbar
	review [rɪ'vju:]	Überprüfung, Testphase
	closure date ['kləʊʒə deɪt]	Auslauffrist
	promote sth [prə'məʊt]	etw fördern, für etw sein
	proxy ['prɒksi]	Vertretung

UNIT 10

100	**ruin** ['ru:ɪn]	Zusammenbruch
	arise [ə'raɪz]	entstehen
	off the shelf [ˌɒf ðə 'ʃelf]	von der Stange, Standard-
	customized ['kʌstəmaɪzd]	maßgeschneidert, individuell zugeschnitten
	Commercial Manager [kəˌmɜ:ʃl 'mænɪdʒə]	Kaufmännische/r Leiter/in
	plant [plɑ:nt]	Fabrik
	tender ['tendə]	Ausschreibung
	submission [səb'mɪʃn]	Angebot
	outline ['aʊtlaɪn]	Übersicht
	approximate [ə'prɒksɪmət]	ungefähr
	Finance Director [ˌfaɪnæns də'rektə]	Finanzvorstand
	scope [skəʊp]	Umfang
	completion [kəm'pli:ʃn]	Abschluss
	authority [ɔ:'θɒrəti]	Vollmacht

	agreement [ə'gri:mənt]	Zustimmung
	outline ['aʊtlaɪn]	(grob) beschreiben
	corner shop ['kɔ:nə ʃɒp]	Tante-Emma-Laden
	turnover ['tɜ:nəʊvə]	Umsatz
101	**kidnap** ['kɪdnæp]	entführen
	ransom ['rænsəm]	Lösegeld zahlen, jdn freikaufen
	business interruption insurance ['bɪznəs ɪntərʌpʃn ɪnʃʊərəns]	Betriebsunterbrechungs-versicherung
	fidelity insurance [fɪ'deləti ɪnʃʊərəns]	Vertrauensschaden-versicherung
	product tamper ['prɒdʌkt tæmpə]	Produktmanipulation
	officer ['ɒfɪsə]	leitende/r Angestellte/r
	variable costs *pl* [,veəriəbl 'kɒsts]	Betriebskosten
	cargo ['kɑ:gəʊ]	Fracht
	foodstuffs *pl* ['fu:dstʌfs]	Nahrungsmittel
	threat [θret]	Gefahr, Bedrohung
	key man [ki: 'mæn]	Schlüsselfigur
	partnership ['pɑ:tnəʃɪp]	Personengesellschaft
	wrongful act [,rɒŋfl 'ækt]	unrechtmäßige Handlung
	bad debt [bæd 'det]	uneinbringliche Forderung
	insolvency [ɪn'sɒlvənsi]	Insolvenz
	gradual ['grædʒuəl]	allmählich
	pollution [pə'lu:ʃn]	Umweltverschmutzung
	dishonesty [dɪs'ɒnəsti]	Unehrlichkeit, Unredlichkeit
	pirate ['paɪrət]	Pirat
	capture ['kæptʃə]	gefangen nehmen
	release [rɪ'li:s]	freilassen
	accounting clerk [ə'kaʊntɪŋ klɑ:k]	Buchhalter/in
	brake [breɪk]	Bremse
	workshop ['wɜ:kʃɒp]	Werkstatt
	guidelines *pl* ['gaɪdlaɪnz]	Richtlinien
	seep [si:p]	sickern
	poison ['pɔɪzn]	vergiften
	crop [krɒp]	Feldfrucht
	partner ['pɑ:tnə]	Gesellschafter/in
102	**cut** [kʌt]	*(Rasen)* mähen
	trim [trɪm]	stutzen
	propose [prə'pəʊz]	vorschlagen, vorlegen
	get down to business [,get 'daʊn tə 'bɪznəs]	zur Sache kommen
	renew [rɪ'nju:]	verlängern
	storm [stɔ:m]	Sturm, Unwetter
	Production Manager [prə'dʌkʃn mænɪdʒə]	Produktionsleiter/in
	forklift truck [,fɔ:klɪft 'trʌk]	Gabelstapler
	varnish ['vɑ:nɪʃ]	Lack
	valuation [,vælju'eɪʃn]	Bewertung, Schätzung
	on a reinstatement basis [ɒn ə ,ri:ɪn'steɪtmənt beɪsɪs]	zum Neuwert
	stock [stɒk]	Warenbestand
	raw materials *pl* [,rɔ: mə'tɪəriəlz]	Rohstoffe, Rohmaterial
	estimate ['estɪmət]	Schätzung
	subtract [səb'trækt]	abziehen, subtrahieren
103	**indemnity period** [ɪn'demnəti pɪəriəd]	Haftungszeitraum
	occasionally [ə'keɪʒənəli]	gelegentlich
	recall [rɪ'kɔ:l]	zurückrufen
	sue [su:]	verklagen
	stroll [strəʊl]	Spaziergang
104	**findings** *pl* ['faɪndɪŋz]	Ergebnis(se)
	fire hazard ['faɪə hæzəd]	Brandgefahr, Feuerrisiko
	site plan ['saɪt plæn]	Lageplan
	compromise ['kɒmprəmaɪz]	Kompromiss
	storage ['stɔ:rɪdʒ]	Lagerung. Vorrats-
	perimeter fence [pə'rɪmɪtə fens]	Begrenzungszaun, Einzäunung
	unprotected [,ʌnprə'tektɪd]	ungeschützt
	arson ['ɑ:sn]	Brandstiftung
	intruder [ɪn'tru:də]	Eindringling
	look into sth [,lʊk 'ɪntə]	sich um etw kümmern
	fleet [fli:t]	Fahrzeugflotte, -park
	fire alarm ['faɪə əlɑ:m]	Feuermelder
	improvement [ɪm'pru:vmənt]	Verbesserung
T	**steady** ['stedi]	stetig, kontinuierlich
	stream [stri:m]	Strom
	take the rough with the smooth [teɪk ðə ,rʌf wɪð ðə 'smu:ð]	etw nehmen, wie es kommt
	all concerned [,ɔ:l kən'sɜ:nd]	alle Beteilgten
	The proof of the pudding is in the eating. [ðə ,pru:f əv ðə ,pʊdɪŋ ɪz ɪn ði 'i:tɪŋ]	Probieren (geht) über Studieren.
	curious ['kjʊəriəs]	neugierig
	respond [rɪ'spɒnd]	reagieren, antworten
	underwriting [,ʌndə'raɪtɪŋ]	Risikoeinschätzung, Risikoprüfung, Risikoannahme
105	**rearrange** [,ri:ə'reɪndʒ]	*(Termin)* verlegen
	crop up [,krɒp 'ʌp]	auftauchen
	cancel ['kænsl]	*(Termin)* absagen
	postpone [pə'spəʊn]	*(Termin)* verlegen
	fix [fɪks]	*(Termin)* ausmachen
106	**preparation** [,prepə'reɪʃn]	Vorbereitung
	clause [klɔ:z]	Klausel
	piped water [paɪpt 'wɔ:tə]	Wasserleitung
	random sample [,rændəm 'sɑ:mpl]	Stichprobe
	clean up expenses *pl* [,kli:n 'ʌp ɪkspensɪz]	Reinigungskosten
	retention [rɪ'tenʃn]	Selbstbehalt
107	**pro rata** [,prəʊ 'rɑ:tə]	anteilig
	escalator clause ['eskəleɪtə klɔ:z]	Gleitklausel, Index-vereinbarung
	underinsurance [,ʌndərɪn'ʃʊərəns]	Unterversicherung
	contingent [kən'tɪndʒənt]	Rückwirkungsschadenver-sicherung, Rückwir-kungsschäden-versicherung
	supplier [sə'plaɪə]	Lieferant, Zulieferer
	market value [,mɑ:kɪt 'vælju:]	Marktwert

	contingency cover [kən'tɪndʒənsi kʌvə]	Veranstaltungs-ausfallversicherung
108	fear [fɪə]	Angst, Furcht
	weakness ['wi:knəs]	Schwäche, Schwachpunkt
	persuade [pə'sweɪd]	überzeugen
	relation [rɪ'leɪʃn]	Beziehung
	present ['preznt]	gegenwärtig, aktuell
	recommendation [ˌrekəmen'deɪʃn]	Empfehlung
	bother ['bɒðə]	Sorgen bereiten
	output ['aʊtpʊt]	Produktion
	extension [ɪk'stenʃn]	Ausweitung, Ergänzung
	blade [bleɪd]	Klinge
	wiring ['waɪərɪŋ]	Elektrik, Leitungen
	inevitable [ɪn'evɪtəbl]	unvermeidlich
	ruin ['ru:ɪn]	ruinieren
109	expertise [ˌekspɜ:'ti:z]	Fachwissen, Fach-kenntnisse
	appoint [ə'pɔɪnt]	ernennen, berufen
	Frankonian [fræŋ'kəʊniən]	fränkisch
110	up front [ʌp 'frʌnt]	offen
	a case of swings and roundabouts [ə keɪs əv ˌswɪŋz ənd 'raʊndəbaʊts]	gehupft wie gesprungen
	reverse [rɪ'vɜ:s]	umkehren
	burden of proof [ˌbɜ:dn əv 'pru:f]	Beweislast
	demand [dɪ'mɑ:nd]	Nachfrage
	supply [sə'plaɪ]	Angebot
	market cycle ['mɑ:kɪt saɪkl]	Marktzyklus
111	be fond of sth [bi 'fɒnd əv]	etw mögen

UNIT 11

112	reinsurance [ˌri:ɪn'ʃʊərəns]	Rückversicherung
	reinsurer [ˌri:ɪn'ʃʊərə]	Rückversicherer
	reinsure [ˌri:ɪn'ʃʊə]	rückversichern
	go bankrupt [gəʊ 'bæŋkrʌpt]	Pleite gehen
	lay off [ˌleɪ 'ɒf]	abgeben
	rate [reɪt]	*hier:* Prämie
	adequate ['ædɪkwət]	angemessen
	book of business [ˌbʊk əv 'bɪznəs]	Portfolio
	risk of random loss [ˌrɪsk əv ˌrændəm 'lɒs]	Zufallsrisiko
	underrated [ˌʌndə'reɪtɪd]	unterbewertet
	price [praɪs]	*(Preis, usw.)* festlegen, ansetzen
113	catastrophe [kə'tæstrəfi]	Katastrophe
	accumulation [əˌkju:mjə'leɪʃn]	Häufung, Akkumulation
	underwrite [ˌʌndə'raɪt]	tarifieren, Risiko annehmen
	coach [kəʊtʃ]	Reisebus
114	balanced ['bælənst]	ausgewogen, ausgeglichen
	unbalanced [ˌʌn'bælənst]	unausgewogen, unausgeglichen
	cedant ['si:dənt]	Zedent
	(loss) severity ['lɒs sɪverəti]	Schadengrad
	endanger [ɪn'deɪndʒə]	gefährden
	cede [si:d]	*(Rechte, usw.)* abtreten
	cession ['seʃn]	Abtretung
	for the sake of simplicity [fə ðə ˌseɪk əv sɪm'plɪsəti]	der Einfachheit halber
	cap sth [kæp]	*(Schäden)* deckeln
115	loading ['ləʊdɪŋ]	(Prämien-)Zuschlag
	non-proportional reinsurance [ˌnɒn prəˌpɔ:ʃnəl ri:ɪn'ʃʊərəns]	nichtproportionale Rückversicherung
	risk excess of loss [ˌrɪsk ekses əv 'lɒs]	Einzelschadenexzedent
	bear in mind [ˌbeər ɪn 'maɪnd]	daran denken
	treaty ['tri:ti]	Vertrag
	renegotiate [ˌri: nɪ'gəʊʃieɪt]	neu verhandeln
116	survivor [sə'vaɪvə]	Überlebende/r
	funds *pl* [fʌndz]	Gelder, Geldmittel
	line [laɪn]	Selbstbehalt
	capacity [kə'pæsəti]	Kapazität
	rate [reɪt]	(Prämien-)Satz
117	marginal ['mɑ:dʒɪnl]	gering(fügig), unwesentlich
	respective [rɪ'spektɪv]	entsprechend
118	concession [kən'seʃn]	Zugeständnis
	admittedly [əd'mɪtɪdli]	zugegebenermaßen
	deny [dɪ'naɪ]	leugnen
	play for time [pleɪ fə 'taɪm]	Zeit gewinnen, auf Zeit spielen
	look closely [ˌlʊk 'kləʊsli]	genau hinsehen
120	proportional reinsurance [prəˌpɔ:ʃnəl ri:ɪn'ʃʊərəns]	proportionale Rück-versicherung
	quota share ['kwəʊtə ʃeə]	Quote
	favourable for ['feɪvərəbl fə]	günstig für, vorteilhaft für
	retain [rɪ'teɪn]	behalten, einbehalten
121	surplus ['sɜ:pləs]	Summenexzedent
	provided that [prə'vaɪdɪd ðət]	vorausgesetzt dass; unter der Voraussetzung, dass
	monetary ['mʌnɪtri]	monetär
	obligatory [ə'blɪgətri]	obligatorisch
	acceptance [ək'septəns]	Akzept
	analogue to ['ænəlɒg tə]	analog zu

UNIT 12

122	apply (for a job) [əˌplaɪ fər ə 'dʒɒb]	sich (um eine Stelle) bewerben
	vocational qualification [vəʊˌkeɪʃnəl kwɒlɪfɪ'keɪʃn]	Berufsausbildung
	course [kɔ:s]	Verlauf, Lauf
	challenge ['tʃælɪndʒ]	Herausforderung
	rare [reə]	selten
	actuarial [ˌæktʃu'eəriəl]	versicherungs-mathematisch
	recruit [rɪ'kru:t]	*(Personal)* einstellen
	accountancy [ə'kaʊntənsi]	Buchhaltung, Rechnungswesen
	employment agency [ɪm'plɔɪmənt eɪdʒənsi]	Arbeitsvermittlung
	applicant ['æplɪkənt]	Bewerber/in
	vacant ['veɪkənt]	*(Stelle)* frei

	jobseeker ['dʒɒbsiːkə]	Arbeitssuchende/r
	dedicated ['dedɪkeɪtɪd]	gewidmet
	curriculum vitae (CV) [kəˌrɪkjələm 'viːtaɪ]	Lebenslauf
	range [reɪndʒ]	Spielraum
	approach [ə'prəʊtʃ]	Herantreten
	encourage sb to do sth [ɪn'kʌrɪdʒ]	jdn ermuntern/bewegen, etw zu tun
	application [ˌæplɪ'keɪʃn]	Bewerbung
123	**covering letter** [ˌkʌvərɪŋ 'letə]	Bewerbungsschreiben
124	**qualify** ['kwɒlɪfaɪ]	den Abschluss machen
	(claims) negotiator ['kleɪmz nɪgəʊʃieɪtə]	Schaden(s)regulierer/in
	permanent ['pɜːmənənt]	*(Arbeit)* unbefristet
	driven ['drɪvn]	engagiert
	hardworking [ˌhɑːd'wɜːkɪŋ]	fleißig
	deadline ['dedlaɪn]	Frist
	fast paced [fɑːst 'peɪst]	temporeich
	toughness ['tʌfnəs]	Hartnäckigkeit, Zähigkeit
	stand sb in good stead [ˌstænd ɪn gʊd 'sted]	jdm gute Dienste leisten
	contribute [kən'trɪbjuːt]	beitragen
	delivery [dɪ'lɪvəri]	Erfüllen (von Zielvorgaben)
	resolve [rɪ'zɒlv]	lösen
	authority limit [ɔː'θɒrəti lɪmɪt]	Kompetenzbereich
	further ['fɜːðə]	fördern
125	**pursue** [pə'sjuː]	verfolgen
	certify ['sɜːtɪfaɪ]	anerkennen, bestätigen
	chamber of commerce [ˌtʃeɪmbər əv 'kɒmɜːs]	Handelskammer
	education [ˌedʒu'keɪʃn]	Schulbildung
	fluent ['fluːənt]	*(Sprache)* fließend
	oral ['ɔːrəl]	mündlich
	conversational French [kɒnvəˌseɪʃənl 'frentʃ]	Alltagsfranzösisch
	on request [ɒn rɪ'kwest]	auf Anfrage
126	**capture** ['kæptʃə]	*(Aufmerksamkeit)* fesseln
	reverse [rɪ'vɜːs]	umgekehrt
	grade [greɪd]	Note
	referee [ˌrefə'riː]	Referenz *(Person)*
128	**examination** [ɪgˌzæmɪ'neɪʃn]	Prüfung
	diploma [dɪ'pləʊmə]	Abschlusszeugnis
	grammar school ['græmə skuːl]	Gymnasium
	be raised [bi 'reɪzd]	aufwachsen
	bilingual [ˌbaɪ'lɪŋgwəl]	zweisprachig
	have appeal [həv ə'piːl]	attraktiv sein
129	**screen sb** [skriːn]	jdn überprüfen
	keep a record [ˌkiːp ə 'rekɔːd]	aufzeichnen, dokumentieren
	confident ['kɒnfɪdənt]	selbstbewusst
T	**accomplishment** [ə'kʌmplɪʃmənt]	Leistung, Fertigkeit
	table etiquette ['teɪbl etɪket]	Tischmanieren
	manners *pl* ['mænəz]	Manieren

Alphabetical word list

Diese Liste enthält alle Wörter in alphabetischer Reihenfolge. Hier sind jedoch die Wörter, die zum Grundwortschatz gehören, nicht aufgeführt.

P = das Wort befindet sich im *Partner file*.
T = das Wort befindet sich im *Transcript*.

Die Zahl nach dem Stichwort bezieht sich auf die Seite, auf der das Wort zum ersten Mal erscheint.

A

abbreviation *28* Abkürzung
ability *52* Fähigkeit
abroad *6* im/ins Ausland
accept *16* akzeptieren
acceptance *121* Akzept
access sb *17* an jdn herantreten, jdn erreichen; *99* zugreifen auf
accident annuity *56* Unfallrente
accident *7* Unfall; **scene of an ~** 56 Unfallort
accidental *31* zufällig; **~ damage** *31* unbeabsichtigte Beschädigung; **~ death** *56* Unfalltod
accommodation *31* Unterkunft
accomplishment *129T* Leistung, Fertigkeit
according to *20* gemäß, nach
account *13* Konto; **National Savings ~** *95* staatliches Einlagenkonto *(vergleichbar mit Bundeswertpapieren)*; **account, term ~** *90* Festgeldkonto; **~ of the incident** *73* Schilderung des Vorfalls; **take into ~** *25T* berücksichtigen
account for *17* ausmachen
accountancy *122* Buchhaltung, Rechnungswesen
accounting clerk *101* Buchhalter/in
Accounting Department *15* Rechnungswesen
accumulation *113* Häufung, Akkumulation
accurate *34T* genau, exakt
acquire *6* erwerben, akquirieren, kaufen
acquisition *17* Akquisition
act *90* fungieren
actuarial *122* versicherungsmathematisch
Actuarial Department *15* Mathematische Abteilung
actuary *14* Aktuar/in
acute *65* akut
adapt *57* anpassen, umbauen
adapted *51* bearbeitet
addicted *50T* abhängig
addiction *50T* Sucht
addition, in ~ *7* darüber hinaus, außerdem
additional *14* zusätzlich, Zusatz-
address *9* Anrede; *26* ansprechen
addressee *48* Adressat, Empfänger/in
adequate *112* angemessen
adjust *18* anpassen
administration *73* Verwaltung
administrative *8* Verwaltungs-
admit *80* zugeben, eingestehen
admittedly *118* zugegebenermaßen
advance, in ~ *90* im Voraus
advantage *45T* Vorteil; **take ~ of** *46* sich etw zunutze machen
advice *12* Beratung, Rat
advise *15* beraten, raten
adviser *12* Berater/in
aerial *31* Antenne
affect sth *14* sich auf etw auswirken
affected, be ~ by sth *63* von etw betroffen sein
afford sth *63* sich etw leisten
affordable *96T* erschwinglich
afraid, be ~ of *63* Angst haben vor, sich fürchten vor
after-school care centre *53* Hort
age, for ~s *50T* eine Ewigkeit
ageing reserve *62* Alterungsrückstellungen
agency *9* Agentur
agent *7* Agent/in, Vertreter/in; **tied ~** *7* Einfirmenvertreter/in
aggregator *17* Vergleichsrechner
agree on sth *46* sich auf etw einigen, etw vereinbaren
agreed *43* vereinbart
agreement *13* Vereinbarung, Abkommen; *100* Zustimmung
aid *17* Hilfe
aids *69* Hilfsmittel
aim *24* Ziel
aircraft *31* Flugzeug
alcohol level *79* Alkoholspiegel
all concerned *104T* alle Beteilgten
alternative accommodation *31* Ausweichunterkunft, -quartier
alternative *17* andere/r/s, alternative/r/s
ambulance *89* Krankenwagen
amount to *7 (Geldsumme)* sich belaufen auf
analogue to *121* analog zu
ankle *53* Knöchel
anniversary *58* Jahrestag
annual percentage rate (APR) *96T* effektiver Jahreszins
annually *27* jährlich
annuity *42* (Kapital-)Rente, Annuität
answering machine *88* Anrufbeantworter
anxiety *61* Sorge
apart from *8* außer, abgesehen von
apologize *10* sich entschuldigen
appeal, have ~ *128* attraktiv sein
appendicitis *65* Blinddarmentzündung
applicable, not ~ *18* nicht zutreffend
applicant *122* Bewerber/in
application *16* Antrag; 122 Bewerbung
apply to *25T* zutreffen auf; *31* gelten; *90 (Gebühren)* anfallen; *122* sich (um eine Stelle) bewerben
appoint *109* ernennen, berufen
appointment *9* Termin, Verabredung
appreciate *29* zu schätzen wissen, schätzen
approach *122* Herantreten
appropriate *11* passend, angemessen
approved repairer *82* Vertragswerkstatt
approximate(ly) *49* ungefähr
area *12* Gebiet, Bereich; **~ code** *34* Vorwahl
arise *79 (Tatbestand)* vorliegen, *(Fall)* eintreten; *100* entstehen
arrange *30* vereinbaren, abmachen
arrest *19* verhaften
arrival *10* Ankunft
arson *104T* Brandstiftung
asap = as soon as possible *28* so bald wie möglich, baldmöglichst
aspect *12* Aspekt
assess *59* schätzen, einschätzen, bewerten, feststellen
assessment *30* Schätzung, Bewertung
assets *41* Vermögen, Vermögenswerte
assist *14* behilflich sein, unterstützen
assistance *47* Hilfe, Unterstützung
association *17* Verband
assumption *85T* Annahme, Vermutung
asthma *65* Asthma
at all *9T* überhaupt
ATM *91* Geldautomat
attach *82* befestigen, anhängen
attachment *28 (Brief)* Anlage, *(E-Mail)* Attachment
attempt *89* versuchen
attempted *31* versucht
attend *6 (Schule, usw.)* besuchen, *(Veranstaltung)* teilnehmen
attention: draw sb's ~ to sth *24* jds Aufmerksamkeit auf etw lenken; **for the ~ of** *48 (Brief)* zu Händen
attitude *18* Einstellung, Haltung
audience *26* Publikum
authority *100* Vollmacht; **~ limit** *124* Kompetenzbereich
Automobile Association (AA) *39 brit. Automobilklub*
available *17* erhältlich, verfügbar; *35* (Telefon) zu sprechen sein
average *27* Durchschnitt, durchschnittlich
avoid *25T* vermeiden; 72 *(Auto)* jdm ausweichen
avoider *42* Vermeider
award *89* Entschädigung(ssumme); *74* zusprechen, zuerkennen

awkward *50T* peinlich, unangenehm; **~ly** *55* ungeschickt

B

back *88 (Auto)* zurücksetzen; **~ off** *27* nachgeben
bad debt *101* uneinbringliche Forderung
balance *92* Kontostand, Saldo
balanced *114* ausgewogen, ausgeglichen
bank, ~ clerk *44* Bankangestellte/r; **~ loan** *41* Kredit
bankrupt, go ~ *112* Pleite gehen
bargain *20* Schnäppchen
based, be ~ in *6* seinen Sitz haben in
basic *63* Grund-; **~ account** *90* Standardkonto
Bavarian *9T* bayerisch
bear in mind *115* daran denken
behave *19* sich verhalten
behaviour *74* Verhalten
belongings *28* Eigentum, Besitz, Sachen
beneficiary *40* Nutznießer, Begünstigte/r; *93* (Zahlungs-)Empfänger/in
benefit *37* (Versicherungs-)Leistung; *73* profitieren; **daily accident ~** *56* Unfalltagegeld; **disability ~** *56* Invaliditätsleistung; **hospital daily ~** *56* Krankenhaustagegeld; **top-up ~** *62* Zusatzleistung
bilingual *128* zweisprachig
bill *66* Rechnung
billion *7* Milliarde
blade *108T* Klinge
blame sb *80* jdm die Schuld geben, jdm (für etw) verantwortlich machen
blameless *89* schuldlos, unschuldig
bleed *55* bluten
blood circulation *59* Blutkreislauf
bodily injury *59* Verletzung
body *30* Haupttext; **(industry) ~** *99* (Branchen-)Verband
bond *15* Wertpapier, Anleihe
bone *65* Knochen
bonnet *88* Motohaube *(BE)*
bonus *43* Prämie, Bonus
book of business *112* Portfolio
boot *88* Kofferraum *(BE)*
borrow *96* leihen
bother *108T* Sorgen bereiten
brake *101* Bremse
branch *91* Filiale, Zweigstelle; **~ office** *6* Niederlassung; **~ out** *6* das Geschäftsfeld erweitern
break *30* Zeilenumbruch; **~down** *21* Aufschlüsselung; *82* Panne; **~ down** *31* kaputtgehen; **~-in** *19* Einbruch
breakage *37* Bruch; **~ of glass** *82* Glasbruch
bribe *79* bestechen
bridging benefit *56* Übergangsleistung
brief *25* kurz, knapp, bündig
briefcase *75* Aktenkoffer
broken pipe *81* Rohrbruch
broker *7* Makler/in
budget *45T* Budget, Etat
building *28* Gebäude; **~ society** *6* Bausparkasse
built-in kitchen unit *34T* Einbauküche
bumper *88* Stoßstange
bumpy *10* holprig, unruhig
burden of proof *110* Beweislast
burglar alarm *39* Alarmanlage
burglary *27* Einbruch
burial *40* Beerdigung
burn *55* (sich) verbrennen
burst pipe *30* Rohrbruch
business *6* Geschäft, Geschäfts-; **~ interruption insurance** *101* Betriebsunterbrechungsversicherung; **business trip** *9T* Geschäftsreise; **book of ~** *112* Portfolio; **get down to ~** *102* zur Sache kommen
businessman *6* Geschäftsmann
busy *35* (Leitung) belegt

C

cable *37* Kabel
calculate *28* berechnen
calculation *59* Rechnung, Berechnung
calculator *34T* Rechner
call *9* nennen, rufen; anrufen
campaign *15* Werbekampagne
camper van *84* Wohnmobil *(BE)*
cancel *14 (Vertrag, usw.)* kündigen; *105 (Termin)* absagen
cancellation *14* Kündigung; *70* Stornierung
cap sth *114* (Schäden) deckeln
capacity *116* Kapazität; **earning ~** *52* Erwerbsfähigkeit
capital *43* Kapital; **~ letter** *30* Großbuchstabe
capture *101* gefangen nehmen; *126 (Aufmerksamkeit)* fesseln
car dealer *17* Autohändler/in
caravan *82* Campingwagen
care, take ~ *14* dafür sorgen
careless *72* unbedacht, fahrlässig
carelessness *71* Unachtsamkeit, Nachlässigkeit, Fahrlässigkeit
cargo *101* Fracht
carpenter *40* Tischler/in
carry out *12* ausführen, durchführen
case *13* Fall
cash: in ~ *44T* bar; **~ back** *90* Bargeldauszahlung; **~ card** *90* Geld-karte; **~ dispenser** *91* Geldautomat; **~ value** *40* Barwert; **~-in value** *43* Rückkaufswert
casualty *56* Verletze/r, Unfallopfer; *81* Haftpflicht *(AE)*
catastrophe *113* Katastrophe
catch *34T* verstehen; *45T* Haken
Catch-22 (situation) *89* Dilemma, Teufelskreis
category, (insurance) ~ *85* (Versicherungs-)Klasse
cause *27* verursachen
cedant *114* Zedent
cede *114 (Rechte, usw.)* abtreten
certain *12* bestimmte/r/s
certainty *43* Gewissheit, Sicherheit
certificate of deposit (CD) *94* festverzinsliches Wertpapier, *hier:* Einlagenzertifikat
certify *125* anerkennen, bestätigen
cession *114* Abtretung
chain *28* Kette
chairman *99* Vorsitzender
challenge *122* Herausforderung
challenging *12* fordernd, anspruchsvoll
chamber of commerce *125* Handelskammer
chamber of handicraft *6* Handwerkskammer
change *22* Veränderung; **~ your mind** *14* seine Meinung ändern
channel of distribution *7* Vertriebskanal
charge *90* Gebühr; **free of ~** *34T* kostenlos, gebührenfrei, gratis; **in ~ of** *12* zuständig für
chartered surveyor *34* Bausachverständige/r
chemist *69* Apotheker/in
cheque *90* Scheck
chest *55* Brust
Chief Executive Officer (CEO) *9* Vorstandsvorsitzende/r
chin *55* Kinn
choice *44* Wahl
chronic *65* chronisch
circumstances *39* Umstände
citizen *62* Bürger/in
civil servant *62T* Beamte/r
claim *13* Schadensfall, Versicherungsanspruch; **~ report** *60* Schadenbericht, *88* Schadenanzeige; **~s Department** *15* Schadenabteilung; **~s history** *85T* Schadenverlauf; **~s procedure** *18* Schadensbearbeitung, -abwicklung; **no ~(s) discount** 82 Schadenfreiheitsrabatt; **~s negotiator** *124* Schaden(s)regulierer/in; **~ on sth** *32* eine Versicherung in Anspruch nehmen; *80* behaupten
claimant *72* Anspruchsberechtigte/r, Antragsteller/in
class *6* Art, Kategorie, Klasse
clause *106* Klausel
clean up expenses *106* Reinigungskosten
clenched fist *26* geballte Faust
clerk *44* Angestellte/r, Sachbearbeite/r
client *12* Kunde/Kundin
close *29 (Brief)* Schlussformel
closure date *99* Auslauffrist
coach *113* Reisebus
coalition *27* Bündnis
collapse *81* einstürzen

collateral *43* Sicherheit, Kollateral
colleague *9* Kollege/-in
collect *13* kassieren, einziehen
collection *13* Inkasso
collide *79* kollidieren, zusammenstoßen
collision *27* Zusammenstoß, Kollision
combine *7* zusammenschließen, vereinigen; *25* kombinieren
come across sb *80* jdn (zufällig) treffen, jdn (zufällig) finden
comfort, cold ~ *89* schwacher Trost
Commercial Manager *100* Kaufmännische/r Leiter/in
commission *72* Provision
commit *27 (Straftat)* begehen
common *27* verbreitet, häufig; **have in ~** *48* gemeinsam haben
company *6* Gesellschaft, Unternehmen, Firma; **~ car** *85* Firmenwagen; **in-~** *54* betriebsintern
compare *12* (miteinander) vergleichen; *69* sich vergleichen lassen
comparison *39* Vergleich
compensate *31* entschädigen
compensation *13* Entschädigung
competent *18* kompetent
competition *12* Wettbewerb
competitive *12* konkurrenzfähig; *34T* konkurrierend; *46 (Preis, usw.)* günstig
competitor *14* Konkurrent/in, Konkurrenz
completion *100* Abschluss
comprehensive *7* umfassend; *62* Vollkasko-; **~ cover** *82* Vollkaskoversicherung
comprise *51* ausmachen
compromise *104* Kompromiss
compulsory *31* obligatorisch
concern *99* Sorge, Besorgnis
concerned *61* besorgt
concerning *49* bezüglich, betreffend
concession *118* Zugeständnis
concise *30* knapp, prägnant
conclusion *24* Schluss
concussed, be ~ *75* eine Gehirnerschütterung haben
concussion *55* Gehirnerschütterung
condition *59* Leiden; *86* Zustand; **on ~ that** *13* unter der Bedingung, dass
condolences *59* Beileid
condominium/condo *33* Eigentumswohnung *(AE)*
conduct *27 (Studie, usw.)* durchführen
confidence *18* Vertrauen
confident *129T* selbstbewusst
confined to a wheelchair *55* an den Rollstuhl gefesselt
confirm *58* bestätigen
Congratulations. *44T* Herzlichen Glückwunsch!
connection *35* Verbindung
conscious *26* bewusst
consequence *65* Folge, Konsequenz
consequently *63* folglich, deshalb
consider *19* erachten, halten für; *45* erwägen, in Betracht ziehen; *64* betrachten; **be ~ed sth** *85T* als etw gelten
considerable *22* beträchtlich; *51* erheblich
consist of *24* bestehen aus
constant *22* konstant, gleich
consultant *63* Chefarzt/-ärztin
consumer goods *27* Konsumgüter
contact lenses *69* Kontaktlinsen
contact sb *14* sich mit jdm in Verbindung setzen
contain *29* enthalten
content *30* Inhalt
contents: ~ insurance *19* Hausratversicherung; **home ~** *31* Hausrat
contingency cover *107* Veranstaltungsausfallversicherung
contingent *107* Rückwirkungsschadenversicherung, Rückwirkungsschädenversicherung
continue *9* weitergehen, (sich) fortsetzen
contract *14* Vertrag
contraction *29* Kurzform
contractual relationship *72* vertragliche Beziehung
contrast, in ~ (to) *17* im Gegensatz zu/dazu
contrasting *26* kontrastierend, Kontrast-
contribute *124* beitragen
contribution *65T* Beitrag
contributory negligence *79* Mitverschulden
control *8* kontrollieren, führen, leiten
convenience *20* Komfort
convenient *34T* angenehm; *90* praktisch, günstig
conversational French *125* Alltagsfranzösisch
conversion option *42* Umtauschoption
convert *43* umwandeln
convertible *84* Cabrio(let)
convince *12* überzeugen
cope *94* bewältigen, zurechtkommen
corner shop *100* Tante-Emma-Laden
cost, variable ~s *101* Betriebskosten
counselling *45* Beratung
counter *91* Schalter
course *122* Verlauf, Lauf
court *27* Gericht
courtesy car *82* Ersatzwagen, Mietwagen *(auf Kosten des Versicherers)*
cover *12* Versicherungsschutz; *13* decken, versichern; **~ note** *87* Deckungsbestätigung; **contingency ~** *107* Veranstaltungsausfallversicherung; **partial ~** *82* Teilkaskoversicherung; **top-up ~** *62T* Zusatzdeckung
coverage *17* Deckung, Versicherungsschutz, Versicherung
covering letter *123* Bewerbungsschreiben
crack *32* Riss; *88 (Glas)* Sprung
credit *93* einzahlen, gutschreiben
crime *27* Verbrechen
criticism *65* Kritik, Kritikpunkte
crook *27* Gauner/in, Kriminelle/r
crop *101* Feldfrucht
crop up *105* auftauchen
crossed arms *26* verschränkte Arme
crowded *75* voll (besetzt)
curious *104T* neugierig
currency *45T* Währung
current *28* aktuell
current account *90* Girokonto
curriculum vitae (CV) *122* Lebenslauf
curtailment *70* (Urlaubs-)Abbruch
customer *12* Kunde/Kundin
customized *100* maßgeschneidert, individuell zugeschnitten
cut: ~ *102 (Rasen)* mähen; **~ (costs, risk)** *39* (Kosten, Risiko) senken; **~ off** *35* unterbrechen; **~** *53* abschneiden; **~ sth short** *70* etw plötzlich abbrechen
cyclist *79* Radfahrer/in

D

damage *30* Schaden, Beschädigung, Schädigung; **~s** *74* Schadenersatz
danger *32* Gefahr,
dash *29* Binde-/Gedankenstrich
dead body *56* Leichnam
deadline *124* Frist
deal: a great ~ *62T* eine Menge, viel
deal with *7* zu tun haben mit, umgehen mit
death *30* Tod
debit *93* abbuchen, belasten; **~ card** *90* Kundenkarte, Bankkarte; **direct ~** *13* Einzug(sverfahren), Lastschrift
debt(s) *40* Schulden; **bad ~** *101* uneinbringliche Forderung
deceive *27* täuschen
decline *15* ablehnen; *99* Abstieg
decrease *16* sinken, zurückgehen
dedicated *122* gewidmet
deductible *85T* Selbstbeteiligung, Abzugsfranchise
deer *88T* Hirsch, Reh
define *19* definieren
degree *56* Grad
delay *10* Verspätung, Verzögerung
delayed *10* verspätet
delete *49* löschen, tilgen
deliberate *78* absichtlich, bewusst, vorsätzlich
delicate *88T* heikel
delivery *124* Erfüllen *(von Zielvorgaben)*
demand *73* fordern, verlangen; *110* Nachfrage
demanding *14* anstrengend, anspruchsvoll
demographic *15* demographisch
denote *93* bezeichnen, anzeigen
dent *88* Beule
dental *63* zahnärztlich, Zahn-
dentist *69* Zahnarzt/-ärztin

deny *118* leugnen
department *9* Abteilung
depend on *34T* davon abhängen, darauf ankommen; *40* abhängig sein von, abhängen von
dependant *40* (finanziell abhängige/r) Angehörige/r
dependent on *39* abhängig von
deposit *91* Kaution, Anzahlung; *93* Einzahlung; **certificate of ~** (CD) *94* festverzinsliches Wertpapier, *hier:* Einlagenzertifikat
design, be ~ed to *43* dafür gedacht sein, dass
desk bound *60* am Schreibtisch
despite *61* trotz
detached house *33* freistehendes Haus
determine *85T* bestimmen
development *17* Entwicklung
diabetes *65* Diabetes
dial *35* *(Telefon)* wählen
differ *25T* sich unterscheiden
difficulty *6* Schwierigkeit, Problem
digit *34* Ziffer
diploma *128* Abschlusszeugnis
direct: ~ debit *13* Einzug(sverfahren), Lastschrift; **~ intention** *78* Vorsatz; **~ selling** *7* Direktvertrieb
direction *88T* Richtung; **~s** *9T* Wegbeschreibung
disability: ~ benefit *56* Invaliditätsleistung; **~ pension** *27* Invaliditätsrente
disabled *43* behindert
disablement benefit *56* Invaliditätsleistung
disappear *88T* verschwinden
disaster *40* Katastrophe
discount *34T* Rabatt; **no claim(s) ~** *82* Schadenfreiheitsrabatt
discover *96T* entdecken
discuss *30* diskutieren, erörtern, besprechen
disease *50T* Krankheit
dishonesty *101* Unehrlichkeit, Unredlichkeit
dissatisfied *65T* unzufrieden
distribution *7* Vertrieb, Versand; **channel of ~** *7* Vertriebskanal
distributor *81T* (Zwischen-)Händler, Vertreiber
diver *60* Taucher/in
divide *24* teilen, unterteilen
division *85* *(Sport)* Liga; *9T* Abteilung
divorced *44* geschieden
documentation *18* Unterlagen, Dokumentation
domestic appliances *31* Haushaltsgeräte
double *56* sich verdoppeln
down, be ~ to sth *61* an etw liegen
drain *37* Abwasserleitung
dramatic *22* dramatisch
draw sb's attention to sth *24* jds Aufmerksamkeit auf etw lenken
drawback *34T* Nachteil, Haken
dresser *76* Garderobier/e
drill *37* bohren
drive *37* Zufahrt, Auffahrt; *89* antreiben; **four-wheel ~** *84* Vierradantrieb
driven *124* engagiert
driving: ~ licence *87P* Führerschein; **~ test** *85* Fahrprüfung
drop *22* zurückgehen
due to *16* aufgrund von
durable *31* langlebig
duration *40* Dauer, Laufzeit
duty *14* Aufgabe, Pflicht

E

early retirement *44* Vorruhestand
earning capacity *52* Erwerbsfähigkeit
earthquake *31* Erdbeben
education *125* Schulbildung
effective *25T* effektiv
effort *39* Mühe, Aufwand
elbow *55* Ellbogen
(the) elderly *61* ältere Menschen
electric kettle *68* Wasserkocher
elsewhere *89* anderswo
embezzlement *19* Veruntreuung, Unterschlagung
emergency department *89* Notaufnahme
emergency evacuation *63* Notevakuierung
emphasize *61* betonen, hervorheben
employ *56* beschäftigen, anstellen
employee *7* Angestellte/r, Mitarbeiter/in
employer *43* Arbeitgeber
employment agency *122* Arbeitsvermittlung
enable *12* in die Lage versetzen, ermöglichen, befähigen
enclosed *28* (Brief) beigefügt
enclosure *47* (Brief) Anlage
encourage *27* fördern; **~ sb to do sth** *122* jdn ermuntern/bewegen, etw zu tun
endanger *114* gefährden
endowment insurance *42* kapitalbildende Lebensversicherung, auch gemischte Versicherung
engaged *35* (Leitung) belegt; **~ in sth** *60* mit etw beschäftigt
engineer *81T* Ingenieur/in
enormous *62* enorm
enquire about *49* sich erkundigen nach
enquiry *28* Anfrage
ensure *98* gewährleisten, sicherstellen
entire *58* gesamte/r/s, ganze/r/s
entitle *13* berechtigen
entitled *63* mit dem Titel; **be ~ to** *58* Anspruch haben auf
entitlement *87* Anspruch, Anrecht
entrance *33* Eingang
entry *28* Eintrag
environmental impairment insurance *81T* Umwelthaftpflichtversicherung
equivalent *31* gleichwertig; *63* Gegenstück, Pendant
error *63* Fehler, Irrtum
escalator clause *107* Gleitklausel, Indexvereinbarung
escape *31* entweichen; **~ of water** *34T* Wasseraustritt
essential *12* unabdingbar, wesentlich
establish *6* gründen
estate (car) *84* Kombi *(BE)*
estimate *27* schätzen; 102 Schätzung
etiquette, table ~ *129T* Tischmanieren
even out *22* sich einpendeln
event, in the ~ of sth *64* bei etw, im Falle von etw
evidence *43* Nachweis
exaggerate *27* übertreiben
examination *128* Prüfung
exceed *62T* überschreiten
except for *31* außer, ausgenommen
exception *9* Ausnahme
excerpt *64* Auszug, Ausschnitt
excess *31* Selbstbeteiligung, Abzugsfranchise
excessive prices *61* überhöhte Preise
exchange rate *45T* Wechselkurs
exchange *20* austauschen
excluded *73* ausgeschlossen, ausgenommen
exclusion *25* Ausschluss(klausel)
expect *25* erwarten
expense(s) *30* Kosten, Auslagen
experience *12* Erfahrung, Berufserfahrung
expertise *109* Fachwissen, Fachkenntnisse
expire *43* *(Vertrag, usw)* auslaufen
express *26* ausdrücken, äußern
extend *43* ausdehnen, erweitern
extension *34* Durchwahl; *108T* Ausweitung, Ergänzung
extinguish *38* (Feuer) löschen

F

face sth *12* mit einer Sache zu kämpfen haben; *65T* sich einer Sache stellen (müssen)
facial expression *26* Gesichtsausdruck
facility *90* Möglichkeit, Einrichtung
factory *33* Fabrik
fail *63* versäumen, nicht schaffen
fake *27* vortäuschen; *99* fälschen
false teeth *69* Zahnprothese
fare *70* Fahrpreis
fashionable *99* in Mode
fast paced *124* temporeich
fatal *79* tödlich, fatal
fault *78* Schuld, Verschulden; **partial ~** *79* Teilschuld; **be at ~** *82* Schuld haben; **own-~** *85* selbst verschuldet
faulty *81T* fehlerhaft, defekt
favour: ~ sth *62* sich für etw aussprechen; **find in ~ of sb** *89* zu jds Gunsten urteilen
favourable for *120* günstig für, vorteilhaft für
fear *108* Angst, Furcht

feature *31* Merkmal, Eigenschaft
fence *34T* Zaun
fender *88* Kotflügel *(AE)*
fidelity insurance *101* Vertrauensschadenversicherung
fierce *16 (Wettbewerb)* hart
figure *7* Zahl, Ziffer
final exam *98* Abschlussprüfung
Finance Director *100* Finanzvorstand
financial: ~ crisis *95* Finanzkrise; **~ services** *6* Finanzdienstleistungen; **~ Services Authority (FSA)** *61 brit. Aufsichtsbehörde für Finanzdienstleistungen*
find in favour of sb *89* zu jds Gunsten urteilen
findings *104* Ergebnis(se)
fine *92* Geldbuße, Geldstrafe
fire: ~ alarm *104T* Feuermelder; **~ away.** *50T* Schießen Sie los!; **~ brigade** *38* Feuerwehr; **~ hazard** *104* Brandgefahr, Feuerrisiko; **~ insurance** *6* Feuerversicherung
first-time(r) *85* Anfänger/in
fit *39* einbauen
fitted *37* eingebaut
fittings *34T* (sanitäre) Installationen
fix *105* (Termin) ausmachen
fixed *31* fest
fixture *34* eingebautes Inventar, dauerhafte Ausstattung
flat, owner-occupied ~ *33* Eigentumswohnung *(BE)*
fleet *104T* Fahrzeugflotte, -park
flood *31* Überschwemmung
flooding *31* Überschwemmung
flow chart *26* Flussdiagramm
fluent *125 (Sprache)* fließend
focus *26* Mittelpunkt
folder *47* Mappe
fond, be ~ of sth *111* etw mögen
font size *26* Schriftgröße
foodstuffs *101* Nahrungsmittel
force *65T* zwingen; 96T erzwingen
forecast *98T* vorhersagen, voraussagen
forefinger *58* Zeigefinger
forehead *75* Stirn
foreseeable *79* vorhersehbar
forklift truck *102* Gabelstapler
former *33* ehemalige/r/s
fortuitous *79* zufällig
fortuity *79* Zufall
fortune *86* Vermögen
found *6* gründen
founder *6* Gründer/in
four-wheel drive *84* Vierradantrieb
fracture *55* (sich etw) brechen
Frankonian *109* fränkisch
fraud *15* Betrug
fraudulent *27* betrügerisch
frayed *79* abgewetzt, zerschlissen
free of charge *34T* kostenlos, gebührenfrei, gratis
freebie *61* Werbegeschenk
frequency *71* Häufigkeit
from ... onwards *22* von ... an
front end *88T (Auto)* Front
funds *116* Gelder, Geldmittel
funeral *40* Trauerfeier
fur coat *79* Pelzmantel
further *124* fördern
furthermore *51* außerdem, darüber hinaus

G

gain *13* erwerben
garage *83* (Kfz-)Werkstatt
gardening tool *32* Gartengerät
gas cylinder *72* Gasflasche
gate *34T* Tor, Tür
general practitioner *69* Allgemeinarzt/-ärztin, Hausarzt/-ärztin
generic term *17* Gattungsbegriff, Oberbegriff
gesture *26* Geste
get: ~ caught *27* erwischt werden; **~ down to business** *102* zur Sache kommen; **~ overdrawn** *90* das Konto überziehen; **~ to know** *9T* kennen lernen
give away *61* verschenken
glasses *69* Brille
goal *96T* Ziel
goldsmith *99* Goldschmied/in
government: ~ bond *98* Staatsschuldverschreibung; **~ paper** *95* staatliches Wertpapier
grade *126* Note
gradual *101* allmählich
graduate *12* einen Abschluss machen
grammar school *128* Gymnasium
grant *34T* gewähren, einräumen
graph *22* Diagramm
groceries *56* Lebensmittel
gross *69P* brutto, Brutto-; **~ negligence** *78* grobe Fahrlässigkeit
growth *22* Wachstum; **~ rate** *22* Wachstumsrate
grumble *89* murren, meckern
guarantee *43* garantieren; 63 Garantie
guide *89* Ratgeber
guidelines *101* Richtlinien

H

hail *82* Hagel
hand: on the one ~ *25T* einerseits; **on the other ~** *25T* andererseits; **~ in** *68* einreichen
handy *34T* praktisch
hardworking *124* fleißig
hardly *73* kaum
harm *74* Schaden
hassle *73* Schwierigkeiten, Ärger
hatchback *84* Schrägheck, Fließheck
hazardous *60* gefährlich, riskant
head *9* Leiter/in, Chef/in; **~ office** *6* Zentrale
headache *96T* Kopfschmerz(en)
headlight *88* Scheinwerfer
headquarters *7* Zentrale
health: ~ care *62* Gesundheitswesen; **~ insurance** *7* Krankenversicherung; **state of ~** *16* Gesundheitszustand
healthy *50T* gesund
hearing *56* Gehör
heel *55* Ferse
hesitate *28* zögern
hidden *27* verborgen
high-performance *85T* leistungsstark
high-profile *27* in der Öffentlichkeit stehend
hip *55* Hüfte
hire sb *17* jdn einstellen; *34T* jdn engagieren
hit *55* stoßen, schlagen
Hold the line. *34T* Bleiben Sie am Apparat.
home contents *31* Hausrat
homeowner *27* Hausbesitzer/in
honest *27* ehrlich; **to be ~** *40* ehrlich gesagt
honesty *18* Ehrlichkeit
hood *88* Motohaube *(AE)*
hospital daily benefit *56* Krankenhaustagegeld
hospitality *11* Gastfreundschaft
housekeeper *56* Haushälterin
hub-cap *88* Radkappe
human *72* menschlich; **~ resources** *9T* Personal-(abteilung)
hyphen *29* Bindestrich

I

idea *30* Gedanke
identify yourself *35* sich zu erkennen geben
ignorance *72* Unwissenheit
ignore *88* ignorieren
imagine *12* sich vorstellen, annehmen, glauben
immediate *51* sofort zahlbar
immediately *49* sofort, unmittelbar
impairment *59* Beeinträchtigung
implant *69* Implantat
implication *85T* Konsequenz, Auswirkung
impression *49* Eindruck
improve *14* verbessern
improvement *104T* Verbesserung
incident *73* Vorfall; **account of the ~** *73* Schilderung des Vorfalls
include *14* einschließen, umfassen
income *7* Einkommen
in-company *54* betriebsintern
increase *17* steigen, zunehmen; *31* Steigerung; *32* erhöhen
increased *25T* gesteigert, vermehrt
incur *70 (Kosten)* haben, anfallen
indemnification *78* Entschädigung
indemnify *78* entschädigen
indemnity *7* Entschädigung; **~ insurance** *7* Schadenversicherung; **~ period** *103* Haftungszeitraum; **professional ~ insurance** *81T*

Berufshaftpflichtversicherung
independent *7* unabhängig
indicate *24* zeigen, hindeuten auf
indicator *88* Blinker
individual *12* Einzelperson
industry *14* Branche
inevitable *108T* unvermeidlich
inflate *27* aufblähen
influence *19* beeinflussen
influenza *65* Grippe
inform *29* informieren
information desk *91* Informationsschalter
inheritance *40* Erbe
initial *43* erste/r/s, anfänglich
injure *31* (sich) verletzen
injured party *73* Geschädigte/r
injury *27* Verletzung; **personal ~** *89* Verletzung
innocent *27* unschuldig
in-patient *64* stationäre/r Patient/in; **~ treatment** *63* stationäre Behandlung
insight *9T* Einblick
insist on *40* bestehen auf
insolvency *101* Insolvenz
install *39* installieren
instalment *96T* Rate
instance, for ~ *73* zum Beispiel
instant access *94* Sofortzugang
insurance *6* Versicherung; **~ category** *85* Versicherungsklasse; **~ fraud** *15* Versicherungsbetrug; **business interruption ~** *101* Betriebsunterbrechungsversicherung; **contents ~** *19* Hausratversicherung; **endowment ~** *42* kapitalbildende Lebensversicherung, auch gemischte Versicherung; **environmental impairment ~** *81T* Umwelthaftpflichtversicherung; **fidelity ~** *101* Vertrauensschadenversicherung; **fire ~** *6* Feuerversicherung; **health ~** *7* Krankenversicherung; **life ~** *6* Lebensversicherung; **motor ~** *7* Kfz-Versicherung; **professional indemnity ~** *81T* Berufshaftpflichtversicherung; **term life ~** *17* Risikolebensversicherung; **under~** *107* Unterversicherung; **take out ~** *34T* einer Versicherung abschließen
insured *17* Versichterte/r; **over-~** *28* überversichert; **under-~** *28* unterversichert
insurer *6* Versicherer
intend *69* beabsichtigen, vorhaben
intended for *43* gedacht für, dazu gedacht
intention *78* Absicht; **direct ~** *78* Vorsatz; **qualified ~** *78* bedingter Vorsatz
intentional *27* absichtlich
interest *44T* Zinsen
interference *62T* Einmischung
intermediary *17* Mittelsmann
interrupt *24* unterbrechen
intervene *89* eingreifen
introduce *9* vorstellen, (miteinander) bekannt machen; *46* einführen
intruder *104T* Eindringling
invent *27* erfinden
invest *43* investieren
investigate *13* untersuchen
investment: ~ Department *15* Abteilung Vermögensanlagen; **~ fund** *12* Investmentfonds; **~ risk** *42* Investitionsrisiko
invisible *12* unsichtbar
invite *6* einladen
involve *13* umfassen, mit sich bringen
involved *72* beteiligt; **be ~ in sth** *12* sich mit etw befassen, mit etw zu tun haben; *61* an etw beteiligt sein
involving *31* mit, unter Beteiligung von
irreversible *99* unumkehrbar
issue *65T* Frage, Problem; 68 *(Dokument, usw.)* ausstellen
item *67* *(Liste)* Punkt

J

jargon *25T* Jargon, Fachchinesisch
jewellery *31* Schmuck
jobseeker *122* Arbeitssuchende/r
joined to *33* verbunden mit
journey *10* Reise, Fahrt
jump *55* Sprung

K

keep: ~ sth up *96T* etw aufrechterhalten; **~ a record** *129T* aufzeichnen, dokumentieren
key man *101* Schlüsselfigur
kidnap *101* entführen
kidney *65T* Niere
knee *55* Knie
know, get to ~ *9T* kennen lernen
knowledge, to the best of your ~ *28* nach bestem Wissen

L

lack *61* Mangel, Nichtvorhandensein; **~ of imagination** *72* Phantasielosigkeit
landline *34* Festnetz
landlord *33* Vermieter
last *65* dauern
later on *9* später, nachher
law *32* Gesetz
lawn mower *31* Rasenmäher
lawyer *81T* (Rechts-)Anwalt/Anwältin
lay off *112* abgeben
lead *79* Kabel
leading *6* führend
leaflet *91* Prospekt, Broschüre
leak *32* *(Wasser)* austreten
leave sb alone *20* jdn in Ruhe lassen
left (over) *10* übrig
legal *27* rechtlich, gesetzlich; **~ assistance** *70* Rechtsbeistand; **~ Department** *15* Rechtsabteilung; **legal liability** *31* gesetzliche Haftpflicht; **~ly liable** *70* gesetzlich haftbar
leisure *52* Freizeit
lend *41* leihen
lender *96T* Kreditgeber
level *33* Etage, Geschoss; *43* Höhe; **~ term** *43* mit gleichbleibender Versicherungssumme
liability: ~ insurance *6* Haftpflichtversicherung; **legal ~** *31* gesetzliche Haftpflicht; **motor third party ~** *81T* Kfz-Haftpflicht; **product ~** *81T* Produkthaftpflicht; **public ~** *81T* Betriebshaftpflicht
liable: legally ~ *70* gesetzlich haftbar; **be ~ to sth** *41* mit etw (einer Steuer) belegt werden können; **be made ~** *80* haftbar gemacht werden, in Haftung genommen werden
license *83* zulassen
life: ~ expectancy *62* Lebenserwartung; **~ insurance** *6* Lebensversicherung; **term ~ insurance** *17* Risikolebensversicherung
liftback *84* Schrägheck, Fließheck
lightning *31* Blitzschlag
likely *65T* wahrscheinlich
limb *58* Gliedmaß
limit *26* beschränken, begrenzen; *30* Obergrenze, Limit
limitation *61* Beschränkung, Grenze
limousine *84* Limousine
line *116* Selbstbehalt; **~ manager** *68* Vorgesetzte/r, Abteilungsleiter/in
linen *31* Bettwäsche
litigation *89* Gerichtsverfahren, Rechtsstreitigkeiten
little white lies *27* Notlügen
load *72* Ladung
loading *115* (Prämien-)Zuschlag
loan *41* Kredit, Darlehen; **secured loan** *96T* Abgesichertes Darlehen; **take out a ~** *96T* einen Kredit aufnehmen
local: ~ office *8* Bezirksdirektion; **~ proximity** *18* räumliche Nähe
located, be ~ in *8* seinen Sitz haben in
location *88T* Ort, Schauplatz
lock up *76* abschließen
long-term *43* langfristig, Langzeit-
look: ~ closely *118* genau hinsehen; **~ forward to** *28* sich freuen auf; **~ into sth** *104T* sich um etw kümmern
loss *13* Verlust; **~ adjuster** *14* Schadensachverständige/r, Gutachter/in; **~ of earnings** *27* Verdienstausfall; **~ of life** *72* Todesopfer; **~ severity** *114* Schadengrad
lower *27* senken
lump sum *42* Pauschalbetrag

M

machinery *60* Maschinen
maintain *39* warten, unterhalten
majority *8* Mehrheit
make: ~ up *60* sich ausdenken; **~ up for**

27 ausgleichen, wiedergutmachen; **~ sure** *60* sicherstellen, sich vergewissern
male *44* männlich
malicious *31* mutwillig
manage *12* es schaffen
Managing Director *9* Geschäftsführer/in
manners *129T* Manieren
manual work *60* körperliche Arbeit, Handarbeit
manufacturer *81T* Hersteller
marginal *117* gering(fügig), unwesentlich
marine insurance *6* Transportversicherung
market: ~ cycle *110* Marktzyklus; **~ share** *51* Marktanteil; **~ value** *107* Marktwert
marten *83* Marder
Mathematical Department *15* Mathematische Abteilung
matter *63* Sache, Angelegenheit
maturity *95* Fälligkeit
means of payment *92* Zahlungsmittel
meant, be ~ to *26* dazu dienen
meantime, in the ~ *42* in der Zwischenzeit
measure *39* Maßnahme
medical: ~ complaints *50T* gesundheitliche Beschwerden; **~ report** *45T* ärztliches Attest
medication *50T* Medikamente
medicine *63* Medizin
member of staff *9* Mitarbeiter/in
membership fee *92* Mitgliedsbeitrag
mentally ill *79* geisteskrank
mention *13* erwähnen, nennen
merchant *99* Kaufmann
merge *6* fusionieren
message *26* Botschaft
method of payment *13* Zahlungsweise
mille, per ~ *79* Promille
mind *10* etwas dagegen haben
misleading *63* irreführend, missverständlich
miss *58* vermissen
monetary *121* monetär
money market *94* Finanzmarkt
monotonous *14* monoton
moral hazard *71* subjektives Risiko
mortgage *12* Hypothek
motor: ~ insurance *7* Kfz-Versicherung; **~ third party liability** *81T* Kfz-Haftpflicht
motorhome *84* Wohnmobil
motoring *86* Autofahren
motorist *85* Autofahrer/in
mountaineering *61* Bergsteigen
move *6* verlegen
MPV (multi-purpose vehicle) *84* Minivan *(AE)*
multi-car bonus *85T* Rabatt für mehrere Fahrzeuge, Mehrvertragsrabatt
mutual insurance company *6* Versicherungsverein auf Gegenseitigkeit (VVaG)

N

national: ~ Health Service (NHS) *63 staatlicher Gesundheitsdienst Großbritanniens*; **~ Savings account** *95* staatliches Einlagenkonto *(vergleichbar mit Bundeswertpapieren)*
nationwide *39* landesweit
naturopath *69* Naturheilkundler/in
naturopathy *69* Naturheilkunde
necessary *12* nötig
neck *55* Hals
needs *12* Bedarf, Bedürnisse
negligence *72* Fahrlässigkeit; **gross ~** *78* grobe Fahrlässigkeit
negligible *22* vernachlässigbar
negotiate *16* verhandeln
(claims) negotiator *124* Schaden(s) regulierer/in
neighbourhood *39* Nachbarschaft
net *69P* netto, Netto-
newly-qualified *85T* frisch qualifiziert
no claim(s) discount *82* Schadenfreiheitsrabatt
non-existent *27* nicht existierend
non-proportional reinsurance *115* nichtproportionale Rückversicherung
not applicable *18* nicht zutreffend
notice *81T* Hinweisschild; *94* Mitteilung, Ankündigung; **~ account** *94* Festgeld-, Termingeldkonto
nurse *44T* Krankenschwester/ -pfleger
nursery school *53* Kindergarten, Kindertagesstätte

O

objection *73* Einwand, (Gegen-) Argument
objective *24* Ziel, Zweck
obligatory *121* obligatorisch
obtain *17* erzielen, erlangen, erhalten
occasional(ly) *82* gelegentlich
occupation *46* Beruf, Beschäftigung
occupational *43* beruflich, berufsbedingt
occupier *31* Bewohner/in
occur *27 (Tatbestand)* vorliegen, *(Fall)* eintreten; *32* geschehen
offer *21* Angebot
office clerk *60* Büroangestellte/r
officer *101* leitende/r Angestellte/r
off-road vehicle *84* Geländewagen
OHP transparency *26* Overheadfolie
one-off payment *90* Einmalzahlung
onwards, from ... ~ *22* von ... an
operate *8* betreiben, unterhalten, operieren, geschäftlich tätig sein; *53* bedienen, arbeiten mit
operations *7* Geschäftsbereiche, -felder
ophthalmic surgeon *59* Augenarzt/ -ärztin, Augenchirurg/in
opinion *26* Meinung, Ansicht
opposite party *89* Gegenpartei
opt: ~ out of sth *63* aus etw aussteigen
optician *69* Optiker/in
oral *125* mündlich
order *49* Reihenfolge; *74* anordnen, befehlen; **in ~ to** *28* um ... zu
organized crime *27* organisiertes Verbrechen
oriented *20* orientiert
osteoporosis *65* Osteoporose
out of date *63* veraltet, überholt
outbuilding *31* Nebengebäude, Anbau
outcome *99* Ergebnis
outlet *17* Verkaufsstelle
outline *100* (grob) beschreiben; Übersicht
output *108T* Produktion
outside circumstances *89* äußere Umstände
overall *18* insgesamt
overdraft facility *96T* Dispositionskredit
overdrawn *90* (Konto) überzogen; **get ~** *90* das Konto überziehen
overdue *80* überfällig
overhear *79* (zufällig) hören
over-insured *28* überversichert
overlap *81T* sich überschneiden
overspend *90 (Etat, usw.)* überziehen
overtake *88* überholen
owe *96T* schulden
own *8* besitzen; **be ~ed by sb** *8* jdm gehören; **on one's ~** *11* allein; **~-fault** *85* selbst verschuldet
owner-occupied flat *33* Eigentumswohnung *(BE)*

P

pace *26* Geschwindigkeit, Tempo
package *61* im Paket anbieten
pad *27 (Rechnung, usw.)* fälschen
painful *59* schmerzhaft
pan *55* Pfanne
panel *28* Liste
parachuting *61* Fallschirmspringen
paralyse *55* lähmen
parent company *6* Muttergesellschaft
part, take ~ in *9* teilnehmen an
partial: ~ cover *82* Teilkaskoversicherung; **~ fault** *79* Teilschuld
participant *64* Teilnehmer/in
particular *34T* bestimmte/r/s, spezielle/r/s, besondere/r/s; **in ~** *9* insbesondere
partner *101* Gesellschafter/in
partnership *101* Personengesellschaft
part-time *17* Teilzeit
party *72* Partei
pass: ~ (a law) *63 (ein Gesetz)* verabschieden; **~ (a test)** *85 (einen Test)* bestehen; **~ sth on** *27* weiterreichen, weitergeben
passenger *27* Mitfahrer/in, Beifahrer/in
patio *37* Terrasse
pavement *72* Gehsteig
pay *34T* sich auszahlen; **~ out** *39* auszahlen

payable *43* zahlbar
payment *13* Zahlung
payout *51* Auszahlung
penalty fee *94* Strafgebühr
penetration rate *72 hier:* Marktdurchdringung
pension *27* Rente; **~ funds** *51* Rentenfonds; **state ~** *41* staatliche Pensionskasse, gesetzliche Rente
pensioner *40* Rentner/in
people carrier *84* Minivan *(BE)*
per mille *79* Promille
percentage *15* (prozentualer) Anteil, Prozentsatz; **annual ~** rate (APR) *96T* effektiver Jahreszins
perception *18* Wahrnehmung
peril *30* Gefahr, Risiko
perimeter fence *104T* Begrenzungszaun, Einzäunung
period of payment *50T* Zahlungszeitraum
permanent *34* dauerhaft; *124 (Arbeit)* unbefristet
permit *65T* zulassen
persist *98T* anhalten, fortbestehen
personal *12* privat, persönlich; **~ injury** *89* Verletzung
personalized *20* persönlich zugeschnitten
Personnel Department *15* Personalabteilung
persuade *108* überzeugen
petrol *86* Benzin
phase sth out *99* etw auslaufen lassen
phenomenon *98T* Phänomen
physical well-being *71* leibliches Wohl(ergehen)
pick-up *84* Pritschenwagen
pick up the tab *89* für die Kosten aufkommen
pie chart *21* Tortendiagramm
piped water *106* Wasserleitung
pirate *101* Pirat
pitch *26* Tonhöhe, Tonlage
plant *100* Fabrik
plastic surgery *56* kosmetische Operationen, plastische Chirurgie
play for time *118* Zeit gewinnen, auf Zeit spielen
pleasant *10* angenehm
pleasure *9* Vergnügen, Freude
plumber *60* Klempner/in
point: ~ of view *26* Standpunkt, Perspektive, Sicht; **to the ~** *30* treffend, sachbezogen; **~ out** *26* deuten auf, hinweisen auf; *61* darauf hinweisen
poison *101* vergiften
police station *88T* Polizeiwache
policy *7* Police; **~ administration department** *68* Policenverwaltung(sabteilung); **stand-alone ~** *61* unabhängige Police, selbstständige Police
policyholder *6* Versicherungsnehmer/in
polite *34* höflich
pollution *101* Umweltverschmutzung
population *65T* Bevölkerung
portability *65T* Portabilität
portion *31* Teil
postcode *34* Postleitzahl
postpone *105 (Termin)* verlegen
potential *17* potenziell
power cut *38* Stromausfall
predict *99* vorhersagen, voraussagen
prefer *9* vorziehen
preferred *50T* bevorzugt
pregnant *40* schwanger
premature *43* vorzeitig
premium *7* Prämie
preparation *106* Vorbereitung
prepared, be ~ to *39* bereit sein
prescription *66* (ärztliches) Rezept
present *11* vorstellen, präsentieren; *108T* gegenwärtig, aktuell
pressure *62* Druck
prevent *53* verhüten, verhindern
prevention *53* Prävention
previous *19* vorherig
price *112 (Preis, usw.)* festlegen, ansetzen
price-sensitive *20* preisbewusst
principle *32* Prinzip
prior *94* vorherig
priority *20* Priorität
pro rata *107* anteilig
procedure *28* Verfahren, Vorgehen
process *72* Verfahren, Ablauf
product: ~ liability *81T* Produkthaftpflicht; **~ tamper** *101* Produktmanipulation
Production Manager *102* Produktionsleiter/in
profession *81T* Beruf, Berufsgruppe
professional: ~ indemnity insurance *81T* Berufshaftfplichtversicherung; **~ training** *12* Berufsausbildung
profile *6* Porträt, Profil
profit *15* Gewinn, Profit
promising *9T* vielversprechend
promote sth *15* etw bewerben; *99* etw fördern, für etw sein
prompt *30* Stichwort; **~ card** *26* Moderationskarte
prone, be ~ to sth *62T* zu etw neigen, für etw anfällig sein
pronunciation *26* Aussprache
proper *61* richtig
property *27* Eigentum; *44T* Immobilie(n); **~ damage** *72* Sachschaden; **~ owner** *81T* Grundbesitzer/in
proportion *17* Anteil
proportional reinsurance *120* proportionale Rückversicherung
proposal form *14* Antrag(s)formular
propose *102* vorschlagen, vorlegen
proposer *14* Antragsteller/in
pros and cons *61* Für und Wider
prosecutor *27* Strafverfolger/in
protect *31* schützen
protected *82 hier:* garantiert
proven *59* erwiesen
provide *6* bieten, anbieten; *12* liefern, sorgen für
provided that *121* vorausgesetzt dass; unter der Voraussetzung, dass
provider *6* Anbieter
proxy *99* Vertretung
public *6* Öffentlichkeit; **~ liability** *81T* Betriebshaftpflicht; **~ limited company (plc)** *6* Aktiengesellschaft (AG)
pudding, The proof of the ~ is in the eating. *104T* Probieren (geht) über Studieren.
purchase *17* kaufen; 91 Kauf, Erwerb
pure *65T* rein
purpose *24* Zweck, Absicht
pursue *125* verfolgen
put *31* formulieren; **~ away** *44 (Geld)* sparen, ansparen; **~ sb through** *34T (Telefon)* jdn durchstellen; **~ money aside** *91* Geld (an)sparen

Q
qualification *12* Abschluss
qualified *12* qualifiziert; **~ intention** *78* bedingter Vorsatz
qualify *124* den Abschluss machen
quarterly *43* vierteljährlich
query *76* Anfrage
question of principle *65T* Grundsatzfrage
questionnaire *11* Fragebogen
queue *61* (Warte-)Schlange
quota share *120* Quote
quotation *16* Angebot, Kostenvoranschlag
quote *12* Angebot, Kostenvoranschlag; **~ sb for sth** *46* jdm ein Angebot für etw machen

R
rack *91* Regal, Ständer
raise *63* (Tarif, usw.) anheben; **be ~d** *128* aufwachsen
random sample *106* Stichprobe
range *7* Angebot, Palette; *90* Reihe, Auswahl; *122* Spielraum
rank (second) *19* den (zweiten) Platz belegen
ransom *101* Lösegeld zahlen, jdn freikaufen
rare *122* selten
rate *90* (Prämien-, Zins-)Satz; *112* Prämie
rather *10* ziemlich
ratio *61* Verhältnis
raw materials *102* Rohstoffe, Rohmaterial
reach *35* erreichen
rearrange *105 (Termin)* verlegen
rear-view mirror *88* Rückspiegel
reason *14* Grund

reasonable 45T vernünftig
rebuilding 34T Wiederaufbau
recall 103 zurückrufen
receive 18 erhalten, bekommen
recent 89 neueste/r/s; ~ly 62 in letzter Zeit
reception 9 Empfang, Rezeption
recipient 29 Empfänger/in
reciprocal 69P gegenseitig
recklessness 78 grobe Fahrlässigkeit
reckon with 78 rechnen mit
recommend 34T empfehlen
recommendation 108T Empfehlung
record, keep a ~ 129T aufzeichnen, dokumentieren
recover 86 zurückbekommen, wiedererlangen
recovery 59 Genesung
recruit 122 (Personal) einstellen
reduce 31 reduzieren
reduction 32 Abzug
redundant, be made ~ 70 den Arbeitsplatz verlieren
refer to sth 41 von etw sprechen, auf etw verweisen
referee 126 Referenz (Person)
reference 48 (Brief) Zeichen
refuse 16 sich weigern
regard 43 betrachten
regarding 30 betreffend, bezüglich
regardless of 43 ungeachtet, egal
regional office 8 Landesdirektion
register 30 Ton
registration 85T Anmeldung
regulator 61 Regulierungsbehörde
reimburse 66 erstatten
reimbursement 66 Erstattung
reinforce 26 verstärken
reinstatement, on a ~ basis 102 zum Neuwert
reinsurance 112 Rückversicherung; non-proportional ~ 115 nichtproportionale Rückversicherung; proportional ~ 120 proportionale Rückversicherung
reinsure 112 rückversichern
reinsurer 112 Rückversicherer
reject 14 ablehnen
relation 108T Beziehung
relationship 20 Beziehung, Verhältnis
relative 44T Verwandte/r
release 101 freilassen
relevant 25T relevant, wichtig
reliable 19 zuverlässig
reliant on 41 angewiesen auf, abhängig von
relieve sb of sth 65T jdm etw abnehmen
rely on 65T angewiesen sein auf
remain 22 bleiben
remaining 17 verbleibend, übrig
remark 49 Bemerkung
remove 31 entfernen
renegotiate 115 neu verhandeln
renew 102 verlängern
renewal 43 Verlängerung
renovate 44T renovieren
rent 28 mieten; 56 Miete
repair 31 reparieren
repayment 44 Rückzahlung, Ratenzahlung
repeat 35 wiederholen
repetition 74 Wiederholung
replace 31 ersetzen
replacement 31 Ersatz; ~ cost 28 Wiederbeschaffungskosten; ~ value 86 Wiederbeschaffungswert
report 19 anzeigen; 88T melden; ~ to sb 8 jdm unterstehen
represent 17 vertreten, repräsentieren
reputation 39 Ruf
request: ~ sth 28 um etw bitten, etw anfordern; on ~ 125 auf Anfrage
require 19 verlangen, vorschreiben
requirement 25T Wunsch, Anforderung
rescue 56 Rettung; ~ operations 56 Rettungsmaßnahmen
research 39 Nachforschungen, Recherche; 89 Untersuchungen
resident 66 Bewohner/in, Einwohner/in
residential area 34T Wohngegend
resolve 124 lösen
resources 53 Mittel, Ressourcen
respective 117 entsprechend
respond 104T reagieren, antworten
response 11 Reaktion, Antwort
responsibility 40 Verantwortung, Verantwortlichkeit
responsible 12 zuständig, verantwortlich; 19 verantwortungsbewusst
restoration work 38 Reparaturarbeiten
restore 52 wiederherstellen
restrict 65 beschränken, einschränken
restriction 43 Einschränkung
result 18 Ergebnis
retail 28 Einzelhandel
retailer 17 (Einzel-)Händler
retain 120 behalten, einbehalten
retention 106 Selbstbehalt
retire 61 in den Ruhestand treten
retirement 40 Ruhestand; early ~ 44 Vorruhestand
return 28 zurückschicken; 95 Ertrag
revenue 15 Einkünfte, Einnahmen
reverse 110 umkehren; 126 umgekehrt
review 14 prüfen, überprüfen; 61 Bericht; 99 Überprüfung, Testphase
rider 42 Zusatzversicherung
ridiculous 65T lächerlich
right of way 88 Vorfahrt
rights and duties 14 Rechte und Pflichten
risk 27 Risiko; ~ excess of loss 115 Einzelschadenexzedent; ~ of random loss 112 Zufallsrisiko
roadster 84 Sportwagen
rock climbing 61 Felsklettern
rough 34T ungefähr, grob; take the ~ with the smooth 104T etw nehmen, wie es kommt
row 33 Reihe
ruin 19 zerstören; 108 ruinieren; 100 Zusammenbruch
rule 32 Vorschrift, Bestimmung, Regel
RV (recreational vehicle) 84 Wohnmobil

S

safety-conscious 95 auf Sicherheit bedacht
sake, for the ~ of simplicity 114T der Einfachheit halber
salary 44T Lohn, Gehalt
sales 16 Vertrieb; 22 Umsatz; ~ and Marketing Department 15 Marketing und Vertrieb
saloon 84 Limousine (BE)
salutation 29 (Brief) Anrede
satisfied 18 zufrieden
satisfying 14 befriedigend, erfüllend
savings 42 Ersparnisse; ~ account 90 Sparkonto
saw 53 Säge
Saxonian 6 sächsisch
scald 55 (sich) verbrühen
scar 56 Narbe
scene of an accident 56 Unfallort
scheme 39 Plan, Projekt
scooter 85 Motorroller
scope 100 Umfang
scratch 88 Kratzer
screen sb 129T jdn überprüfen
seat, take a ~ 9T Platz nehmen
section 89 Abschnitt
secure 42 sichern
secured loan 96T abgesichertes Darlehen
securities 95 Wertpapiere
security 39 Sicherheit
sedan 84 Limousine (AE)
sedentary 60 sitzend
seek 20 suchen
seep 101 sickern
segment 24 Segment
select 43 wählen, auswählen
self-employed 40 selbstständig
semi-detached house 33 Doppelhaushälfte
sender 29 Absender/in
senior 9 vorgesetzt, ranghöher
sense, make ~ 82 sinnvoll sein
separation 58 Trennung, Abtrennung
serve 7 versorgen; 8 dienen
services 27 Dienstleistungen
set up 13 gründen; 64 einrichten
settle (a claim) 13 (Schaden) regulieren
settlement (of claims) 13 (Schaden-)Regulierung
several 6 einige, mehrere
severity 27 Schwere; loss ~ 114 Schadengrad
share 6 Aktie, Anteil
sharp 22 drastisch, rapide
shed 31 Schuppen

shelf, off the ~ *100* von der Stange, Standard-
shin *55* Schienbein
shop around for *20* sich umsehen nach
shop assistant *40* Verkäufer/in
shorten *71* kürzen
short-term *62T* Kurzzeit-, befristet
shrink *65T* schrumpfen
sickness *44* Krankheit; **~ benefit** *69* Krankengeld
sight *9T* Sehenswürdigkeit; *58* Sehvermögen
signature *30* Unterschrift
significant *22* bedeutend, signifikant, erheblich
similarity *81T* Ähnlichkeit
single parent *54* Alleinerziehende/r
site plan *104* Lageplan
skid *88* schlittern
skills *12* Fähigkeiten, Fertigkeiten, Kenntnisse
slash *29* Schrägstrich
slight *22* leicht, gering
slightly *19* ein bisschen, etwas
slip *81* ausrutschen
slippery *88* rutschig, glatt
slow down *22* (sich) verlangsamen
smoke alarm *39* Rauchmelder
soar *89* *(Kosten)* in die Höhe schießen
social security *69P* Sozialversicherung
solicitor *75* (Rechts-)Anwalt/Anwältin
solution *12* Lösung
sort code *92* Bankleitzahl
sound *9T* klingen
speak up *35* lauter sprechen
specify *31* (genau) angeben, spezifizieren
speculative spekulativ
spill *38* verschütten
sponsoring company *12* Ausbildungsbetrieb
spouse *50T* Gatte/Gattin
sprain *55* verstauchen
spread *23* Verteilung; *96T* Überziehungsprovision, -zins; *96T* verteilen
spring up *17* aus dem Boden schießen
stable *22* stabil
staff *9* Personal, Mitarbeiter; **member of ~** *9* Mitarbeiter/ -in
stage *24* Abschnitt; *27* inszenieren
staircase *81* Treppe
stake *8* Anteil, Beteiligung
stand-alone policy *61* unabhängige Police, selbstständige Police
standing order *90* Dauerauftrag
state *48* angeben, sagen, erklären; *62* Staat, staatlich; **~ of health** *16* Gesundheitszustand; **~ pension** *41* staatliche Pensionskasse, gesetzliche Rente
(bank) statement *91* Kontoauszug
station wagon *84* Kombi *(AE)*
statistics *15* Statistik
statutory *52* gesetzlich (vorgeschrieben)
stay *9* bleiben; wohnen, übernachten; *9T* Aufenthalt
stead, stand sb in good ~ *124* jdm gute Dienste leisten
steady *61* stabil; *104T* stetig, kontinuierlich
steering wheel *88* Lenkrad
step, take ~s *53* Schritte unternehmen, Maßnahmen ergreifen
stock *102* Warenbestand
storage *104T* Lagerung. Vorrats-
storm *102* Sturm, Unwetter
stream *104T* Strom
strict *62* streng, strikt
strike *32* treffen, erschlagen
striking *99* erstaunlich, hervorstechend
stroll *103* Spaziergang
structure *24* strukturieren; *8* Struktur; *34T* Bau(werk), Konstruktion
studio flat *33* Einzimmerwohnung
subject *30* Thema, *(E-Mail)* Betreff; **~ to** *70* abhängig von, je nach; **be ~ to sth** *62T* einer Sache unterliegen
submission *100* Angebot
subsidence *31* Absacken (eines Gebäudes)
subsidiary *8* Tochtergesellschaft
subsidize *65T* subventionieren
subtract *102* abziehen, subtrahieren
success *12* Erfolg
sue *103* verklagen
suffer *27* erleiden, leiden
sufficient(ly) *26* ausreichend, genügend
suggest *61* andeuten; *89* darauf hindeuten
suggestion *54* Vorschlag
suit *54* passen
suitable *19* geeignet, passend; **make ~** *33* *(Haus, usw.)* umbauen
sum *28* Summe; **~ insured/assured** *28* Versicherungs-summe
superior to *69P* besser als
supplier *107* Lieferant, Zulieferer
supply *110* Angebot
support *12* Unterstützung
sure, make ~ *26* sicherstellen, gewährleisten, sich vergewissern
surgeon *69* Chirurg/in
surgery *50T* Operation, chirurgischer Eingriff
surname *9* Nachname
surplus *121* Summenexzedent
survey *18* Umfrage, Befragung
surveyor *88T* Gutachter/in; **chartered ~** *34* Bausachverständige/r
survive *13* überleben
survivor *116* Überlebende/r
suspicious *27* verdächtig
SUV (sports utility vehicle) *84* Geländewagen, -limousine
swerve *72* einen Schlenker machen, ausscheren
swindler *27* Betrüger/in
swing, a case of ~s and roundabouts *110* gehupft wie gesprungen
sympathy *59* Mitgefühl

T

tab, pick up the ~ *89* für die Kosten aufkommen
table *20* Tabelle; **~ etiquette** *129T* Tischmanieren
tabletop *31* Tischplatte
tailor-made *12* maßgeschneidert
take: ~ over *6* übernehmen; **~ out a loan** *96T* einen Kredit aufnehmen; **~ out insurance** *34T* einer Versicherung abschließen; **~ a seat** *9T* Platz nehmen; **~ advantage of** *46* sich etw zunutze machen; **~ care** *14* dafür sorgen; **~ into account** *25T* berücksichtigen; **~ part in** *9* teilnehmen an; **~ steps** *53* Schritte unternehmen, Maßnahmen ergreifen
talk *24* Vortrag
tamper, product ~ *101* Produktmanipulation
target *25* zielen auf
tariff *15* Tarif
task *13* Aufgabe
tax *27* Steuer; **~ benefits** *40* Steuervergünstigungen, -vorteile; **~ break** *51* Steuererleichterung; **~ credit** *90* Steuer(rück)erstattung; **~ deferred** *40* latente Steuer, aufgeschobene Steuer; **~ relief** *65* Steuervergünstigung, -erleichterung, -nachlass; **~-free** *40* steuerfrei
technician *44* Techniker/in
temporary *31* befristet, vorübergehend
tempting *89* verlockend
tend to *42* dazu neigen
tender *100* Ausschreibung
term *40* Laufzeit; **~ account** *90* Festgeldkonto; **~ life insurance** *17* Risikolebensversicherung; **generic ~** *17* Gattungsbegriff, Oberbegriff, **in ~s of ...** *61* was ... angeht, was ... betrifft; **long-~** *43* langfristig, Langzeit-
terminal illness *42* tödliche/unheilbare Krankheit
terminate *57* enden, auslaufen
terms *13* Bedingungen, Konditionen; **~ and conditions** *47* Allgemeine Geschäftsbedingungen
terraced house *33* Reihenhaus
text message *99* SMS
theoretical *12* theoretisch
thigh *55* Oberschenkel
thoughtlessness *79* Nachlässigkeit, Unaufmerksamkeit
threat *101* Gefahr, Bedrohung
thumb *53* Daumen
tick *50T* ankreuzen, mit einem Häkchen versehen
tied agent *7* Einfirmenvertreter/in
tied up *54* beschäftigt
tight *45T* eng, knapp

till *91* Schalter
time: on ~ *10* pünktlich; **play for ~** *118* Zeit gewinnen, auf Zeit spielen; **~ switch** *39* Zeitschalter
tire *88* Reifen *(AE)*
toes *55* Zehen
tool *60* Werkzeug
top-up: ~ benefit *62* Zusatzleistung; **~ cover** *62T* Zusatzdeckung
tough *12* *(Wettbewerb)* hart
toughness *124* Hartnäckigkeit, Zähigkeit
tow *83* ziehen, (ab)schleppen
trade fair *9* (Handels-)Messe
traffic *10* Verkehr
trailer *82* Anhänger
trainee *9* Auszubildende/r, Trainee
traineeship *12* Ausbildung
transaction *93* (Geschäfts-)Vorgang, Überweisung
transfer *13* überweisen; *63* wechseln
transparency *25* Transparenz
treat *64* behandeln
treatment *52* Behandlung
treaty *115* Vertrag
trim *102* stutzen
trip sb up *81* jdm ein Bein stellen
trouble *9T* Schwierigkeiten, Probleme
trunk *88* Kofferraum *(AE)*
trust *12* vertrauen; *20* Vertrauen
trustworthiness *18* Vertrauenswürdigkeit
turn: ~ down *68* ablehnen; **~ one's back to sb** *26* jdm den Rücken zuwenden; **~ out to be** *6* sich (als etw) erweisen, sich (als etw) herausstellen; **~ to sth** *24* sich einer Sache zuwenden
turnover *100* Umsatz
tyre *88* Reifen *(BE)*

U
unable *56* unfähig; **~ to work** *56* arbeitsunfähig
unbalanced *114* unausgewogen, unausgeglichen
uncertain *12* unsicher; *43* ungewiss
unchallenged, go ~ *99* nicht bestritten werden, nicht angegriffen werden
uncomplicated *18* unkompliziert
undemanding *14* anspruchslos
underinsurance *107* Unterversicherung
under-insured *28* unterversichert
underrated *112* unterbewertet
underscore *29* Unterstrich
underwrite *113* tarifieren, Risiko annehmen
underwriter *14* Versicherer; Risikoprüfer/in, Antragsprüfer/in
underwriting *104* Risikoeinschätzung, Risikoprüfung, Risikoannahme; **~ Department** *15* Antragsabteilung
underwritten *62* gezeichnet
unexpected *32* unerwartet
uninsurable *60* nicht versicherbar, nicht versicherungsfähig
uninterested *20* desinteressiert
unit trust *43* Anlagefond, Investmentfond
unit-linked *42* fondsgebunden
universal *62* allgemein
unless *48* es sei denn, außer (wenn)
unlikely *72* unwahrscheinlich
unprotected *104T* ungeschützt
unsatisfying *14* unbefriedigend
unsuitable *82* ungeeignet
up front *110* offen
urban area *85T* Stadtgebiet, Ballungsraum
use *32* Gebrauch

V
vacant *122* (Stelle) frei
valid *71* gültig
valuable *19* wertvoll; **~s** *31* Wertsachen
valuation *102* Bewertung, Schätzung
value *18* Wert
van *84* Lieferwagen
vandal *38* Vandale
variable costs *101* Betriebskosten
variation *25T* Unterschied, Schwankung
varied *14* abwechslungsreich
various *12* verschieden
varnish *102* Lack
vary *25T* variieren, schwanken; **~ with** *60* sich richten nach
vehicle *31* Fahrzeug; **off-road ~** *84* Geländewagen
veterinary *30* tierärztlich
viable *99* machbar, durchführbar
victim *27* Opfer
victimless *27* ohne Opfer
view *26* Ansicht; *27* sehen, betrachten
violence *27* Gewalt
vision *59* Sehkraft
visitor *10* Gast, Besucher/in
visual aids *26* visuelle Hilfsmittel
visually impaired *69P* sehbehindert
visuals *24* visuelle Hilfsmittel
vocational: ~ qualification *122* Berufsausbildung; **~ school** *12* Berufsschule; **~ training** *57* Berufsausbildung
voice *20* Stimme
volume *26* Lautstärke
voluntary *31* freiwillig
vulnerable *61* verwundbar, anfällig

W
wage *91* Lohn, Gehalt
waist *55* Taille
waive *85T* verzichten auf, *(Gebühren)* erlassen
warehouse *33* Lagerhaus
warning *61* Warnung, Warnhinweis; *80* Mahnung
washbasin *37* Waschbecken
waste: ~ of money *61* Geldverschwendung; **~ of time** *16* Zeitverschwendung
watch *39* Wache
water damage *30* Wasserschaden
weakness *108* Schwäche, Schwachpunkt
wear and tear *31* Abnutzung, Verschleiß
well-off *65T* wohlhabend
wheel *88* Rad
wheelchair *55* Rollstuhl; **confined to a ~** *55* an den Rollstuhl gefesselt
whereas *17* während, dagegen
whether *14* ob
whiplash *27* Schleudertrauma
wide range *12* große Auswahl
widespread *27* verbreitet
widow *44* Witwe
wig *79* Perücke
willing *20* bereit
windscreen *88* Windschutzscheibe *(BE)*
windshield *88* Windschutzscheibe *(AE)*
wing *88* Kotflügel *(BE)*
wipers *88* Scheibenwischer
wiring *108T* Elektrik, Leitungen
wish *28* Wunsch
withdraw *90* *(Geld)* abheben
withdrawal *93* Abhebung
within *7* innerhalb
work out *28* ausrechnen, herausfinden
workman *81T* Arbeiter
workshop *101* Werkstatt
worry *10* sich Sorgen machen; **Don't ~.** *10* Keine Sorge.
worth *85* wert, im Wert von
wrist *55* Handgelenk
wrongful act *101* unrechtmäßige Handlung

X Y
X-ray *55* Röntgenstrahlen, -bild
yield *94* Ertrag, Zinsertrag

Irregular verbs

be – was/were – been	*sein*
beat – beat – beaten	*schlagen, besiegen*
become – became – become	*werden*
begin – began – begun	*anfangen, beginnen*
bleed – bled – bled	*bluten*
break – broke – broken	*brechen*
bring – brought – brought	*bringen*
build – built – built	*bauen*
burn – burnt – burnt	*(ver)brennen*
buy – bought – bought	*kaufen*
catch – caught – caught	*fangen*
choose – chose – chosen	*wählen*
come – came – come	*kommen*
cost – cost – cost	*kosten*
cut – cut – cut	*schneiden*
do – did – done	*tun, machen*
draw – drew – drawn	*zeichnen*
dream – dreamt/dreamed – dreamt/dreamed	*träumen*
drink – drank – drunk	*trinken*
drive – drove – driven	*fahren*
eat – ate – eaten	*essen*
fall – fell – fallen	*fallen*
feed – fed – fed	*füttern, ernähren*
feel – felt – felt	*(sich) fühlen, empfinden*
fight – fought – fought	*kämpfen*
find – found – found	*finden*
fit – fit/fitted – fit/fitted	*passen*
fly – flew – flown	*fliegen*
forget – forgot – forgotten	*vergessen*
freeze – froze – frozen	*frieren*
get – got – got (*AE* gotten)	*bekommen*
give – gave – given	*geben*
go – went – gone	*gehen, fahren*
grow – grew – grown	*wachsen*
hang – hung – hung	*hängen*
have – had – had	*haben*
hear – heard – heard	*hören*
hide – hid – hidden	*(sich) verstecken*
hit – hit – hit	*schlagen*
hold – held – held	*halten, festhalten*
keep – kept – kept	*behalten*
know – knew – known	*kennen, wissen*
lay – laid – laid	*legen*
lean – leant/leaned – leant/leaned	*(sich) lehnen, neigen*
learn – learnt/learned – learnt/learned	*lernen*
leave – left – left	*abfahren, verlassen, weggehen*
let – let – let	*lassen*
lie – lay – lain	*liegen*
light – lit – lit	*anzünden, beleuchten, anmachen*
lose – lost – lost	*verlieren*
make – made – made	*machen*
mean – meant – meant	*meinen, bedeuten*
meet – met – met	*treffen*
pay – paid – paid	*bezahlen*
put – put – put	*setzen, stellen, legen*
quit – quit/quitted – quit/quitted	*verlassen, aufhören*
read – read – read	*lesen*
ride – rode – ridden	*reiten, fahren*
rise – rose – risen	*(an)steigen*
run – ran – run	*laufen, rennen*
say – said – said	*sagen*
see – saw – seen	*sehen*
sell – sold – sold	*verkaufen*
send – sent – sent	*senden, schicken*
set – set – set	*setzen, stellen*
show – showed – shown	*zeigen*
shut – shut – shut	*schließen*
sing – sang – sung	*singen*
sit – sat – sat	*sitzen*
sleep – slept – slept	*schlafen*
smell – smelt/smelled – smelt/smelled	*riechen*
speak – spoke – spoken	*sprechen*
spell – spelt/spelled – spelt/spelled	*buchstabieren*
spend – spent – spent	*ausgeben, verbringen*
stand – stood – stood	*stehen*
steal – stole – stolen	*stehlen*
swim – swam – swum	*schwimmen*
take – took – taken	*nehmen*
teach – taught – taught	*unterrichten, beibringen*
tear – tore – torn	*zerreißen*
tell – told – told	*sagen, erzählen*
think – thought – thought	*denken*
throw – threw – thrown	*werfen*
understand – understood – understood	*verstehen*
wake – woke – woken	*aufwachen/ aufwecken*
wear – wore – worn	*tragen (Kleidung)*
win – won – won	*gewinnen*
write – wrote – written	*schreiben*

Wir danken allen Instituten, Firmen und Personen, die bei der Erstellung dieses Lehrwerks mit Materialien und Informationen behilflich waren.

RF-Fotos:
Corbis: S.90/Rachel Frank;
Istockphoto: S.33/1/2/3/4, S.39/1, S.53, S.68, S.84/2/5/9, S.85/4, S.89, S.92;
Shutterstock: S.11, S.26, S.28, S.33/5/ 6. S.34/2, S.40/2, S.51, S.62, S.82, S.85/3, S.103, S.123.

RM-Fotos:
Alamy: S.34/1/Nikreates, S.37/Nick Turner, S.39/2/Libby Welch, S.41/1/Francis Roberts, S.41/2/Calathea Photo, S.54/I love images, S.64/KablonkRM, S.81/2/Martin Jenkinson, S.84/1/National Motor Museum, S.84/2/EvoxProductions, S.84/4/izmostock, S.84/6/National Motor Museum, S.84/8/National Motor Museum, S.84/10/EvoxProductions, S.84/11/DBURKE, S.84/12/EvoxProductions, S.84/13/National Motor Museum, S.85/2/B.Bachmann, S.85/5/H. Lam, S.94/S.May, S.95/Net Pics, S.96/GlowimagesRM, S.98/GlowimagesRM, S.104/IS356, S.122/2/M.Richardson;
Corbis: S.24/Helen King, S.50/1/Sullivan;
Fotofinder: S.49/Stock4B/Ian Mammey, S.52/Keystone, S.53/2/docStock/M.Rennertz, S.122/F1online/denkou images;
Masterfile: S.6/Westend61, S.12/David Hall, S.19/Westend61, S.40/Masterfile, S.44/MTPA Stock, S.50/2/Masterfile, S.72/Masterfile, S.76/1/Masterfile, S.81/1/Masterfile, S.108/Masterfile, S.112/Masterfile, S.117/Mark Leibowitz, S.118/Masterfile, S.124/Masterfile;
PictureAlliance: S.8/Uwe Gerig, S.73/A.Limbach, S.76/2/Eisner, S.79/Daniel Beltra, S.107/N. MacInnes, S.110/Mousse, S.113/L.Smith;
UllsteinBild: S.71, S.84/7.

Textquellen:
S.39: 'Cutting costs on home insurance' adapted from www.moneysupermarket.com/c/home-insurance/money/saving/tips/;
S.51: : 'Life insurance trends' adapted from *GDV Yearbook 2008*;
S.52/53: 'Statutory accident insurance in Germany' adapted from www.dguv.de/content/about/index.jsp;
S.61: 'Is accident cover just a waste of money?', *The Guardian*, 17 November 2007;
S.70: : 'Axa Travel Insurance', www.axa.co.uk/insurance/travel/policy;
S.82: adapted from www.moneysupermarket.com/car-insurance/guide/2/;
S.89: 'What drives the cost of car insurance?' adapted from www.moneysupermarket.com/car-insurance/guide/3/;
S.90: 'Basic bank accounts in Britain' adapted from www.direct.gov.uk/en/MoneyTaxAndBenefits/ManagingMoney/BankAccountsAndBankingProducts/DG_10035164;
S.94/95: 'Types of savings accounts' adapted from www.moneyinstructor.com/banking.asp;
S.96: 'Der Kredit, der nur Vorteil kennt', www.easycredit.de/vorteile.jsp;
S.99: 'How we will pay in the future', news.bbc.co.uk/1/hi/business/7398327.stm.

KMK exam practice – Textquellen
S. 135: 'How to use comparison sites' abridged from https://www.moneyadviceservice.org.uk/en/articles/how-to-buy-insurance-using-comparison-sites
S. 138: 'Which policy is right for me?', http://www.privatehealth.co.uk/healthinsurance/personal-accident-insurance/guide/choosing-policy/
S. 141; 'Young women to see insurance premiums 'double'', abridged from http://www.telegraph.co.uk/finance/personalfinance/insurance/motorinsurance/9760222/Young-women-to-see-insurance-premiums-double-html
S. 143; '5 ways to save money on business insurance', abridged from Susan Ward, About.com Guide, http://sbinfocanada.about.com/od/insurance/a/bizinsurance1.htm
S. 144, based on information from, GDV, S. 74
S. 146: 'TR Insurance offers working abroad travel insurance', http://www.endsleigh.co.uk/Travel/Pages/work-abroad-insurance.aspx

KMK exam practice – Bildquellen
S.135/Shutterstock/Pablo Calvog; S. 136/Shutterstock/Burnel; S. 138/Shutterstock/mangostock; S. 140/Shutterstock/JanVloek; S. 143/Shutterstock/Astragal; S. 14/Shutterstock/ElenaElisseeva, shutterstock/BlajGabriel; S. 148/Shutterstock/CandyBoxImages